RED SUN RISING

GREAT BATTLES OF HISTORY

HANSON W. BALDWIN, General Editor

Also by REGINALD HARGREAVES

THE NARROW SEAS
THE ENEMY AT THE GATE
THIS HAPPY BREED
WOMEN AT ARMS
ONLOOKER AT WAR

In collaboration with Lewis Melville

'MR. CROFTS THE KING'S BASTARD'
IN THE DAYS OF QUEEN ANNE
FAMOUS DUELS AND ASSASSINATIONS
JOHN GAY

RED SUN RISING:

THE SIEGE OF PORT ARTHUR

REGINALD HARGREAVES

J. B. LIPPINCOTT COMPANY

PHILADELPHIA & NEW YORK

For

Don Hittle,

Brigadier General

United States Marine Corps,

In Friendship

CONTENTS

Preface · ix

1. PRELUDE TO CONFLICT · 1
2. CHALLENGE TO THE WEST · 11
3. THE YELLOW FLOOD · 31
4. DIVIDED COUNCILS · 54
5. TIGER AT THE GATES · 75
6. THE TROUGH OF THE WAVE · 97
7. THE HORNS OF DILEMMA · 116
8. THE SPIRIT OF YAMATO DAMASHII · 132
9. THE SANDS RUN OUT · 149
10. THE PORTENT · 167

Notes and Bibliography · 185
Appendices · 196
Index · 205

MAPS

The Fortress of Port Arthur, August, 1904 · xii-xiii
The Russo-Japanese Campaign · *facing p. 1*

"Red sun in the morning,

Shepherd's warning."

—*Old Adage*

PREFACE

It has been said that history is philosophy-teaching by example. The Russo-Japanese campaign of 1904–5 was generous in examples that embodied invaluable lessons for the soldier and the sailor, while the political implications of Japan's victory over the Russians are still in process of crystallization.

The struggle was fought in the territory of Manchuria and its adjacent waters. This is a region in which nearly all the place names are Chinese, and, when written down, they are rendered in Chinese characters. Throughout the war the Japanese adapted a number of these place names, transcribing them in hieroglyphics that to the untutored Western eye are no less incomprehensible. The Russians also evolved a version of them in equally unhelpful Cyrillic script. Any rendering of them in English can only be phonetic; and phonetic renderings are apt to vary widely. In the following narrative what is known as Wade's System of Transcription has been employed throughout, and Appendix C, at the end of the book, shows his version of these place names, together with certain alternatives in equally common use.

Port Arthur's fortifications were constructed under the inspiration of the Crimean veteran General Edouard Ivanovitch Todleben, an obvious disciple of that seventeenth-century master of fortress engineering Marshal Sebastien le Prestre de Vauban. Since reference to these defence works involves the use of a number of archaic technical terms with which the present-day reader may be unfamiliar, a short explanatory list of them is given in Appendix E.

In general, casualty returns, parade states, and the like have been found to differ widely from one account to another. The figures published by H. Fischer in *Kriegschirurgische Rück- und Ausblicke vom Asiatischen Kriegsschauplatze* have been accepted, with some reserve, as approximately accurate, although they are often at variance with the returns collated by Matignon, Kinai, and Rozlovski.

ACKNOWLEDGMENTS

I am under the very greatest obligation to Miss Kathleen M. Withy, B.A., for her invaluable work in preparing the manuscript, the index, and the bibliography. For unfailing interest and help my sincere thanks are due to the General Editor, Mr. Hanson W. Baldwin; to Col. Sidney Williams, Department of the Army, Office of the Chief of Information, Washington; to Brig. John Stevenson, O.B.E., Librarian, Royal United Service Institution; to Mr. D. W. King, O.B.E., F.L.A., Librarian, the War Office, and to his Assistant, Mr. C. A. Potts; to R. R. Lawson, F.L.A., County Librarian, Winchester; to F. M. L. Peppin, Borough Librarian, Bournemouth; to A. Longworth, F.L.A., City Librarian, Salford; and to Capt. Y. Takahashi, of the Embassy of Japan to the Court of St. James's.

To the following publishers I am greatly indebted for permission to quote from the works indicated: to Constable and Co. for permission to quote from Tadayoshi Sakurai's *Human Bullets*, William Greener's *Secret Agent in Port Arthur*, and Col. F. E. Whitton's *Decisive Battles of Modern Times;* to John Murray, Publishers, for extracts from E. K. Nojine's *The Truth about Port Arthur*, Gen. A. N. Kuropatkin's *The Russian Army and the Japanese War*, Brig. Gen. W. H.-H. Waters' *Secret and Confidential*, Capt. Vladimir Semenoff's *Rasplata*, and Capt. R. Grant's translation of the anonymous work *Before Port Arthur in a Destroyer;* to Hutchinson and Co. for extracts from Lt. Gen. A. A. Ignatyev's *A Subaltern in Old Russia;* to Longmans, Green and Co. for extracts from Frederick Villiers' *Port Arthur;* to Methuen and Co. for extracts from B. W. Norregaard's *The Great Siege;* to William Blackwood and Son for extracts from Ellis Ashmead-Bartlett's *Port Arthur, the Siege and Capitulation;* to the Liquidator, Hugh Rees, Ltd., for extracts from Lt. Gen. N. A. Tretyakov's *Nan-Shan and Port Arthur;* to Edward Arnold (Publishers) for extracts from Gen. Sir Ian Hamilton's *Staff Officer's Scrap Book;* and to the Controller, Her Majesty's Stationery Office, for extracts from the *Official History (Naval and Military) of the Russo-Japanese War.*

REGINALD HARGREAVES

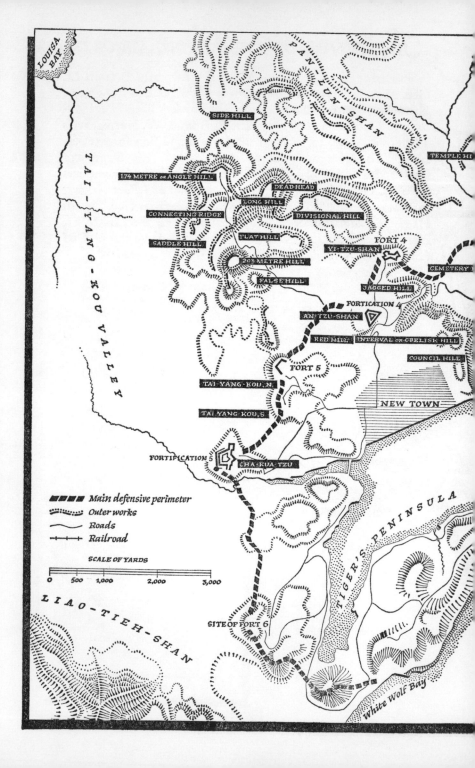

LOUISA BAY

PAN-LUN-SHAN

SIDE HILL

TEMPLE HI

TAI-YANG-KOU VALLEY

174 METRE or ANGLE HILL

DEAD HEAD

LONG HILL

CONNECTING RIDGE

DIVISIONAL HILL

SADDLE HILL

FLAT HILL

FORT 4

YI-TZU-SHAN

203 METRE HILL

CEMETERY I

FALSE HILL

JAGGED HILL

FORTICATION 4

AN-TZU-SHAN

RED HILL

INTERVAL or OBELISK HILL

FORT 5

COUNCIL HILL

TAI-YANG-KOU, N

NEW TOWN

TAI-YANG-KOU, S

FORTIFICATION 5

CHA-KUA-TZU

━━━ Main defensive perimeter

⋯⋯⋯ Outer works

—— Roads

—+—+— Railroad

SCALE OF YARDS

0   500   1,000   2,000   3,000

TIGER'S PENINSULA

LIAO-TIEH-SHAN

SITE OF FORT 6

White Wolf Bay

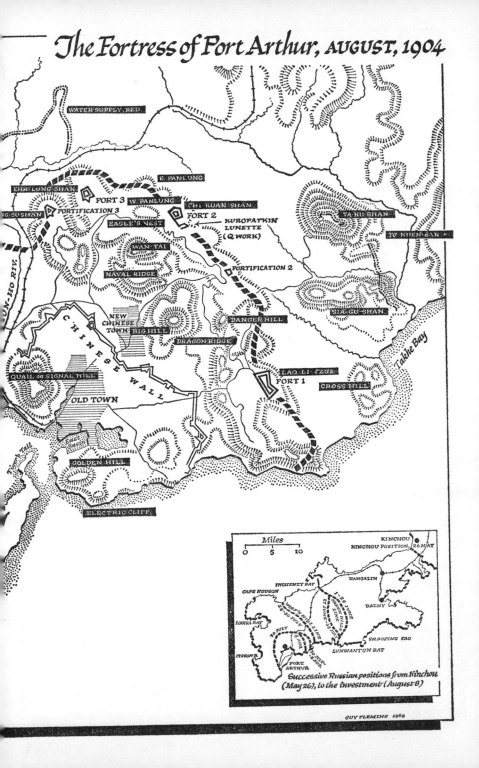

The Fortress of Port Arthur, AUGUST, 1904

WATER SUPPLY, RED

E. PANLUNG

EHR-LUNG SHAN
FORT 3
W. PANLUNG
CHI-KUAN-SHAN
IG-SU-SHAN
FORTIFICATION 3
FORT 2
TA-KU-SHAN
EAGLE'S NEST
KUROPATKIN
LUNETTE
(Q WORK)
TO KUEN-SAN

WAN-TAI

NAVAL RIDGE
FORTIFICATION 2

UN-HO RIV

SIA-GU-SHAN

NEW
CHINESE
TOWN
BIG HILL
DANGER HILL

DRAGON RIDGE

QUAIL OR SIGNAL HILL

OLD TOWN
LAO-LI-TZUL
FORT 1
CROSS HILL

CHINESE WALL

Takhe Bay

GOLDEN HILL

ELECTRIC CLIFF

Successive Russian positions from Kinchou (May 26), to the Investment (August 8)

Miles

0   5   10

KINCHOU
KINCHOU POSITION, 26 MAY

INCHENZY BAY
NANGALIN

CAPE HUDSON
DALNY

LOUISA BAY

SHAOPING TAO

PIGEON B.
LUNWANTUN BAY

PORT
ARTHUR

GUY FLEMING 1962

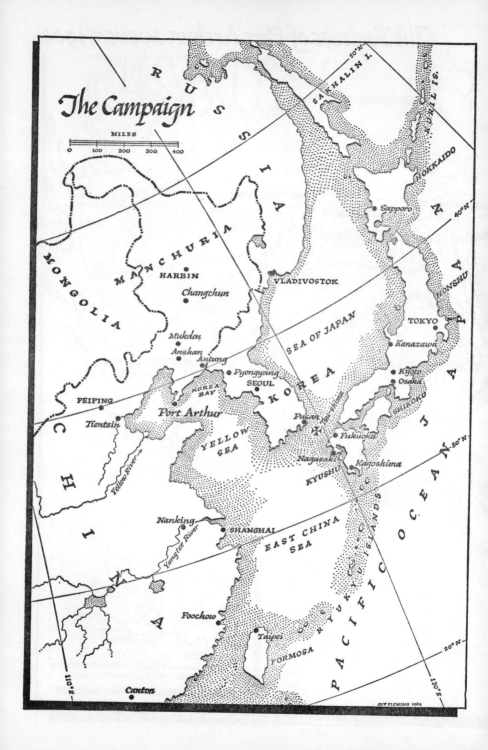

The Campaign

MILES
0 100 200 300 400

PRELUDE TO
CONFLICT

"TWO STARS KEEP NOT THEIR MOTION IN ONE SPHERE"
—SHAKESPEARE

1   IN THE 3,640 YEARS of its recorded history, the world has known only 292 years that were free from the clash of arms.

For many centuries warfare was pursued on extremely primitive lines. Even the introduction of missile weapons—first the sling and the bow and then the firearm—and an elementary logistics system scarcely affected the simplicity of the means and methods by which war was conducted.

It was the American Civil War, the first of the modern wars, which witnessed the initial large-scale appearance on the battlefield of the breech-loading magazine rifle, the machine gun, the breech-loading rifled cannon, the searchlight, the incendiary shell, and the electrically exploded mine and torpedo. Furthermore, the railroad was employed for the first time to accelerate troop movements; information and orders were transmitted by electric telegraph, and the military balloon was frequently used for purposes of observation. Naval vessels acquired protective armour plating, and a Confederate submarine proved its worth by sinking a Federal warship. Above all, the struggle clearly demonstrated that superior industrial and financial resources had become the determinative factor in any major conflict.

Throughout the balance of the century the scientists and the engineers of the West took an increasing hand in the extension of warfare's armoury. They little thought that the day was not far distant when, at the hands of an Oriental race, the West, as represented by Imperial Russia, would be defeated with its own weapons.

The military facts of life, as underscored by the rapid progress in the pursuit of warfare during the era 1861–1902, were digested nowhere with more eager appetite than in the aggressively emergent country of Japan.

From the days of Marco Polo onward, the island of Cipango had intrigued the Western voyager's imagination. Actual contact with the kingdom was first made in 1542, when three Portuguese sailors found themselves stranded on the offshore island of Tanehashima. But it was not until 1853 that Commodore Matthew Calbraith Perry, in command of four United States warships, entered Yedo Bay, bearing a letter from President Millard Fillmore to the Mikado. Since the Presidential note somewhat pointedly drew attention to the "powerful squadron" that had accompanied it, Perry's demand for the friendly treatment of shipwrecked whalers was no more to be ignored than the additional request for permission to establish a coaling station and generally to open up Japanese ports to trade.

In due course acknowledgment of President Fillmore's message was conveyed to Perry, who promptly announced his intention of returning in the following April or May for the Emperor's considered reply. "With all the ships?" queried the interpreter anxiously. "Yes," replied the commodore, "and probably with more"—a broad hint that seemed to give the Japanese deputation much food for thought.

In the spring, faithful to his word, Perry once more appeared in Yedo Bay, and in command of an even more impressive armament. Within a very short time a pact was signed granting all the concessions that had been demanded. As Nelson once drily commented, "A fleet of men-of-war are the best negotiators in the world"!

The agreement which opened the ports of Shimoda and

Hakodate to American vessels was followed by similar concessions to Britain, Holland, and Russia; and in 1859 a comprehensive treaty with the United States was concluded, on his own responsibility, with the Shogun, the Mikado's chief representative in Yedo. The Emperor's unconcealed resentment at this further encroachment on a realm hitherto almost hermetically sealed off from the rest of the world split the country into two warring factions—those who sought to encourage free intercourse with the West and those who were determined to prevent it.

As one way of reinforcing their resolve the reactionaries lost no time in victimizing such foreign nationals as had the misfortune to fall into their clutches. In retaliation, an outraged Britain promptly resorted to the traditional gunboat diplomacy. A powerful fleet subjected the coastal towns of Kagoshima and Shimonoseki to punishing bombardment.

The lesson was simple even for the most stubborn mind to absorb—that something less archaic than spears, swords, and lacquered armour was required to cope on equal terms with gunpowder, shells, and steam-driven ships. It would be necessary to assimilate the technology that gave mastery of such potent instruments of war; a task for which the receptive Japanese people, more imitative than inventive, were peculiarly predisposed.

Thus while the Mikado grudgingly accorded extraterritorial rights to a swarm of traders eager to do business within his Empire, the contemporary Shogun and his supporters were at pains to identify themselves with a drive for the westernization of Dai-Nippon[1]* which gathered such force and momentum as to constitute a revolution virtually without parallel in modern times. Hundreds of youthful Japanese were sent to Europe and the United States to learn the principles of Western technology, while Britain furnished Naval instructors and France sent a mission to supervise army training and remodel the country's feudal military system on thoroughly up-to-date lines. The contradiction between a surging spirit of nationalism and submission to Western tutelage was reconciled by the

* Superior numbers refer to Notes at end of text.

reservation that outside influence would be rejected the moment the assimilative process had been completed.

By 1872, when military service was declared universal and obligatory, the Gallic system of army reform had been found both too brittle and too doctrinaire. In consequence, Germany was called upon to weld an ardent but heterogeneous army into a balanced, fully integrated fighting force modelled on the organization which had made such contemptuously short work of Gallic warlike pretensions in the recent Franco-German War. The task presented few fundamental difficulties. For "in the days of Japan's seclusion she had owned a system beside which the militarism even of Prussia would have paled. Each feudal chief maintained what was nothing less than a small army. A puissant *daimyo's* retinue often amounted to as many as a thousand armed men; and at the appearance of this military procession all commoners who happened to be abroad had to prostrate themselves with uncovered heads."[2] With the warrior held in such high esteem, and with such a virile and disciplined spirit to work on, all that was required was to establish the principle of combined effort under central control, plan the strategic deployment of the forces available, train them on sound tactical lines, and ensure their mastery of the new technical means by which wars would be fought. It was not a question of having to stimulate the spirit of patriotism, but of directing its impulse along lines whose worth had already been proven in the uncompromising crucible of war.

In 1899 Japan found herself confronted with another urgent problem—the pressing need for lebensraum. So mountainous was her terrain that no more than one-fifteenth could be put under cultivation. Yet the appalling, unremitting fecundity of the people acknowledged no restraint. In 1872 the island population was given at approximately 33,000,000. Twenty years later it had reached the 41,000,000 mark, with an annual increase of over 700,000. Congestion was so acute that even wholesale emigration to the neighbouring realm of Formosa was unable adequately to relieve it. Since Russian pressure in 1875 had compelled the Emperor to surrender most of the island of Sakhalin in return for recognition of his title to the negligible islets of the Kuriles, it was comprehensible that Japanese eyes should turn longingly to the sparsely inhabited regions of Korea. For Japan had continued to claim a general suzerainty over this hermit kingdom even after the withdrawal of her troops from the territory in 1598. Since Chinese pretensions to dominance over the coveted land were no less exigent, tension between Tokio and Peking mounted steadily until, in 1894, the dispute merged into an appeal to arms which has aptly been described as "a contest between Japanese progress and Chinese stagnation."

For Japan the ensuing campaign was an unbroken succession of triumphs, which ended with her outright acquisition of Formosa and the occupation of Wei-hai-wei and the valuable haven of Port Arthur. In addition, China paid over an indemnity of $25,000,000, the money being raised by a combination of French and Russian interests animated by the coldly calculating consideration that the Western powers' "open door" policy in the Far East could best be advantaged by a doorstop made of gold.

By the terms of the Shimonoseki Treaty, which brought hostilities to a close, Korea was declared independent, and a slice of southern Manchuria, in the form of the Liao-tung peninsula, including Port Arthur, was ceded to the victors.

To prosecute and win a war by the employment of an entirely alien technique represented a very considerable achievement for a race of agriculturists and simple but accomplished handicraftsmen, with no prior knowledge of or sympathy for the machine. The only thing which had remained unaffected by the change in their fighting method was the fundamental Orientalism of their outlook.

The upsurge of an assertive Japanese nationalism had in no way gone unnoticed by a concert of European powers more interested in exploiting trade openings in the Far East than in fostering an Eastern country's pretensions to domination of the Pacific. A joint note from Russia, Germany, and France was presented to Japan protesting against her occupation of Chinese territory. In vain the Mikado looked about him for support. The United States had still to cope with the repercussions of Emilio Aguinaldo's insurrection in the Philippines—in essence, the reincarnation of the age-old struggle between East and West—and no one else appeared to be interested. Japan was therefore forced to evacuate the Liao-tung peninsula, her military authorities having ruefully to accept the fact that their warlike resources had not yet reached the point at which they could confidently risk defiance of a major European power, let alone a combination of them.

Japan's concession to what Russia cynically euphemized as "the dictates of humanity" had involved considerable loss of face, a political intangible to which the Oriental mind attached an overwhelming importance. But the authorities in Tokio impassively swallowed the bitter pill of humiliation—and resolutely set about doubling the size of their army and trebling that of their fleet. In 1893 Japan's military budget had been a mere $10,000,000. By 1900 it had risen to $65,000,000. The day of reckoning would come, a day when Japan, having ensured the noninterference of the other European powers, would be free to challenge the clay-footed colossus that most nearly threatened her vital interests—Imperial Russia.

From the day when Ivan III (1462–1505) first set about expanding a Grand Duchy of Moscow too "cabin'd, cribb'd, confin'd and bound in" to satisfy his soaring dynastic ambitions, Russian leaders of all political persuasions have consistently followed a policy of insatiable and ruthlessly enforced colonial expansion. In something under four hundred years they contrived to enlarge their territory from a constricted satrapy covering less than 500,000 square miles into a vast empire extending to well over 8,660,000 square miles. Peter the Great (1672–1725) was the first to set about the search for a warm-water port to improve maritime communications that were even more primitive and restricted than those hampering movement on the land. Ultimately, his eye came to rest on the Kamchatka peninsula, which separates the Bering Sea from the Sea of Okhotsk. It was a quest his successors never abandoned.

In the mid nineteenth century, Russia's defeat in the

Crimean War finally frustrated her attempt to conquer Constantinople and establish herself on the Mediterranean. She was impelled, therefore, once more to turn her face to the East, in the hope of securing a warm-water port on the Pacific. The vast area separating European Russia from Far Eastern waters was speedily occupied by a chain of Russian posts; and without recourse to military action Peking was persuaded to cede to her voracious neighbour the greater part of the Amur basin. Then, taking full advantage of China's exhaustion after her war with Britain and France in 1857–60, Russia hustled through a treaty by whose terms she acquired Usuri, the maritime province of Siberia, from the Amur to the Korean frontier. But her new and excellent port of Vladivostok suffered from the handicap of being icebound for at least three months in the year. It was not long, therefore, before Russian eyes turned longingly to the south, to dwell acquisitively on the area still under Chinese sway in Manchuria—the Liao-tung peninsula and the secluded, unwelcoming, but alluring feudatory of Korea.

With Russian diplomacy paramount in Peking and a Russian bank exhibiting a lenity in the matter of loans of which the Chinese government took every possible advantage, permission was readily forthcoming for the final section of the Trans-Siberian railway to straddle Chinese Manchuria; a concession which conveniently poised the interlopers for a further move towards the south.

In 1897 the anti-foreign risings in the Chinese province of Shan-tung furnished the European powers with a heaven-sent excuse for demanding that the Peking government should lease them certain of its ports. This was Russia's prime opportunity to settle the problem of an ice-free haven and at the same time permanently establish her predominance throughout the Far East. In December warships of the Imperial navy appeared at Port Arthur, and the following year a convention was signed by which that strategic harbour, together with Ta-lien-wan on the deeply indented bay to the northeast, was leased to the Tsarists for a period of twenty-five years.

With the lease—which was renewable—went the right to fortify this Russian port of egress to warm water; a concession secured to offset the admittance of Britain to Hong-kong and Germany to Kaio-chao.

When the news of the exceptionally favourable conditions embodied in the Russo-Chinese treaty reached the West, it was received with an incredulity that argued a complete incomprehension of the intransigent Russian character. Those who are oblivious to the lessons of the past are invariably condemned to relive it. Thus the European chancelleries were still seeking to recover from their outraged sense of astonishment as the construction of the branch line linking Port Arthur with the trunk Siberian railway was brazenly pushed through. Thereafter, the Boxer Rebellion of 1900 offered a perfect excuse for pouring Russian troops into Manchuria until practically the whole area was in Russian hands, with only the Germans openly protesting at a move that no one was prepared to stop.

Since it was clear that with the Russians in full occupation of Manchuria it could only be a matter of time before Korea disappeared in the Russian maw, and with it the bulk of Japan's foreign trade, both the United States and Britain eventually came to Japan's support, extracting a promise that the Tsarist forces would progressively be withdrawn from Manchurian soil. Instead of fulfilling the pledge, however, the Moscow government put forward alternative proposals clearly designed, under a mask of accommodation, to strengthen its grip on the province. With some reluctance Japan offered to recognize Russia's position in Manchuria in return for Moscow's acknowledgment of Tokio's interest in Korea, with all nations enjoying equal commercial rights in both territories.

For a time there seemed every hope of a successful outcome to the protracted bargaining. The Russian War Minister, Gen. Alexei Nicholaevitch Kuropatkin, with a sense of reality unusual in a Slav, counselled the abandonment of Russian designs in southern Manchuria and the restoration of Port Arthur to China, in return for further concessions on the side of Vladivostok. What he had overlooked, however, was that a Russian speculator by the name of Alexander Mikhailovich Bezabrazoff had secured a concession from the Korean administration to cut timber along the Turmen and Yalu Rivers—

a project in which a number of nobles and court officials had been given substantial grounds for taking a warmly sympathetic interest. When money is the measure of worth, it is remarkably easy to come to the wrong decision. To afford protection for this financial complot, strong pressure was brought to bear on the Russian government, not only to strengthen the Manchurian garrison and the Far Eastern Fleet, but to send troops to the Yalu. And this despite the agreement guaranteeing Korean inviolability, to which both Japan and Russia had set their hands.

Throughout the South African War, Continental sympathies, particularly those expressed in France and Germany, had been strongly in favour of the Boers. Britain's reaction was as effective as it was bizarre—a five-year treaty with Japan, designed "to maintain the *status quo* and general peace in the extreme East." Within two months France and Russia published the terms of an agreement unctuously affirming that the principles expressed in the Anglo-Japanese concordat were fundamentally the same as those actuating French and Russian policy. With a great air of rectitude Russia then proceeded to conclude a treaty with China by which she agreed to evacuate Manchuria within eighteen months. But there was no noticeable movement on the part of her troops.

By the terms of the Anglo-Japanese alliance each nation was pledged to observe neutrality if the other were attacked by a *single* opponent, but was under obligation to come to the assistance of its ally should another power join the enemy. By implication, this meant that if Russia should be afforded military help by France or Germany, then Britain would render the Japanese forces immediate support.

It was a strange concatenation of East and West, but perfectly in line with Britain's abiding policy—to maintain by all possible means a world-wide balance of power. For it had not been overlooked that prior to the conclusion of the Franco-Russian treaty a Gallic squadron had paid a ceremonial visit to Kronstad, or that in 1893 a Russian military mission had been entertained in Paris. With the likelihood of trouble between Russia and Japan, it was well for everyone to be made fully aware beforehand that the ring would be kept clear for the two contestants to fight it out on their own.

As the months dragged by and Russia continued to return evasive replies to Japanese enquiries and demands while effecting no more than token withdrawals of her troops from southern Manchuria, it was clear that Moscow had no intention of conducting negotiations to a satisfactory conclusion. The handwriting was on the wall. The Japanese Ambassador's stern request for a definite answer to his government's representations by Feb. 4, 1904, having been ignored, Japan prepared for war. All too thoroughly had Tokio learned the Western principle that a country's army and navy exist to advance by force, or the threat of force, civil policies that cannot be advanced by civil means. And the Japanese Fighting Services were only too ready and eager to put that doctrine into practice.

CHALLENGE TO
THE WEST

"... NATURE DID
DESIGN US TO BE WARRIORS, AND TO BREAK THROUGH
OUR RING, THE SEA, BY WHICH WE ARE ENVIRONED."

—PHILIP MASSINGER

2   IN WARFARE *Twice is he armed who hath his quarrel
just,/And three times he who gets his blow in fust.* To this
intensely practical belief no one adhered more closely than the
Japanese. In their war with China they had struck the first blow
and gone through the motions of declaring war afterwards.

The Japanese believed the outcome of the coming struggle
would depend on their ability to win naval supremacy and
with it the freedom of movement necessary for their plans.
Although strong land forces would be required to drive the
Russians from the Manchurian territory where they were so
strongly established, Japanese victory would require the im-
mobilization of the reinforced Tsarist Pacific Ocean Squadron,
based on Port Arthur, before it could be further reinforced
from Europe, and while it was still scattered. For seven battleships and six cruisers, with some gunboats and auxiliary craft,
were at the main base, while four cruisers—the *Gromboy,
Rossia, Rurik,* and *Bogatyr*—were at Vladivostok, and two
other warcraft at the Korean haven of Chemulpo. Should the
Russian vessels refuse to come out and fight, Port Arthur would
first have to be blockaded and then attacked and reduced from
the landward side. The warships sheltering in its Basin, if not
previously scuttled, could then be taken over.

To take Port Arthur by land assault would necessitate putting ashore four army corps in the neighbourhood of Pi-tzu-wo, some sixty miles east by northeast of the ultimate objective. While three of these engaged the Russian forces concentrated between Hai-cheng, Mukden, and Liao-yang, the remaining corps would fight its way down the peninsula until it was in a position to close in on Port Arthur. With the Russian field armies thrown back or held, the besiegers could progressively be reinforced. Once the build-up had been completed, Yorktown could be re-enacted on the shores of the Gulf of Chihli.

At the outset every effort would be made to dispose of the Pacific Ocean Squadron by bringing it to action and defeating it. Thus on the night of Feb. 6, 1904, while negotiations were still theoretically being pursued in the respective chancelleries, Admiral Heihachiro Togo's fleet lay with steam up at Sasebo, above Nagasaki on the Strait of Tsu-shima. On the following day it stood out to sea in search of the Russian fleet, while a torpedo boat flotilla took the opportunity to convoy General Kuroki and three transports crammed with troops to Chemulpo, a handy port to the westward of the Korean capital of Seoul. In the harbour was an old unarmoured Russian gunboat, the *Koreëts*, and the 6,500-ton first-class protected cruiser *Variag* from Vladivostok, which tried to make a run for it. Having got to sea and been heavily attacked by a Japanese squadron, these two vessels put back to Chemulpo—the cruiser badly damaged—and were then deliberately set on fire, their crews taking refuge in certain sympathetic neutral craft standing by in the port.

By six o'clock on the night of Feb. 8, Admiral Togo was on passage past Round Island, sixty miles from Port Arthur. Japanese agents had reported the Russian fleet anchored in the roadstead; and as Togo's vessels stealthily made toward the haven, it could be seen that the Russian ships, like the town itself, were brilliantly illuminated. The authorities must have been perfectly well aware that war was imminent, that it would be advisable to be on the alert. But "Monday February 8th was the name-day of Port Admiral Starck's wife and daughter. The invitations were out and the reception was in full swing."[1]

It was a little before midnight when the boom of *Novik's* guns and the sight of three rockets snaking into the inky sky from the signal station on Golden Hill brought the garrison and many of the townsfolk hurrying to their doors in bewilderment and a growing sense of unease. With the bugles shrilling the alarm, the men in the barracks stumbled out onto their parade grounds as their officers straggled in to join them from the restaurants and cabarets in the town.

At first there was a tendency to treat the whole commotion as no more than a practice "Alert." It was a delusion that was borne out by the discovery that the alarm posts were furnished neither with ammunition nor with rations. None of the regimental officers having been permitted to familiarize themselves with the layout of the defence system, a number of units went astray; and such orders as did reach them were mostly contradictory or were countermanded before they could be carried out.

With morning light the town was humming with rumours, despite the threat to punish those guilty of spreading false intelligence which the governor, Gen. Baron Anatole Mikhailovitch Stössel, was swift to announce. But the naked truth was not to be disguised—the *Tzesarevitch*, the *Pallada*, and the *Retvisan* had been hit and in attempting to re-enter the harbour had run aground. The first two, it was said, could be hauled off, but the *Retvisan* was stuck fast, with water pouring in through the gash in her bows and spreading all through the ship.

As the townsfolk streamed out to take up positions on the commanding heights of Quail Hill and Liao-tieh-shan, overlooking the sea, there could no longer be room for doubt. For the *Retvisan* lay in full view at the mouth of the harbour, and her helplessness was apparent even to a layman's eyes. Later it became generally known that in the course of the night encounter the Japanese destroyer *Shirakuma* had been sunk by the guns of the *Tzesarevitch* and considerable damage inflicted on other vessels of the enemy fleet, which had made off—unpursued—in the direction of the Elliot Islands. But there was no escaping the conclusion that had the Japanese torpedoes' net-cutters functioned properly, the damage inflicted on the Russian fleet would have been far heavier. The *Tzesarevitch* had found no less than four "yellow cigars" caught up in her nets.

So far no word of war had appeared in the local *Novy Kry*, but the bustle and confusion at the governor's headquarters was not to be misinterpreted. Nothing but the actual outbreak of hostilities could account for the pandemonium raging in that cackling military hencoop, where only Colonel Khvostoff, Chief of the Fortress Staff, and his immediate subordinates appeared to have kept their heads.

While the troops of the garrison eddied to and fro in confusion the bulk of the Pacific Ocean Squadron lay in the outer harbour with steam up and decks cleared for action. At 10 A.M. the *Boyarin* signalled that the Japanese fleet was approaching in force. "A little later the *Askold*, which was already in action, with the Japanese cruisers chasing her, closed and reported 'The enemy's main body is approaching.' . . . Soon there was no need for signals. The entire Japanese fleet appeared above the horizon, and yet the Russian fleet remained lying there. The Admiral had been sent for by the Viceroy in the morning to receive instructions, and had not yet returned. Yet Golden Hill could take in all signals, as it could see much further than the ships in the roads. The signal station was in direct telephonic communication with the Viceroy's palace. Presumably he said: 'No, not yet,' and continued the discussion. . . . When the Chief of Staff saw that the enemy would soon be within range, he signalled: 'Weigh and form single line ahead.' He did not wait for the Admiral, and when the latter came out at last he had to follow in his steam barge. He boarded the flagship after she had already begun to go ahead."[2]

The progress of events was anxiously observed by the milling crowds on the heights, and by General Stössel, supported by a *sotnia* of Cossacks and a numerous staff, from a vantage point on Golden Hill.[3]

As the coastal batteries fired in support of their ships—although for want of live ammunition several of them were firing blank—Port Arthur quivered to the shock of the guns, the streets and harbour rocking to the explosion of the Japanese 12-inch shells.

In the town itself "goods had been hurled hither and thither by the force of the explosions; the double glass windows of the buildings along the waterfront had scarcely a whole pane remaining. On the Bund near the water-edge a shell had burrowed a hole large enough to hold an omnibus and team, the gravel and earth had been scattered everywhere and mixed up with a heap of coal dust being discharged from lighters. Walls were down here, the plastering from house-sides there, and in the garden of a house built on a terrace cut in the hillside a spent 13-inch live shell had dropped and was guarded by a sentry. It was a long-range bombardment from eight to twelve miles out to sea, and was in fact excellent shooting."[4]

In something less than forty minutes the terror was over, as the badly hammered Russian vessels put about and ran for the shelter of the port. The myth of the Pacific Ocean Squadron's invincibility had been destroyed by the very individuals who had been loudest in proclaiming it; and the faith of both junior officers and men in their leaders had suffered irreparable damage. "We had just ceased fire," one of them recorded, "when our good-natured, fat little friend S—— turned towards Golden Hill with clenched fists. Tears of rage stood in his eyes and with a choking voice he cried: 'Did they expect this, these infallible, high and mighty gentlemen?'"[5] Nor was his complaint without justification. A nation that had undergone no more than thirty-two years' training in the Western technique of maritime war had successfully challenged an Imperial navy founded two centuries before by Peter the Great.

February 10 brought news of the formal declaration of war, and with it the re-endorsement of Admiral Eugene Alexeieff's appointment as viceroy and generalissimo of all the sea and land forces within the Manchurian theatre of conflict. At the same time Lt. Gen. Konstantine Nikolaevitch Smirnoff was ordered to proceed from Warsaw to Port Arthur to take over the command of the defences. Stössel would then be free to attend to his duties as military governor of the entire Kuantun Province, an area which included the subsidiary but important harbour of Kin-chou on the bay of that name, and all the likely beachheads on which the Japanese might be expected to attempt landings. Until relieved of his present command, he of course remained responsible for Port Arthur and its defence.

On Feb. 12 the Japanese fleet again sought to grapple their opponents in a general action. Failing in this design, they began mine-laying and harbour-blocking operations. On the night of Feb. 24–25 five black-painted blockships, escorted by twelve destroyers, cautiously made their way toward Port Arthur. But the shore defences were on the alert. "The *Retvisan* was the first to have doubts, and opened fire on them. It appeared strange to her that these steamers had formed single line abreast, just as if they were intending to steam altogether into the narrow entrance of Port Arthur. For merchant ships it would have been more natural to form single line ahead, that is, in each other's wake, as at Port Arthur, and especially at night, only one ship at a time could pass through the entrance. The further proceedings of these mysterious craft had strengthened the suspicions of our people. They did not anchor, nor did their syrens shriek, when they were fired upon. Instead of this they resolutely continued their course. However, when suddenly a number of torpedo boats, which had up till then been hiding behind the steamers, dashed out and attacked the *Retvisan*, every doubt vanished. At that moment fire was opened all along the line."[6] With their high elevation on the clifftops, the forts were able to bring plunging fire to bear, while the stranded *Retvisan* served as a useful floating battery. Russian cruisers also came out to join the fight, but "they showed little skill," one Japanese participant recorded, "for they ought to have made a clean sweep of us."[7] One steamer was sunk in the roads; another ran on the rocks at the foot of White Wolf Hill. One went a little too far to starboard and sank under Golden Hill; the fourth went too far to port and ran up on the southern slope of Lighthouse Hill. The fifth was sunk fairly in the roads. The operation, in effect, could claim no more than limited success; but until the early days of May, Admiral Togo persisted in his attempts to block the harbour. Unable or unwilling to put to sea and renew their defiance of the enemy, the Russians allowed themselves to be penned in their anchorage as a fox is stopped up in its lair.

"The essence of strategy is forethought; the essence of tactics is surprise." The Japanese had exhibited both, although they had fallen a good deal short of the swift, decisive result at which they had aimed.

Had General Kuroki and a substantial part of his forces been close at hand, the outcome might have been very different. For "the torpedo attack and subsequent bombardment had astonished the Russians, and they were rendered defenceless by their unlimited bewilderment. A few well-armed, daring troops landed immediately after the torpedo attack, or simultaneously, would have captured the town, the Staff and the heads of the Naval and Military Departments, and might have carried at least one of the forts. At any time during the first week the Russians would have been surprised by an attack, and probably would have succumbed to a well-organised offensive movement."[8] Commander Semenoff, whose outlook on affairs was normally sanguine in the extreme, was of similar opinion, recording in his private journal that "Had the Japanese sent, not four, but forty destroyers, and at the same time disembarked a Division of troops, the town and the rest of the squadron would have fallen into their hands."

To precede land operations by a naval bombardment is only to alert the defenders to prepare against designs yet to be put in motion, as Gallipoli in 1915 was only too eloquently to bear witness.

Japan had entered upon her struggle with the Russian legions under certain handicaps that were not altogether outweighed by a relatively short, though possibly hazardous, line of communications, an intimate knowledge of the terrain over which the armies would be operating, and an Intelligence service that penetrated every nook and cranny of the enemy defences. The standing army, ardent, well equipped, and admirably tutored as it might be, totalled some 270,000, with trained reserves that ran to no more than 530,000. Further expansion under the terms of general conscription would certainly be possible, but would be hampered by a shortage of officers.[9]

The Japanese navy was well furnished with fortified bases, Sasebo, Hakodate, Miyazu, Hiroshima, Maisura, Shimoneseki, and Nagasaki all possessing excellent docks, while there were additional ports fit to take torpedo craft. Three of these bases were situated close to the Korean Straits, midway between Vladivostok and Port Arthur, where the passage was narrowed to a mere thirty miles by the island of Tsu-shima. Thirty-five miles to the west of Tsu-shima lay the Korean mainland. The navy's bigger craft had been built in foreign yards, but under Western supervision the Japanese slips had turned out some of the smaller vessels; and repair facilities were far in advance of the country's ability to pay for the replacement of such losses as her fleet might suffer. For Japan had relatively few industrial assets and a treasury whose coffers would swiftly be drained unless the Mikado's forces achieved a speedy victory. The last of the vessels acquired for the Japanese navy in Europe, the armoured cruisers *Nisshin* and *Kasuga*, completed their passage from Genoa to Sasebo on Feb. 14. Laid down on the order of the Argentinian Government, they had first been offered to Russia, but the offer had disdainfully been refused.[10]

The Russian army was maintained at a strength of over 1,000,000, and if the reserves were called up by district rather than selectively by category, this total could be increased to 3,500,000. Many of these troops, however, including such élite formations as the Guards and Grenadiers, would have to be retained in the West, where it was necessary to keep a watchful eye on an unpredictable Germany and an effervescent Poland. For no Russian administration could possibly forget that Germany had not only sided with Austria against the Tsar at the 1878 Conference of Berlin, which had settled the peace terms that brought the Russo-Turkish War to a close, but had vigorously protested the Russians' attempt to consolidate their position in Manchuria after the Boxer Rebellion. As for Poland —it seemed that for every Kosciuszko that faded from the scene two more firebrands invariably sprang up to keep the flag of rebellion briskly flying.

Moreover, from a practical point of view many of the Russian reservists were men who had left the Colours as long before as 1887; land workers who resented the war since its call on their services would deprive their large and mostly adolescent families of their principal breadwinner. In any case such field training as any of them might recall would be thoroughly out of date, while the new "three line"[11] rifle was a weapon that only the younger men, and barely a tenth of them, had ever handled. Furthermore, a very considerable body of troops would have to be retained in the homeland for purposes of internal security, a preoccupation from which Japan was completely relieved. In general, the conflict with Japan lacked popular support. "In European Russia," one traveller recorded, "I met no one who wanted war; many who were opposed to it."[12] Moreover, the expatriate insurrectionmongers and underground fomenters of revolution within Russia itself had quickly perceived in the general unpopularity of the conflict a magnificent opportunity to intensify their campaign of subversion and subornation. When a country is at war, it is stirred to its depths, and scum rises to the surface. Even the men entraining for the front were not immune from the attentions of those seeking to pervert them from their patriotic duty. "Hundreds of thousands of proclamations were distributed amongst the troops . . . urging the soldiers on to defeat, not victory";[13] and many a man set out to face the perils and privations that lay ahead with troubled spirit, chilled and questioning. The seeds of the *Oktybrskaya Revolutsia* of 1917 had already begun to germinate.

Neither was it possible to leave out of consideration that Port Arthur and the Liao-tung peninsula were over five thousand miles from their Moscow base, to which they were linked by a precarious single-track railway line. Even this was not continuous, since there was a hundred-mile gap at Lake Baikal. Between November and April, when the huge sheet of water was frozen over, all supplies had to be hauled—carefully spaced out—over the treacherous ice, which was not firm enough to carry a locomotive and cars on a temporary line laid across it. The troops, of course, made the passage by route march, dragging their personal equipment on sledges, an ordeal that rarely took less than five days to complete. Even under the most favourable conditions, anything from four to six weeks was required to transport a battalion from Moscow to Mukden. Neither main line, sidings, stations, nor rolling stock were in any way equal to dealing with the additional demands that would be made upon them in time of war; water facilities would never cope even with the modest increase in traffic that might be anticipated, while coal stocks, having been seaborne, were piled up in Dalny, a mere thirty-five miles from Port Arthur and an obvious Japanese objective should the Pacific Squadron ever lose command of the Yellow Sea. Finally, for much of its length the Trans-Siberian railway was bounded by Chinese territory; and the attitude of China towards an opponent of fellow-Asiatics was a matter of uneasy speculation.

In the actual theatre of operations Alexeieff had at his immediate command some 83,000 field troops, 25,000 fortress troops, and 30,000 railway troops, with 196 guns other than those incorporated in Port Arthur's fixed defences. To increase this total would inevitably prove a dangerously lengthy task.

The country over which the troops had to operate was abrupt and mountainous, extremely primitive despite a patchwork of squalid villages, and virtually without anything resembling a passable road. On its open levels and cultivable slopes it was everywhere sown with beans and kaoliang—tall crops of millet growing to a height of from 12 to 15 feet, which had a peculiarly baffling and intimidating effect on the Russian infantryman wandering and lost in its green, whispering maze. Scorchingly hot in the summer months, the Manchurian climate was cold and intensely penetrating in winter; and throughout May, June, July, and August, and often into September, the rain lashed down unmercifully. Throughout this period the valleys were turned into a quagmire, one Russian officer recording that "The mud reaches the breasts of the horses and covers the spokes of the wheels of heavy waggons sinking in the soil. . . . Only Chinese *abbas* (mere platforms on two enormous wheels) survive the swamps and holes of the impassable Manchurian roads."[14]

Fortunately for them, the men of both armies came of sound peasant stock, which is the best military raw material in the world—providing the slow bucolic mind can be trained to master intricate modern weapons. For the man of the soil is bred under harsher conditions than the city dweller, has far greater powers of endurance, more solid fighting qualities, and exhibits much greater stoicism under privation.

These attributes were common to both the ex-moujik and the former coolie. But the Japanese were inspired by a far more intense sense of patriotism. The Russians lacked the real "fire in the belly" that irresistibly drove their opponents forward even in the face of certain death. Shintoism, which counted it a privilege to serve the Fatherland even unto death, and was the spirit of *Yamato Damashii*, which had inspired the medieval samurai, broadened out to exalt a whole people, so that it was not unknown for a mother to commit hara-kiri in shame and dismay at her son's failure, on medical grounds, to gain admittance to his country's fighting forces. Nor should it be forgotten that the Mikado's army already nurtured a strong feeling of tradition, founded on its prowess in the great Satsuma rebellion of 1877 and its successful showing in the war against China. On the other hand, the type of war to which the Russian was committed—standing doggedly on the defensive with his back to the wall, knowing that he must hold his own or perish where he fell—found the hard core of the Russian army at its best. But that hard core of sturdy fighters was perilously small.

The fortress system of Port Arthur the Russian soldier was to defend was materially helped by the rugged nature of the country surrounding the settlement. To the east a range of steep hills, rising in places to well over 600 feet, swung northwestward until, due north, they were abruptly broken by the Lun-ho River valley. This swept down from the village of Shui-shih-ying to the shore line between the Old and New Towns, separated by the conical eminence known as Quail Hill, or alternatively as Signal Hill. Equally abrupt, another range of hills reached out from the north to westward, ultimately curving round to form the Tiger Peninsula, covering the port's West Basin from the sea. Beyond this barrier the barren hog's-back of Liao-tieh-shan, with its solitary lighthouse, thrust its unfortified bulk into the sea.

The range of hills facing up the peninsula towards Liao-yang was straddled by the old Chinese Wall and crowned by three principal forts. Two additional permanent works crested the heights to the west, where a sixth fort had been marked out in the region of 203 Metre Hill but had not been built. In between these major defences lay an intricate but unfinished network of subsidiary fortifications, redoubts, and field entrenchments. They seamed all the slopes and were eventually extended to enclose the temple and the Waterworks to the north. Coastal batteries were built into Golden Hill, to the east of the town, on Tiger Peninsula, and on the knoll known as White Wolf, linking the Tiger Peninsula with Liao-tieh-shan. In itself, the position was one of considerable strength. But the Russian sappers, charged over a period of six years with the erection of the defence works, "had quietly pursued the dogmas of ancient manuals,"[15] and many of the redoubts, lunettes, and caponiers were incomplete, and all were outmoded, while the siting of the guns was quite inept. "Barbed wire was scarce and worth its weight in gold";[16] the system of communications was both immature and extremely faulty. In almost every direction the field of fire was obscured by crops of high-standing kao-liang. There was no fear, however, of any water shortage, even if the outlying Waterworks position should be taken. For a lake was conveniently tucked away between Golden Hill and the Old Town, and there were a number of horse ponds in the hills. The three fortified works of North Fort Chi-kuan-shan (Fort No. 2), Erh-lung-shan (Fort No. 3), and 203 Metre Hill were the keys of Port Arthur. Of almost equal importance were the eminences of Ta-ku-shan and Sia-gu-shan to the east. Retention of the complementary stronghold of Kin-chou, to the northeast, would guard against any enemy advance against the flank. With these defences firmly held, Port Arthur would prove a difficult nut to crack.

Under conditions of modern war, which so often impose remoteness and impersonality on the higher command, a siege offers perhaps the only situation in which the commander's personality can closely influence the morale of both his troops and the civilian population. Given a man with the faculty of inspiring confidence—such as Osman Pasha at Plevna and Baden-Powell at Mafeking—morale will remain high despite occasional setbacks and the progressive deterioration of every-day conditions.

Unhappily for Port Arthur's destiny, no such uplifting quality was to be found in General Stössel, who, even by un-exacting Russian standards, can be accounted as little more than an inflated military manikin overweighted by his epau-lettes. An individual whom active service against the Turks and in the Boxer Rebellion appeared to have taught nothing, he was a compound of textbook pedant and parade-ground martinet. To such a man an unbuttoned pocket or a forage cap set awry was of far greater importance than a breach in his main defences. Although responsible for holding the entire Kuan-tun peninsula, he was too busy reprimanding his subordinates, savagely disciplining his troops, and dictating flamboyant but ambiguous *directives* to strengthen and reorganize the coastal defences and those of Kin-chou and Port Arthur.

Although proudly regarded by its Russian inhabitants as symbolic of successful Muscovite expansion, in reality the town over which Stössel ruled had little enough to recommend it. For the most part its dwellings were poor in appearance and lacking in all the conveniences of modern houses. A vast hotel had been completed but was requisitioned as a hospital before it could be opened. The Viceregal Lodge and the Naval Club had some pretensions to architectural style, but Nikodadze's and Efimoff's hotels were less like reputable, well-run inns than glorified native khans. Saratov's restaurant alone could be regarded as up to middle-class European standards. With the outbreak of hostilities the few places of amusement were im-mediately closed down, including the resident circus, whose trick-riding horses were impounded by the military—which led to some very tricky riding when the band struck up suddenly! "There was no real street or good roadway anywhere; the tracks, unless frozen hard, which was unusual, were just troughs of mud through which horses splashed and jinrickshaws were pushed by two men."[17] Bleak, dusty, and plagued by violent winds, Port Arthur did little credit to the royal prince after whom it had originally been named.[18]

With war hanging over it, Port Arthur was thrown into great confusion, which infected everyone, including the harbour officials and the officer commanding the guardship. In a moment of panic the *Knight Commander* and the *Hipsang*, both sailing under the British flag, were fired on and sunk. The *Wenchow* was detained once because she had Japanese aboard, next because she had *no* Japanese aboard; the *Pleiades*, with many sacks of flour for a consignee who had fled, was allowed to sail chock-full of provisions that were urgently needed in the port itself.

Stössel's handling of the matter of reserve supplies was scarcely more intelligent. Slaughter herds that should have been requisitioned were allowed to be driven off into the interior, many of the cattle subsequently falling into Japanese hands. No effort was made to prevent a swarm of upcountry officers from raiding Port Arthur's shops and carrying away great quantities of flour, sugar, preserved meat and fish, and tinned milk. One commodity, however, was added to rather than diminished: "the rail had not been used as it might have been to bring in food, yet the mountain of packing cases near the station showed that it had not been idle. This mound, which served as a landmark—a sort of triumphal arch by the entrance to the Old Town—was composed entirely of vodka!"[19] But rather than conserve essential supplies against the possibility of enemy victory, Stössel recklessly sent trainloads of them up the line to the Russian forces concentrating in the neighbourhood of Mukden.

Of Port Arthur's civil population of 55,000—which included a large number of Chinese coolies—many had no commercial or sentimental ties to bind them to the town. Had the task been handled in orderly fashion, there would have been ample time in which to evacuate a considerable proportion of them overland. But although refugees crowded the railway station, there was scant accommodation for them on the trains. For these were reserved almost exclusively for so-called military traffic—mostly the removal of commodities of which the port itself would soon be in desperate need. Some of the refugees fled to Dalny, which turned out to be a case of jumping from the frying pan into the fire. Others clubbed together to hire junks to transport them to Chefu or some other neutral city; the few steamers that could boast a nonbelligerent flag were crowded with others in hasty flight. Japanese civilians who remained in Port Arthur were herded, men and women together, in cattle trucks for evacuation by rail, their roundup being attended by every type of barbarity. The local Chinese coolies took swift advantage of the general state of confusion to pilfer the unguarded stores on the wharves, or raid the abandoned houses. Since it seemed impossible for any Russian to differentiate between a Chinese and a Japanese, many Japanese agents were enabled to stay on in the town by the simple expedient of passing themselves off as Chinese.

Bombastic orders continued to flow in an unbroken stream from Command Headquarters; but instead of strengthening his grip on Kin-chou and hurrying to build up the neglected defences on 203 Metre Hill, Stössel busied himself with the construction of an inner wall, with a ditch, to surround the Old Town. Costing all of $100,000, it was quite useless as a defence should the Japanese occupy the commanding hills overlooking the outer ring of fortifications. For from that position the Old Town and its puerile central wall would be completely dominated. This, however, was a consideration the governor obstinately chose to ignore, and work on "Stössel's Folly" was pressed forward with the utmost urgency. In warfare there are few things more dangerous than active ignorance.

General Kuroki's landing at Chemulpo had speedily been followed by his occupation of Pingyang; the Japanese build-up of the forces earlier put ashore proceeded with bland disregard for Alexeieff's "fleet in being," for the simple reason that the intimidating effect of a "fleet in being" is nil unless it is prepared to take risks boldly.

With investment an imminent possibility, on Feb. 29 Stössel issued a General Proclamation which ended on a note whose irony was quite obviously unconscious:

The troops know well, and I now make known to the civilians, that there will be no retirement; in the first place, the Fortress must fight to the last, and I, its Commandant, will never give the order to retreat; in the second, there is no place to which to retreat.

Communications with upcountry were, of course, still intact. But with the Japanese on the march to the Yalu River, it was only a matter of elementary precaution to increase the number of railway troops guarding the line and mount light field artillery on the principal bridges. On the seaward side Rear Admiral Loschinsky set to work to countermine the approaches to Port Arthur and Dalny, farther round the coast, where conditions were excellent for a hostile landing. Then on Mar. 8 the accomplished Vice-Admiral S. O. Makharoff arrived to take over command of the naval forces from Vice-Admiral Starck. From the outset he was kept far busier than his travelling companion, the officer appointed to command the balloon park. For neither balloons nor the material to fabricate them were available, the whole stock—together with a quantity of ammunition—having fallen into Japanese hands with the capture of the S.S. *Manchuria*.

Makharoff had scarcely taken up his duties before the Pacific Ocean Squadron had another taste of action. "In the early hours of March 10th," the newspaper correspondent E. K. Nojine subsequently recorded, "our destroyer division went out scouting. At dawn they were engaged by the enemy, and we lost the *Steresguschy*, which was sunk." Engaged at almost point-blank range by the *Akasuki* the gun duel between the two destroyers veered in the Japanese favour when the Russians' 7.5-cm was put out of action by concentrated fire. Disabled and motionless, with the majority of her crew *hors de combat*, the *Steresguschy*, had no men left to repel the enemy boarding party. This promptly swarmed overside to hunt down the few survivors, who were frantically at work trying to scuttle their craft, which was subsequently found to be too heavily damaged to keep afloat. The Japanese had not escaped unscathed, but Nojine continues, "at 8.18 A.M. the enemy fleet appeared off Liao-tieh-shan. At 8.30 three battleships and two light cruisers separated from the rest and took up their position about a mile from that hill, whose cliffs ran at right angles to our shore line. None of the batteries could fire on them, for they were in 'dead water.' It was impossible for us to use high-angle fire, controlled from the highest point of that hill, against these ships, for the gun-mountings in these seaward batteries did not allow of enough elevation or of all-round fire. Telephone connections to the observation posts also were then only in process of construction. This simple manoeuver of the enemy rendered us absolutely helpless."

In any case proper control of any return fire that might have been brought to bear was quite out of the question. For both private and military lines went through the same central exchange, and obtaining a quick connection was as much out of the question as maintaining the secrecy of communications. Comfortably immune from all interference, the Japanese warships were free to pump 12-inch salvos into the New Town, both Basins, and their adjacent workshops, without the slightest fear of retaliation. At 11 A.M. the first line of warships steamed away, their stations being taken by the vessels of the second line; and punctually at 11.25 the bombardment was resumed. Fire had been switched to the inner harbour, where further damage was done to some of the craft under repair. To elude the rain of shells by putting to sea was out of the question. The smaller vessels dared not go out without the support of the battleships; and in the seven years that Port Arthur had been in Russian hands nothing had been done to deepen the harbour and its entrance. Big ships could go in and out with safety only at high water; and the Japanese had carefully chosen low water as the time for their shoot. Promptly at 1 P.M. the bombardment ended; the Japanese having fired two hundred 12-inch shells into the town and harbour without the Russians being in a position to return a single effective shot.

The garrison had undergone a humiliating ordeal, but the same silly sneers—"A Japanese? He's nothing but a mosquito; we'll stick a pin in him and send him home in a letter!" "They're just yellow apes, with a lust to kill"—were bandied about with a specious air of contempt that was tantamount to a schoolboy whistling in the dark to keep up his courage.

As the outcome of their first encounter with the Japanese and of the subsequent bombardment of the harbour, many of the Russian warships had suffered substantial injury. The *Retvisan* had a gash of over 40 feet by 20 in her side, and seven of her compartments were flooded. The *Tzesarevitch* had lost a propeller and a boss, and could be kept afloat only by constant pumping. There was no dry dock in which to effect repairs, so a big cavity was scooped out of the Basin's shore into which the *Tzesarevitch* was backed so that her damaged stern could be got at above water. But it was impossible, even with the use of cofferdams, to put the damaged vessels in full repair with the limited means available in Port Arthur. The real facilities were all to be found at Dalny; and the waters between the two ports were sown with enemy mines and patrolled by a vigilant enemy fleet. However, by a typical piece of blundering staff work, the shipwrights and artificers sent posthaste from the Baltic and destined for Dalny had been casually decanted at Port Arthur. Although short of many of their requirements, under the direction of the energetic engineer officer Kuteynikoff their skilled work did much to render the damaged warships once more relatively seaworthy. Even the unfortunate *Retvisan* was eventually pumped out, patched up, and refloated, and then brought by tugs to a berth in the West Basin, the divers and artisans of the Reval Salvage Company ably seconding the work of their fellow Balts.

The navy and the coastal artillery were fully on the alert. The more unruly elements of the garrison, on the other hand, bored for want of occupation, speedily took to marauding and petty larceny; the blacked-out streets at night became so dangerous to traverse that darkness found most of the civilian population behind locked doors—and this despite the savage flogging promptly awarded to those caught red-handed by the provost marshal, the heavy-handed martinet Colonel Petrusha.

News that the Japanese had passed on from Pyongyang to Anju on the Chechen River, something under seventy-five miles from the Yalu, reached Port Arthur only a day or two ahead of Lt. Gen. Konstantine Nikolaevitch Smirnoff. With the arrival of the newly appointed fortress commander, Port Arthur's sigh of relief must have made Stössel's ears positively burn. A truly professional soldier of wide experience, with a keen eye in a face that looked as if it had been rough-planed out of well-seasoned hickory, Smirnoff would have been any man's choice to lead a "forlorn hope" or hold a rear guard together like the immortal Marshal Ney. He was accompanied, as his chief of staff, by Maj. Gen. Roman Isidorovitch Kondratenko, all fire and energy, with a head set on his shoulders like a clenched fist. Without a moment's loss of time the two set about making a thorough inspection of the landward defences. It was a survey that left them very far from agreeing with the Order of the Day, circulated by Stössel preparatory to his scheduled departure to take up the command of the III Siberian Army Corps. For the flatulent boast that "Port Arthur is now an impregnable stronghold" bore so little relation to the facts that Smirnoff concentrated all his energies on hastening the construction of the many essential fieldworks that so far had been little more than spitlocked. Chinese coolie gangs—which included a strong infusion of Japanese agents— were roped in to accelerate the work. But they proved highly responsive to the propaganda spread among them by the aforesaid agents and deserted in great numbers when secretly presented with a leaflet which assured them that

> Port Arthur will soon be cut off, and then captured.
> No Chinaman who has in any way assisted the Russians to defend the place will be given quarter.

Far more than Stössel, Smirnoff recognized the strategical importance of Kin-chou, and his orders to the fortress commanding engineer authorized a heavy draft on the defence fund for the outwork's additional strengthening. Toiling as hard as the men who drudged and sweated on the rocky slopes above Port Arthur, all the general asked for was time to complete the herculean task he had taken so vigorously in hand—

time, and the removal to some other sphere of activity of the man whose clumsy, doltish interference baulked and delayed his work at every turn. For Stössel, like most men whose ability is in inverse ratio to their own good opinion of themselves, was as incapable of minding his own business as he was of intervening usefully in another's. But the newcomer at least contrived to fortify Liao-tieh-shan and arrange for high-angle fire over its hump, should the Japanese attempt to repeat their tactics of Mar. 10. As an additional precaution the gunboats *Otvanjy* and *Giliak* were stationed in the narrows as lookouts, and by night the cruisers took it in turn to patrol the outer roads. So long as Smirnoff and Makharoff remained in charge of its defences, Port Arthur would not again be caught napping.

So far the Japanese had gained several of the advantages that accrue to a belligerent who seizes the initiative. By landing troops in Korea, they had secured an intermediate base between the prospective theatre of operations and their main sources of supply. In any case these were far closer to Manchuria than those of their opponents, whose lengthy lines of communication were further handicapped by the limitations imposed by the single-track Siberian railway.

The main danger for the Japanese lay in the possibility of a sortie by the Pacific Ocean Squadron which would disrupt the steady and punctual transportation of the troops to Manchuria by sea. For the alternative was a long, intensely difficult, and wearing march across a countryside devoid of all good roads and abounding in defensive positions of which a resourceful enemy could take punishing advantage.

Furthermore, any interruption or delay in the deployment of the three army corps scheduled to concentrate against General Kuropatkin would present the Russian commander with an excellent opportunity to tackle his antagonists one by one and defeat them in detail. But as James Wolfe once commented, "War is an option of risks"; and there are greater risks involved in not taking any than ever attended boldness.

THE YELLOW FLOOD

"ENERGY, ENERGY—SPEED! APTITUDE FOR
WAR IS APTITUDE FOR MOVEMENT."

—NAPOLEON

3 VLADIVOSTOK'S PREPARATIONS to deal with the enemy had been almost as laggard and haphazard as those at Port Arthur. Additional ordnance for the city's defence had arrived well ahead of the declaration of war. But "when the Japanese made a surprise visit the guns still lay at the foot of the new forts, batteries were unmanned, and thus a very feeble reply could be made to the Japanese bombardment, which fortunately was not heavy."[1] Furthermore, on the remote chance that the Japanese might attempt an amphibious landing in the neighbourhood, two whole divisions and more than twenty squadrons were retained by way of garrison, troops that could have been employed far more advantageously with the field army.

Russian inefficiency was equally in evidence at Port Arthur. The destroyers *Boevoy* and *Silny* collided through sheer bad seamanship; and when the *Yenusei* struck a mine in Ta-lien Bay, the *Boyarin* and four destroyers were sent off pell-mell to investigate. "Before sailing, Captain Sarnichev, the commander of the *Boyarin*, had some conversation with Rear-Admiral Molas, from which it appears that there was some uncertainty as to the position of the mine-field that had been laid by the Russians. The Admiral thought it was probably in one place; Captain Sarnichev thought it was in another."[2] Small wonder that in such circumstances the *Boyarin* also struck a mine. The crew was taken off, and after two attempts to sink the vessel by torpedo had failed, the craft obligingly sank of her own accord. Nonetheless, the Russians continued to sow the sea with mines, some eight hundred being laid in Deep and Kerr Bays, and others in Eight Ships Bay and as far north as Niu-chuang. As they were not covered by shore batteries, it was only a matter of time before they were all swept by the Japanese.

Early on the morning of Mar. 22 the Japanese fleet, made up of six battleships, six armoured cruisers, and six second- and third-class cruisers, with attendant small craft, was sighted steaming toward Port Arthur in three divisions. By 7 A.M. the Russian cruiser squadron, with the *Askold* wearing Vice-Admiral Makharoff's flag, had slipped out into the roads. In their rear ploughed the battleships. At 9.30 the Japanese opened with a salvo from their 12-inch guns. The Russians replied with direct fire from their ships and indirect fire from the land batteries. But on neither side was the shooting anything but indifferent, and by eleven o'clock the Japanese had abandoned the fight and gone on their way unpursued. If it had been Togo's original intention to try and rush the port, the strength and greater alertness of its seaward defences had brought it home to him that the opportunity of a successful attack was past—if, indeed, it had ever existed. As with the Dardanelles expedition of eleven years later, it had to be recognized that conditions had not changed materially since the day when Collingwood had laid it down as axiomatic that "ships' guns unassisted by advancing troops are almost useless to destroy guns suitably mounted ashore." It was clear that Port Arthur could only be taken by sea and land forces acting in co-operation.

Frustrated in their attempt to overwhelm the Russian fleet and seaward defences, the Japanese fell back on an intensified blockade of the port. If the Russian fleet could not be destroyed in a general action, it could be bottled up and rendered ineffectual.

It was at 2.45 A.M. Mar. 27 when the blockers approached the roadstead, the *Yonemaro Maru* contriving to reach the fairway, where her explosive charge was detonated at the very moment she was struck by a torpedo. But her hulk only partially obstructed the gut; and the shore defences promptly sank the other three blockships well out of harm's way.

The jubilation occasioned by this successful defence of the harbour was speedily tempered by the intelligence that Stössel had been confirmed in his joint command of the Kuantun District and the stronghold of Port Arthur, Smirnoff as fortress commander coming under his orders.

Late on Mar. 27 Gen. Alexei Nicholaevitch Kuropatkin arrived at Liao-yang to take up operational command of the troops assembled in Manchuria. Born in 1845, the son of a provincial official, he had been educated at the Pavlosk War School and had first seen service with a Turkestan rifle battalion. Entirely without influence, he had fought his way up to the post of chief of staff to Skobeleff for the Central Asian expedition of 1876; he had taken part in the Turkish campaign of 1877–78, and in 1898 had been appointed Minister of War. Thoughtful and farsighted rather than dynamic, he was consistently hampered by his subordination to the viceroy—as were the activities of the army in the field. A divided command invariably gives rise to half measures; and in this case the blight of compromise, indecision, and tedious ratiocination came to overhang the whole campaign.

It had always been the contention of Viceroy Alexeieff and the naval staff that "the plan of operations should be based upon the assumption that it is impossible for our fleet to be beaten . . . and that a Japanese landing at Niu-chuang or in the Gulf of Korea is impracticable."[3] And despite the unfortunate trend of recent events, for the time being Alexeieff clung to this belief with an obstinacy that was proof against all argument.

It followed that Kuropatkin found himself in command of an extremely modest force of 59 battalions—of which two were sapper formations—39 squadrons and *sotnias*, and 140 guns. With reinforcements arriving from Russia in trickles it is understandable that the field commander should have doubted his ability to hold his ground in southern Manchuria during the first phase of the war, were that region to be invaded by the whole strength of the Japanese army. "We should count on Port Arthur being cut off for a considerable period," he wrote; "and in order to avoid defeat in detail, we should withdraw towards Harbin until reinforcements from Russia enable us to assume the offensive." Here was a fundamental difference of opinion as to the right course to pursue that was long to prevail and effectually bedevil the conduct of the whole campaign.

On the morning of Apr. 13, after a night of groping through relentless fog and rain, there was a sharp encounter between elements of both fleets. Almost surrounded by her enemies, the *Strashny* was sent to the bottom, a shell having struck her after torpedo tube just as the missile was about to be fired, setting the craft ablaze and strewing her decks with dead and injured. Hastening to the rescue of the wounded still struggling in the water, the flagship *Petropalovsk* was torn almost in two by a triple explosion that gutted her and filled the air with a tower of smoke and flame. In something under a couple of minutes the pride of the Pacific Ocean Squadron had vanished beneath the waves, the gallant Makharoff perishing with his ship. "In the opinion of some with a close knowledge of contemporary events, the loss of the flagship was attributable to 'carelessness on board.' "[4] It is far more likely that the *Petropalovsk* fouled some of the mines laid overnight by the newly arrived mine layer *Koryo Maru*. Only seven officers and seventy-three men were saved out of a crew of nearly nine hundred. Among those who went down with the ship was the celebrated war artist Vasili Verestchagin. The *Pobieda* was also damaged severely below the waterline; and with this the Russians lost their heads completely, firing wildly in all directions in the belief that they were under attack by submarine. Eventually the whole armament, including the crippled *Pobieda*, contrived to make harbour without further loss.

The Russians had lost two of their most powerful vessels.

But, of far graver consequence, death had robbed them of a leader it would be impossible to replace. An outstanding strategist and accomplished seaman, Admiral Makharoff had won the respect and personal loyalty of every officer and man who had ever served under him. He had been, moreover, the only man capable of making proper use of the fleet as a mobile aggressive force dedicated to the fulfilment of a navy's traditional task—"to seek out and destroy the enemy wherever he may be found." "It is not the loss of a battleship," one of the foremast hands was heard to lament; "the Japanese are welcome to two of them. It is *he!*"

Yet even without Makharoff to give it inspiration, the Pacific Ocean Squadron, under the protection of the fortress guns, was still a factor to be reckoned with, even under the command of the far less daring and gifted Admiral Witgeft.

On Apr. 14 the viceroy returned to Port Arthur "to organise the defence," although he now openly questioned "whether the place would be able to hold out for more than two or three months, in spite of the steps taken to strengthen the defences."

On Apr. 15 Port Arthur was again under bombardment for two hours by the *Kasuga* and *Nisshin*, firing from Pigeon Bay; and some hastily constructed fieldworks on Liao-tieh-shan were reduced to silence.

Ten days later the Japanese transports *Kinshu Maru* and *Goya Maru* fell foul of three Russian cruisers from Vladivostok, which had managed to elude Vice-Admiral Kamamura's squadron on patrol in the vicinity of Gensan. Both troopers were sunk, with 100 men killed or drowned, and 250 captured.

With every reason to doubt Alexeieff's claim that the Pacific Ocean Squadron had nothing to fear from the Japanese fleet, Kuropatkin's attention was concentrated on Vladivostok, Port Arthur, and his western frontiers, where the disapproving attitude of the Chinese gave rise to increasing uneasiness. In the army commander's view, the Russian force detached to the Yalu in no way committed him to serious operations on the Korean border, a course of action he was most anxious to avoid. In this approach to the problem he was in diametric opposition to Alexeieff, whose prime concern was to preserve the Bezobrazoff timber-cutting enterprise in whose success both he and his influential friends were intimately involved.[5] So as the month of April drew to a close, it was with growing dismay that the admiral learned that General Kuroki and his First Army were steadily approaching Wiju, facing the Russians on the Peking Road at Chiu-lien-cheng, on the far side of the Yalu. Bezobrazoff's sawmills would be fortunate if they did not find themselves in the firing line.

The first round had ended, with the Japanese clearly leading, but only on points. Although they had severely hammered the Russian fleet, they had failed to knock it out. Port Arthur had not been rushed out of hand, as it had been by General Yamaji in 1894, and its siege was the weighty task that now confronted them. Command of the sea, however, had endowed them with the freedom of movement they had so eagerly been awaiting.

General Kuroki's advance on the Yalu, for all that it had been urged with his accustomed energy, had been appreciably slowed down by the damage done to the single makeshift road from Pinyang to Wiju by consistently bad weather. But by May 1 three divisions supported by three reserve brigades, in all a little over 40,000 men, were ready to force the river crossing and sweep the 16,000 Russians confronting them back over the Fen-shui-ling passes.

At Chiu-lien-cheng General Zasulich was at the extremity of Kuropatkin's 400-mile front; and his instructions were to fight no more than a rear-guard action and on no account to become involved in a costly general engagement. Bad lateral communications together with a lack of Chinese carts—the only practicable type of transport—rendered it impossible to reinforce him even had such a course been advisable and the necessary troops available. But with the concentration of Kuroki's entire force, backed by an infinitely superior artillery, Zasulich proceeded obstinately to dig in his heels, fully prepared to fight it out. With the Russian troops dispersed over a twenty-four-mile front along the Yalu and its tributary the

Aiho, and in great uncertainty as to where the Japanese would attempt a crossing, gunboats demonstrating on the estuary first drew attention to the mouth of the river. A wide turning movement by the Japanese 12th Division then switched their opponents' gaze to the extreme left of their line. Under cover of these feints the Imperial Guards and the 2nd Division bridged the subsidiary channels and effected a crossing at the juncture of the Yalu and Aiho which brought them above Chiu-lien-cheng and at close grips with their adversaries.

Zasulich's men had an admirable field of fire, but "the Russian soldier is the worst shot existing in any great army in Europe,"[6] and although the volume of musketry was heavy enough to give pause to assailants undergoing their first ordeal by battle, the Japanese swiftly recovered and vigorously pressed forward. While the struggle raged in the centre, the 2nd Division succeeded in carrying Chiu-lien-cheng and the west side of the steep Suribachi-Yama that overlooked the village. With Zasulich's right crumpled, his exposed centre and left began to give way, and the whole line was forced into retreat.

The Russians were in full flight, but there was no immediate attempt to pursue them despite Kuroki's possession of fresh mounted troops that could well have been utilized for this purpose. "The popping of champagne corks had replaced the rattle of musketry,"[7] and in the intervals of celebrating their success the staff was busy with the regrouping of their disorganized forces. It was not until the last files of the rear guard were spotted hastening over the heights, 3,000 yards west of Chiu-lien-cheng, that word was given which again set the main body of the troops in motion.

The Russians' way of retreat was blocked by an isolated company of the Japanese Twenty-fourth Infantry Regiment. As the pursuit pressed on their heels the rearguard found themselves pinned down in the region of the lonely village of Ha-ma-tong. Trapped in a valley between two razor-back heights, they fought with the desperation of cornered animals; and it was not until they had been reduced to a pitiful, exhausted remnant that the white flag was hoisted to bring the slaughter

to an end. Under cover of this dogged delaying action, however, the rest of Zasulich's defeated force was able to make
good its escape.

At Kuropatkin's headquarters the news of Zasulich's defeat was received with what amounted to stunned incomprehension. It simply could not be true. But the backwash of
shamefaced fugitives told a tale that could not be misinterpreted. "The panic in the baggage train on the night following
the battle came to us in the guise of a panic flight on the part
of the whole detachment," recorded one of the army commander's staff. "None of us, not even on the Staff, was able to
imagine how the Japanese could have contrived not only to
cross an exceedingly wide river without punishment, and to
defeat our vanguard, but even to capture several guns."[8]

What the Russians had yet to grasp was, that when it
came to making war along modern lines they had a great deal
still to learn. Their gunners—always the arm in which the
Russians had taken the greatest pride—had done little to
camouflage their battery positions, dig in, or provide durable
splinter-proof cover for their gun crews. In a tactical sense they
had failed to absorb the lesson that a numerically weaker artillery can survive to play an effective part in the later stages of
the fight only by realizing that at the outset they must hold
back and await their chance. But as Captain Soloviev subsequently commented, "Our artillery had to operate under absolutely new and unknown conditions. Having been taught
during peace-time to select positions on the crest of hills, it
suffered great losses during the first period of the war, almost
useless losses. Our artillerymen are unanimous in saying our
guns are excellent, much better then the Japanese. But the
Japanese had been learning the ways of their guns for many
years, while in our army some of the units made the acquaintance of their guns on the road, and many were taught gunnery
in the railway cars."[9] For their part, the infantry consistently
preferred to construct breastworks and painfully conspicuous
entrenchments rather than make use of the natural cover that
abounded, supplemented by fieldworks well dug in and furnished with loopholes and good overhead protection. In gen-

eral, the Russians had failed signally to afford each other mutual support; while the co-operation of the Japanese formations, and particularly that between the land forces and the navy, had been of the very first order.

Japanese losses had come to a little over 1,000; the Russians reported 1,400 killed, 1,100 wounded, and 500 missing. Eight machine guns and twenty-one guns had been captured out of the eighty allotted to Zasulich's detached force.

From a strategic point of view, Kuropatkin had been woefully hampered by the viceroy's insistence that every effort should be made to hold the Yalu position firmly. Hence the army commander had been forced to assign the watch on his overextended left to a body of infantry and field guns—a course that invariably entails serious fighting—rather than to a holding force of Cossacks, mounted infantry, and horse artillery, who could have harassed, stung, and imposed delay, and still retained an excellent chance of getting away. Alexeieff, in his preoccupation with the Yalu position, had committed himself to dispersion rather than to concentration, forgetful of the fact that he who seeks to defend all, ends up by defending nothing.

But "the importance of this Yalu victory cannot be overestimated, for, though not a great battle, this fight between 40,000 Japanese and a considerably inferior force of Russians was the Valmy of Japan, because it lowered the prestige of Russia in the eyes of the world. This fact alone, that a small Eastern nation had in its first encounter defeated a great Western Power, shot like a glowing meteor over Asia."[10]

The emergence of the Japanese as victors in the Yalu battle not only added enormously to their international prestige, but appreciably enhanced their own fighting morale. In Port Arthur the news from the north was received with undisguised dismay. "We became convinced," Nojine recorded, "that we should be cut off and that the enemy were preparing to transport troops for a landing. There were continual rumours also that they would make another attempt to block the entrance to the harbour." Compared with this grim pros-

pect the sinking of the Japanese battleship *Hatsuse* and the
damage inflicted on the *Yashima* by a mine field laid well out
to sea by the plucky little *Amur*, were of no more than passing
consolation, particularly as Admiral Witgeft feebly let slip
the chance to engage the crippled vessel and its escort while
they were at a disadvantage. The *Yashima* subsequently went
down, but without any sacrifice of life, her loss being successfully concealed for many months, as was that of the second-
class cruiser *Yoshino*, sunk the same day as the result of a
collision in dense fog. The unfortunate *Amur* subsequently
fouled the wreck of a blocker sunk west of Liao-tieh-shan,
damaging herself badly. As it was impossible to dock her, she
had to be abandoned, and her work was taken over by the
Bogatyr and *Reshitelny*.

In general, Witgeft was far more concerned to perfect
an impregnable system of defence than to work out means of
bringing the enemy to battle. The fairway into Port Arthur
was straight, and therefore difficult to safeguard. Such booms
as were floated were not very effective. But the *Chailar* and
Charbin, of the Chinese Railway Company's fleet, were sunk
across the channel, as was the merchant vessel *Shilka* farther
in, so that the course was rendered far more difficult. The
Gilyak and some buoyed gunboats formed the first and second
lines of defence, backed up by the shore batteries at the foot
of Electric Hill. Finally, the *Askold* and the *Bayan* were positioned so that they could sweep the whole fairway with their
guns. Electric contact mines were laid along each side of the
channel, controlled from the shore, and a floating torpedo-net
defence was added subsequently, all of which measures had the
viceroy's unqualified approval.

With troop landings imminent, the Japanese were determined to confine the Russian warships to their harbour. At
midnight on the night of May 3 searchlights lancing out over
the sea picked up the Japanese fleet, and with commendable
speed the shore batteries went into action. A whirlwind of
cross fire set the narrows echoing as the Japanese blockers
were met by the shells of the *Giliak* and the gunboat *Otvanjny*.
On the bridge of the *Otvanjny* Alexeieff, to no one's particular

benefit, took personal charge of the attempt to sink the un-armoured enemy vessels where they would not foul the channel. Thoroughly aroused, "the whole fortress turned all its force to beyond the narrows, to which the doomed vessels, brilliantly lit up in the rays of the searchlights, were dashing at full speed."[11] In the offing the major elements of the Japanese fleet sought vainly to master the fire that had been concentrated on the blockships and their escorts.

"The enemy had doubtless heard from their spies that their previous attempts had miscarried, and similarly what measures we had taken against renewed attempts. They knew that they could no longer reach the entrance on a straight course, but would have to follow an artificially winding fairway. What did they do? Under the furious fire of our batteries and guard-ships they placed destroyers at the turning points. These showed the 'fire-ships' their path. Eye-witnesses described the pluck of these boats as simply fabulous. One of these destroyers was blown up by our mines, another was sunk by gunfire, and probably many were damaged. But they accomplished their task. . . . The 'fire-ships' numbered twelve. Four of these sank or could not face our fire and fled seawards. Eight held on. The whole of these eight steamers sank at a distance from the entrance, but two got through all the turns in the fairway and reached the *Chailar*. Fortunately they did not sink across the fairway. But that was neither their fault nor our merit, but mere chance."[12] Of the 27 officers and 207 seamen who had volunteered for the venture only 63 were rescued, of whom 20 were wounded. A few survivors were captured, taken half frozen from the rigging of their vessels; a few got ashore and, refusing to surrender, died fighting.

Despite the failure to seal off the Russian fleet completely, it gave so little sign of venturing forth that preparations for the troop landings went steadily forward. With Zasulich thrown back onto the Russian centre, any threat to the right flank and rear of a Japanese force landing on the eastern shores of the Liao-yang—Kuan-tun peninsula had finally been dissipated. On May 4, therefore, General Oku began the landing of the 1st, 2nd, 3rd and 4th Divisions of his Second Army at

Pi-tzu-wo and at Ta-lien-wan, a little farther southwest, on Hand Bay; the whole operation screened by naval units working from their forward base on the Elliot Islands. The 5th Division was scheduled to follow close on its predecessors' heels. Each division consisted of twelve battalions of infantry, one regiment (three squadrons) of cavalry, thirty-six guns, and one battalion (three companies) of engineers—approximately 18,000 men. Also put ashore was the First Artillery Brigade, of three regiments, or 108 guns.

Pi-tzu-wo was only a little over sixty miles east by northeast of Port Arthur, Ta-lien-wan even closer. But no serious steps had been taken to oppose a hostile landing, although there was a certain amount of skirmishing with Colonel Tretyakov's troops, pushed out from Kin-chou. The harbour facilities at these two places were not nearly so good as at Dalny, but the Japanese simply could not credit that the best entry port on the whole of the east coast should have been left entirely undefended save for a hastily laid mine field and a handful of Cossacks. In the circumstances, almost three weeks were required to complete the disembarkation, severely handicapped as it was by the continued bad weather. At Ta-lien-wan "innumerable small boats were fastened to steam launches like beads on a rosary. Rolling and tumbling, these rosaries of boats would whistle their way to the shore."[13] So rapid had been Japan's metamorphosis from medievalism to modernity that there were officers in these landing parties who had fought in armour and with two-handed samurai swords.

On the evening of May 4 Captain Pekarsey of the gunboat *Otvanjny* suddenly appeared in his wardroom. "Gentlemen," he said, "I've just got a message to say that the enemy are in process of landing at Pi-tzu-wo. The Viceroy, in accordance with Imperial orders, leaves for Mukden tomorrow." There was a long silence—the silence of shamed and angry men kept idle and impotent when every instinct and tradition urged them to intervene where their enemies were being brought ashore without a finger raised to dispute their landing. "Suppressed indignation prevailed throughout the squadron, and grew from day to day."[14]

Hurriedly relinquishing the naval command to Rear Admiral Witgeft, Alexeieff ordered a special train to take him north before the Japanese could cut the line. With somewhat questionable guile, the viceroy had a car full of wounded attached to the several coaches required to accommodate himself and a staff numbering no less than ninety-three; "and a Red Cross flag was shown when the train was stopped by the enemy's infantry at Pu-lien-ten. They tried ineffectually to stop the train by rifle fire when they found they had been deceived."[15] But Alexeieff got through; and two days later the line was almost entirely in Japanese hands. None the less Kuropatkin called for volunteers to hurl a trainload of ammunition into Port Arthur to help in the stronghold's defence. Under the command of the gallant Colonel Spiradov, the cars were loaded up and the train set off, every precaution having been taken to blow it up rather than let it fall into enemy possession. Since the invaders had not yet found time to block the line securely, the precious consignment got through and was thankfully welcomed by the fortress artillery commander, General Biely.

As a legacy for Port Arthur's defenders Alexeieff left a document—a minute the Council of War had automatically endorsed—which categorically laid it down that "the Pacific Ocean Squadron is momentarily in such a situation that active enterprise has no chance of success. On these grounds, therefore, all its means must be utilised for the defence of Port Arthur until better times come round again." Bitterly resented by the more enterprising officers, this defeatist instruction was universally dubbed "The Great Edict of Renunciation of the Navy." Since the terms of the directive were speedily in Japanese hands, it was all they needed to reassure them that such chance of interference with their landing operations as had previously existed had dwindled to the infinitesimal. The green light had been given them to go ahead without fear of molestation. "They disembarked their army, with guns, transport, provisions, etc., etc., just as at peace manoeuvres," Semenoff sourly recorded. Indeed, except for the foundering of the *Miyaka* in Kerr Bay after striking a mine, the disembarkation was carried through without any serious mishap.

On the western coast of the Kuan-tun peninsula, some

fifteen miles straight across country from Pi-tzu-wo, lay Port Adams. At the urgent request of the lean, tremendously energetic General Oku, thirty escorted troop transports had landed a substantial force there, which immediately linked up with the formations to the east. Without the least loss of time a cordon, steadily strengthened, was deployed across the neck of the isthmus to complete Port Arthur's isolation, the northern face being guarded by the newly landed 5th Division. The whole of the Kuan-tun peninsula was in a state of siege, and in Port Arthur itself the unfortunate troops had already been put on shortened rations.

While the Japanese elements consolidated their grip on Port Adams and the line of posts linking it with Pi-tzu-wo, General Oku steadily completed his arrangements for a dual assault on Kin-chou and the strongly fortified eminence of Nan-shan, some forty miles from Port Arthur. Situated on the narrow neck of the Kuan-tun peninsula—in width, at high tide, no more than 3,500 yards from the eastern to the western shore—Nan-shan, rising to a height of 400 feet, had an air of absolute impregnability. Fully prepared against assault, 20,000 men were available for its defence, although in actual fact no more than 4,000 were actively engaged in the struggle for its retention. The muddle and confusion attendant on the concentration of this force was only too typical of the sorry sense of command common both to Stössel and General Fock, the G.O.C. of the 4th Siberian Rifle Division, as was the fatal indecision which prevailed over Dalny. For although a committee had solemnly deliberated the matter, no comprehensive steps had been taken either to destroy or to dismantle and remove the valuable repair shop and dockside equipment; while the Fifteenth and Sixteenth East Siberian Rifle Regiments were first ordered into the haven for its defence and then entrained and brought back to Port Arthur. In desperation, some of the harassed and bewildered officers took counsel of General Smirnoff. As far as he could, he sought to straighten out the labyrinthine tangle. But there was not a great deal he could do, since his authority did not extend beyond the glacis, and even within the confines of the fortress itself he could be overruled at a word from the consequential Stössel, or even at a hint from the governor's wife, who "interfered in everything."[16]

Oku's first objective was Kin-chou, which obviously had to be taken before any assault on Nan-shan could successfully be mounted. Both Stössel and Fock had hastily revised their assertion that the place was unassailable; and indeed its hurriedly strengthened defences would have inspired few troops with confidence. For some reason unexplained, the Japanese attempted its capture by a night attack, which was met and held, at heavy sacrifice, by the men of the Fifth East Siberian Regiment. Heavy rain and a violent thunderstorm so seriously added to the obscurity and uncertainty in which all night operations are conducted that the attack was broken off before the town had actually fallen. Nonetheless, by the early morning of May 26 the attenuated Russian force had evacuated the place, which was promptly occupied by the Japanese.

The Russians' main defence line was disposed along the hills that crowded the narrow strip of territory lying between Nan-shan Bay[17] and Ta-lien-wan. Between the hills and Nan-shan Bay a strip of flat ground, at low tide about half a mile wide, led round to the rear of the Russian position. To the southeast another stretch of fairly level going gave passage to the road and railway which ran, by way of Nan-kuan-ling junction, to Port Arthur. Since Nan-shan was the obvious cornerstone of the defences, it was the Japanese aim to outflank and ultimately envelop it.

At 5.30 A.M. on May 26 the struggle opened with an artillery duel in which the Japanese gradually gained the upper hand. At 6 A.M. blue-coated infantry[18] started their advance from the westward extremity of the line, emerging from the shelter of the southern wall enclosing the neighbouring township of Tsintchow, a useful cover Stössel had failed to destroy for want of the necessary explosive.[19] The tide was high and many of the troops had to wade through the shallows. At the same time the Japanese field artillery was brought forward, and support fire was opened by the gunboats *Tsukusi, Heiyen, Akaji,* and *Chokai,* operating from Nan-shan Bay.

At 9 A.M. the first consolidated infantry attack was launched against the defences dug at the foot of the hills. Although the many permanent works and the elaborate trench system of Nan-shan were relatively thinly manned, the assault waves were met with vigorous resistance. But the Russians were at a hopeless disadvantage. As the centre of what soon became three-quarters of a circle, the Japanese guns could concentrate on them as a focus, while the Russian artillery had to distribute their shells over the periphery, their lines of fire diverging like the sticks of a fan. But there was plenty of fight in the infantry manning their trenches. The Tokio Division, making a frontal attack on the east face of the position, encountered such a reception as to be halted and thrown back, two companies being wiped out. The Japanese advancing along the Nan-shan Bay foreshore encountered artillery fire at relatively close range. "The tide was falling and the enemy was trying to turn our flank," one participant subsequently reported. "What their strength was at the beginning I can't say. Probably they had already suffered losses on our front. What we had before our guns appeared to be a battalion, but they had Colours and had therefore once been a regiment. The enemy wheels towards the beach and straight at us: the men only advance with difficulty, wading in water up to the chest. The bottom is slippery clay; we open fire; nearly every shot is a hit; whoever is hit in the leg falls and is drowned, none of them rise again. They become fewer and fewer, but on they come. The Colours move about, they pass from one hand to another; still they are advancing. Only with the last man did the Colours sink into the water; only then did I realise what we had felt at the thought—'The enemy will be on top of us at once.' "[20]

On the left an attempt at encirclement had been broken up by vigorous fire from the Russian gunboat *Bobr*, which, with great daring, had put in to Hand Bay and brought all its armament to bear on the men of the Nagoya Division advancing across the neck of the miniature Liu-shu-tun peninsula. Safe behind a mine field that kept the Japanese naval craft from interfering with them, a Russian force was standing by in three transports, temporarily moored in Hand Bay; and with these troops being landed it seemed as if the Japanese must be caught between two fires. On the strength of this exhilarating prospect an excited officer "sent a report to the effect that the Japanese had been repulsed and were on the run. The news of a victory was instantly telegraphed to General Stössel in Port Arthur, and was at once circulated all over the town. In Stössel's Head-quarters a convivial company gathered to drink champagne."[21]

It is always dangerous to start skinning the wolf without first having made sure he is dead. For as it transpired, victory was already veering to the other side. One by one the reck-lessly exposed Russian batteries fell silent, either from shortage of ammunition or as the result of the hammering they had received from the Japanese artillery, among which the handy little mountain guns had accomplished wonders. Like the 7.62-cm mountain gun subsequently developed by the Russians, the Japanese quick-firing weapon and its carriage could be trans-ported on six pack animals and was therefore extremely mobile and adaptable.

At one-thirty the attack worked up to a new intensity, its vortex being the sector in rear of Kin-chou, held with rare tenacity by the remnants of the Fifth East Siberians. In the middle of the onslaught General Fock arrived at Nan-kuan-ling to take over command of his East Siberian Division. He was determined, however, that the 16,000 men of his command, waiting in reserve, should not be embroiled so long as there were others to sustain the fight.

At four o'clock there was a lull, but it was no more than the ominous hush that precedes a storm. The receding tide had left a wider strip of Nan-shan Bay foreshore exposed, and the Japanese made use of this to extend their line against the Russian left, which Fock still obstinately refused to reinforce. With a little more room to manoeuvre, the Osaka Division closed in with such resolution that they were able to obtain a footing on the flank and well around to the rear of the Russian defences. The northern half of the position on Nan-shan had already been carried by the unflinching Tokio Division, and it was the Osaka men's aim to press even farther southward so as to swing round and bar the Russians' escape route by way of Nan-kuan-ling. Away on the Russian right a cavalry contingent, which had been thrown out to protect the flank, "had been surprised from behind; they had no way to retreat, were driven into the sea, and there were almost all drowned."[22]

The assault against the Russian left was pressed home with such determination that the sharpshooters' companies of the centre were in grave danger of being cut off and rolled up from the flank. Yet a general withdrawal during the hours of daylight was out of the question, and the weary men held on under a tempest of rifle fire until, with the sun declining, the core of the defence began to crumple. Instantly the Japanese were upon it, hurling back those who were not surrounded and killed, or taken prisoner. With that the whole front dissolved in chaos as "in the dim light the flashes of the enemy artillery showed up against the dark mass of Mount Samson like long threads of fire, like golden chains swaying up and down, rocking to and fro."[23] With the Rising Sun ensign floating over Nan-shan and the ruptured firing line everywhere stumbling back, panic quickly infected the troops held in the rear. "The din and confusion were awful," Colonel Tretyakov subsequently recorded, "and from the bivouacs behind us shots and volleys were heard. Together with other Officers near me I rushed to the rear to restore order. I also ordered our band to strike up a march, and, thank God, its martial strains restored confidence among the fugitives."

But the hard fact was that the Russians had abandoned the field and with it many of their heavy guns. Moreover, it was clear that their artillery had been hopelessly outmatched. The Japanese batteries had been more cunningly concealed from observation, more alertly served, and more efficiently commanded. The whole battlefield "showed clearly the terrible effect of their fire. The hills presented the appearance of a rabbit warren; there was hardly a square yard which did not show a hole where a shell had burst. In places the entrenchments were entirely destroyed and the gun emplacements blown away. . . . A captured Russian non-commissioned Officer stated that his company, the 8th of the 5th Siberian Sharpshooters, were stationed in the most advanced trench on the east side, facing the 1st Division. At the commencement of the action they were 250 strong, and in the evening 26 men answered the roll."[24]

Japanese losses in this preliminary battle for Port Arthur were heavy—4,885 killed and wounded, out of approximately 43,000 men engaged. But those of the Russians, in proportion to the number of men actually embroiled, were shattering—1,416, or over 40 per cent; while eighty-two guns and ten machine guns fell into the victors' hands. High as the price the Russians had exacted, it was not too much to pay for the capture of Nan-shan, Kin-chou, and the invaluable entry port of Dalny, which, quickly cleared of mines and such rubble as minor sabotage had occasioned, furnished the vital line of communications for subsequent operations against Port Arthur from the landward side.

Nan-shan was the first, but by no means the last, occasion on which the Japanese employed their favourite tactical manoeuvre—a heavy flank attack made simultaneously with a frontal assault, "the latter usually consisting of two distinct and separate attacks from different points; a combination the Russians never resisted with ultimate success."[25]

In this battle it is arguable whether it would have been wiser for the Russians to put all their available resources into a maximum effort to throw the Japanese into the sea, or to have fallen back on Port Arthur without becoming too heavily engaged. As it transpired, compromise and half measures had ruled the day, and exacted their inevitable penalty.

A retreat is always an extremely difficult movement to keep under control even by the most experienced staff. But the withdrawal of the beaten and dejected Russian legions on Port Arthur was a night of maniac pandemonium and bitter, unalleviated agony. "The evacuation had not been prepared for. We had intended to maintain ourselves on the isthmus several weeks longer. The result was utter confusion; the same troops which had only just repulsed the attack of the enemy's best forces like heroes, retired in complete disorder. . . . The result was that we fired on our own supply columns. Once it was still worse; two regiments skirmished against one another and nearly had a battle by themselves."[26] One battery, having taken the road in reasonably good order, "was almost swept away by the other batteries galloping on top of it in the dark."[27] The rail junction at Nan-kuan-ling was an inferno, for the few medical officers available were working under conditions of incredible difficulty, toiling by the dim light of a few storm lanterns among the heaps of wounded and dying, piled into cattle trucks. No proper Red Cross arrangements had been organized, nor any steps taken to furnish the hot meal that the soldier craves above all things in the aftermath of a fight. Some baggage cars were found that yielded a little bread, but its subsequent distribution was haphazard, and it went to the men whose officers exhibited the greatest enterprise in claiming a share of it. There was even a lack of ordinary drinking water; the boiler of one engine being surreptitiously emptied to help eke it out. The injured lay everywhere, racked with thirst, tortured with hunger, and numbed by the piercing cold. "The first and second-class refreshment rooms were filled with Officers, whose numbers were being momentarily increased by fresh arrivals by train, on horseback, on bicycles and on foot. Nobody knew anything or what to do: everyone waited for orders which did not come, for none of the commanders was there. The majority of the senior Officers, having eaten, were lying on the floor."[28]

Men who could still keep their feet or sit a horse crowded the road that swept up hill and down dale to curve into Port Arthur. As always, there were alarmists to raise the cry "The enemy cavalry are coming!" and with their shouts the heaving column would quicken its pace awhile, only to drop back into the dragging shuffle that was its normal gait.

Not far from Nan-kuan-ling station the highway merged with the road from Dalny, which was choked with civilian refugees who had been held in the town on Stössel's direct instruction; some of them having originally left Port Arthur to seek safety in the very place from which they were now in flight. Not till the beaten Russian forces were in full retreat from Nan-shan had belated permission been forthcoming for Dalny's evacuation. By this time all the rolling stock had been requisitioned by the military, while the few horsed carriages to be found in the place were scarcely sufficient to accommodate the sick and aged. A few of the more fortunate were able to hire rickshaws, while Chinese carts were procured to transport such baggage and personal possessions as could be crammed into them. Some of the fugitives had set out along the shore route by way of Shao-ping-tau. But the majority took the better, if longer, Central Road; over thirty-five miles of weary tramping, with the river Tai to cross and the ridge of the Green Hills to negotiate before Port Arthur even came in sight—and with the fear of the Japanese haunting every step.

Stössel's orders to the mayor of Dalny to blow up all the railway cars remaining on the sidings came too late, even had the unfortunate official possessed the explosives and the necessary knowledge of their use to undertake the task. Dalny was just another gift this military dunderhead had handed his opponents on a platter; although it was some twenty-four hours before the Japanese took possession. In the interim the town was thoroughly looted by predatory Chinese from the surrounding villages, and by gangs of Hunhuses—brigands and cattle rustlers—from the surrounding hills.

Known to the more disinterested Russians as the *lishni* (unwanted) haven, Dalny had been designed as a port of commerce, very largely in the interest of Bezobrazoff and his Royal Timber Company, who proposed erecting their principal sawmills where rail facilities were conveniently at hand. Some $17,500,000 had been laid out on the docks, and with the minimum of effort the Japanese were able to restore them to full working order. Their facilities were to prove of the greatest service in landing the 11-inch howitzers eventually brought in for Port Arthur's bombardment.

With panic and inextricable confusion on the roads into Port Arthur, "that same night the first destroyer flotilla was got ready in a great hurry and was sent into Society Bay [Nan-shan Bay]. They were to attack the Japanese gunboats, which had fired on the left flank and thus supported the attack of the right wing of the Japanese Army. This expedition of our destroyers ended disastrously. The gunboats, naturally, were not found; as a matter of course they had gone to the open sea for the night. When the *Vnushitelny* was looking for them amongst the islands, she grounded on a rocky patch. She had to be blown up so as not to fall into the hands of the enemy."[29]

And so it went. At sea as on the land, fumbling, stupidity, and a lack of the most elementary professionalism exacted their inevitable toil.

It was over twenty-four hours before the last of the hungry and worn-out refugees from Dalny reached the temporary sanctuary of the port. And it must stand to the eternal credit of the town's inhabitants that in the midst of their own uncertainty and distress they promptly opened a subscription list to help the wretched folk who, in one night, had lost their homes and everything they possessed. A few of those who had brought away a store of money or valuables joined with some of the wealthier of Port Arthur's residents to charter junks to take them to Chefu, in the Chinese province of Shantung. But many were left behind to share the perils and privations of a garrison that was soon to find itself under close siege.

With the fall of Nan-shan and Kin-chou, the reorganization of the Japanese invasion corps was speedily implemented. With the First and Second Armies faced about to march on Kuropatkin and the armanent mustering in and around Liao-yang and Hai-cheng, General Nodzu's Fourth Army, of two divisions, was landed at Ta-ku-shan to form a connecting link between Kuroki and Oku. The Third Army, of two divisions —later increased to four—was retained under Nogi's command for the capture of Port Arthur. Of the mobile field force Oku's men were the first in motion, marching north along the railway.

All this realignment of the Japanese troops took time— time in which the Russians were accorded an invaluable breathing space in which to reorganize and take up position in defences they had been given even further opportunity to strengthen. But instead of taking advantage of this heaven-sent delay, Stössel proceeded to add to the general confusion by getting at loggerheads with the fortress commander, insisting that although Smirnoff might have been charged with the safekeeping of the fortress as such, his own authority, as governor of the district—what was left of it!—was paramount. To Smirnoff's protest that it was the Tsar's personal order that rendered him directly responsible for Port Arthur's defence, Stössel curtly retorted, "You will remain Commandant, but *I* shall run the Fortress. Whether legal or not is my affair. I will answer for that."

Inevitably, news of Stössel's highhanded self-assertion leaked out, and there were those who suggested that the principal medical officer should invalid the governor and forcibly detain him in hospital. Others swore that the day and the hour had been settled when Smirnoff would surround Stössel's official residence and arrest him, together with Fock and several others. But Smirnoff was a man trained in the school of strict subordination, and however difficult the position in which he found himself, discipline demanded that he should accept it and make the best of it.

"The prime qualities of a soldier," that hard-bitten veteran George Monck had once remarked, "are valour and sufferance." Smirnoff's valour had never been in question; but no man's capacity for sufferance can ever have been put to a more galling test.

DIVIDED COUNCILS

"FORTRESSES ARE USEFUL IN OFFENSIVE AS WELL
AS DEFENSIVE WARFARE. TRUE, THEY WILL NOT IN
THEMSELVES ARREST AN ARMY BUT THEY ARE AN EX-
CELLENT MEANS BY WHICH TO RETARD, EMBARRASS,
WEAKEN AND ANNOY AN ENEMY."

—NAPOLEON

4 ALEXEIEFF'S *stratégie de la bourse* had been founded on the delusive belief that even if Kuroki were successful in crossing the Yalu, he would be committed to the long, exhausting overland march from Chiu-lien-cheng northwestward on Mo-tien-ling and Liao-yang, a course which would afford Kuropatkin ample time to complete the muster of his reserves. What the viceroy had failed to allow for was the possibility that the Japanese would speed up the movement of their troops by employing sea transport to land them at Pi-tzu-wo and Hon-tu-shih, near the mouth of the Ta-sha-Ho in Ta-lien Bay.

With two sharp reverses to lend emphasis to the folly of dispersion, the army commander bent all his energies to the task of redirecting the strategy of the campaign on sounder lines. For the Japanese were rapidly building up their resources, while Alexeieff's "fleet in being" continued to crouch inertly behind its booms and mine fields. Indeed, some of its guns and their personnel had already been brought ashore on the grounds that they would help in strengthening Port Arthur's landward defences. These had already been supplemented by some forty rusty pieces, brought away from the loot of Tientsin in 1900, which had been found mouldering in the dockyard, refurbished, and hauled into position in the lunettes on whose completion Smirnoff was toiling so furiously.

As it appeared to Kuropatkin and his advisers, either a concerted effort must be made to reopen communication with Port Arthur, or, accepting Stössel's qualified assurance as to the stronghold's ability to hold out, the Japanese must be kept in check somewhere forward of Liao-yang while a sufficient body of troops was mustered between Harbin and Mukden to permit the prosecution of a victorious offensive. Time was of the essence, since the Russian War Office calculated that at least six months would be required before a maximum of 145,000 men could be assembled in the theatre of war.[1] Provided Port Arthur could withstand assault, obviously it would be wiser temporarily to adopt a purely Fabian strategy.

Up to the middle of May one only of the twelve formations promised as reinforcements had put in an appearance—the 2nd Siberian Division. Although considerably under strength, its arrival spurred the viceroy to send Kuropatkin a letter, by the hand of his chief of staff, General Jilinsky, suggesting that the time had come for an advance on the Yalu or, alternatively, on Port Arthur. Not unnaturally, Kuropatkin strongly questioned the advisability of embarking on any offensive movement until it could be undertaken with sound prospects of success. At this juncture Stössel suddenly abandoned his former tone of braggadocio to protest to the viceroy that Port Arthur had been provisioned to subsist no more than a dozen battalions for a year. It followed that with the presence within the fortress of twenty-seven battalions the stronghold could scarcely be expected to hold out even for the six months originally predicated.[2] On May 31, therefore, Alexeieff "urgently requested" Kuropatkin to advance to the relief of the fortress and "expressed the wish that four Divisions should be detailed for the operation."

Again the army commander raised cogent objections, whereupon Alexeieff telegraphed that "Port Arthur cannot strictly be called a storm-proof fortress, and it is a question whether it can even stand a siege of the length indicated in my telegram of May 16th"—that is, of two or three months.

The Russian Intelligence service being the faulty organization it was,[3] Kuropatkin had only recently been informed of the landing of the Japanese Fourth Army at Hon-tu-Shih and was still perplexed as to the exact whereabouts of the lines of deployment of the other three. It was incumbent upon him, therefore, to take advantage of the fact that he was working on interior lines and to keep his forces together, ready to meet the attack of two or even three armies. His best hope was that they might prove to be too widely separated to afford each other full support. If any offensive movement were to be undertaken, a diversionary drive on the Yalu, even to draw enemy troops away from Port Arthur, was quite out of the question, sore blow as this might be to Alexeieff and the sponsors of the Royal Timber Company. The terrain was remote from the railway; local food resources had been pretty well exhausted; there was no transport to sustain a large force so far from its base; should the Japanese fall back on the river line, the offensive would come to a standstill, having struck no more than an empty blow in the air.

If any operation were to be risked at all, then the contingent under Gen. Hokyo Oku, said to be advancing along the railway line toward Te-li-ssu, should prove the least hazardous objective, provided a superior force could be swiftly concentrated against him and resolutely employed. But troops had to be found to hold the Fen-shui-ling mountain passes, cover Hai-cheng, and fully protect Liao-yang, "the key of the strategic position of the Russian armies."[4] If any general reserve were to be held in hand, not more than twenty-five battalions could be assigned for an offensive move against Oku and a force estimated to total some 20,000.

It could not be overlooked, moreover, that if Nogi's Third Army were to be taken up from in front of Port Arthur and whipped aboard ship for transportation to Ying-kou, the Treaty Port serving theoretically neutral Niu-chuang,[5] any Russian force operating in the neighbourhood of Te-li-ssu would be caught in the jaws of the Japanese pincers. In any case, to despatch a Russian force 130 miles from its main body was gravely to risk its being cut off by Gen. Itei Kuroki's army moving up from the coast, or by a corps striking due west from Hon-tu-shih.

Kuropatkin's argument in favour of conserving his strength while steadily building it up would seem to be irrefutable. But the viceroy was in a position to overrule him and did not hesitate to exert his authority. Port Arthur, he insisted, was in grave need of help, and something must be done to relieve it. What he entirely failed to realize was, that it was not so much Port Arthur that required to be relieved as the man in ostensible command of it!

Perhaps even stronger than any pseudostrategical considerations put forward by Viceroy Alexeieff in favour of an advance, was the political need for a little encouraging "window dressing" to counteract the depressing effect exerted on the home population by the defeat of Russian arms at Yalu and Nan-shan. Only consistent victory from the very outset would have served to redeem the struggle in the Far East from its general unpopularity with the mass of the Russian people. Alexeieff had no difficulty, therefore, in engineering a message from the highest quarters insisting that "the time is ripe for the Manchurian Army to assume the offensive." In the face of what amounted to an Imperial ukase Kuropatkin had no option but to suppress his reluctance to risk the defeat in detail of yet another detached force, and issue orders to General Shtakelberg, commanding the 35,000 men of his right wing, to assume the offensive toward Port Arthur.[6]

To some extent, to permit a stronghold to come under siege is, in itself, an admission of military failure. Those besieged have surrendered the priceless asset of mobility; the forces of investment, having failed to inflict defeat upon their opponents in the field, have lost the invaluable power of manoeuvre. It is therefore a bludgeoning, head-on affair to which both sides have allowed themselves to be committed, with prepared positions, the concentration of the apparatus of defence, the desperate courage of the cornered animal, and the hope of relief by outside forces as the assets of the besieged, and with famine the spectral ally of the besiegers. To this must be added the waning morale of an ill-supplied, cooped-up civilian population in ever-present danger.

Peril and privation will wear down the stoutest spirit; and in Port Arthur morale was none too high even at the outset. Letters from home reflecting the mood of seething dissatisfaction with the progress of the war and the authorities responsible for its guidance only added to the general demoralization of people whose own prospects afforded them more than sufficient grounds for uneasiness. Furthermore, the local inhabitants were denied the safety valve of criticism and complaint. For Stössel had imposed a strict censorship on all outgoing private mail, and any letters hinting at the true state of affairs prevailing within the fortress were destroyed and their writers sharply punished.

There were already shortages in the shops, accompanied by a sharp increase in prices. Inflation had been checked, so far as staple commodities were concerned, by Stössel's order regulating their price—one of his few sensible measures. A thriving black market catered for those with long purses, however; and there was small satisfaction to be derived from the knowledge that there would be no profiteering on bread when there was remarkably little bread on which to profiteer. There were, of course, a number of vessels plying out of Chefu that were prepared to try and run the blockade with cargoes extending from assorted munitions to articles of everyday consumption. But Stössel "refused all proffers of assistance, saying we required nothing, and this in the face of Smirnoff's protests that big gun ammunition, preserved meat, vegetables, hospital appliances, etc., were urgently needed. . . . One day a steamer owned by a private Frenchman ran into Pigeon Bay with supplies, among which was a large stock of tinned milk. It was with the greatest difficulty that Stössel could be got to take this, yet milk was one of the first things to run out; and he warned the captain not to come again."[7]

To add to the general feeling of unease that overhung Port Arthur, considerable ill-feeling had arisen between the personnel of the army and navy. Under the ineffectual

Witgeft no serious attempt had been made either to challenge the Japanese fleet or to impede the landing of enemy troops and supplies. Criticism of the admiral among the junior officers was bitter and outspoken, and went entirely unrebuked by their immediate seniors. Furthermore, "the Army violently accused the Squadron of having been caught unprepared by the enemy's attack. The Navy, on the other hand, maintained that the Fortress had been taken by surprise by the war. On February 9th only two hastily prepared batteries had been able to support the Squadron. The remainder had not been manned, and the guns were still swaddled up for the winter. It was a case of the kettle and the pot."[8] The only common ground between army and navy was to be found in their mutual detestation of all those of alien race. "A quiet young American, a clerk in one of the firms, was struck by a Naval Officer in Saratoff's restaurant for no other reason than that he was a foreigner."[9] Nor was this the only instance of an almost hysterical xenophobia. But owing to the general dearth of non-Muscovites—other than Orientals—displays of ill-temper had largely to be confined to the two services; and "scarcely a day passed without a conflict between the Officers of the two branches."[10] In the drinking dens of the Old Town there were frequent brawls between soldiers and sailors, which called for the forceful intervention of the military police. Moreover, according to rumour, Stössel, instead of striving to make the two services pull together, tried to gain cheap popularity among his entourage by openly deriding Admiral Witgeft and the "fleet in being" that never left its moorings. In nervous alarm at the numerous instances of bickering in the streets and *bistros*, some of the more responsible residents sought and eventually secured grudging permission to form a Town Guard. This was subsequently transformed into a body of militia, into which all the male inhabitants of the town were forcibly conscripted; the younger men took their turn in the defences, with a certain amount of time allowed them to attend to their own business affairs, while the older members were detailed for duty in the hospitals and stores. All things considered, Port Arthur was scarcely in the right mood to confront an enemy so ruthless and so dedicated as the Japanese.

In the scramble back from Nan-shan the Russians had made no offensive move against a Japanese force they considerably outnumbered, and left no more than outlying pickets on the excellent natural defensive position along the line of the Green Hills, stretching in a seventeen-mile arc from Lun-wan-tun Bay, on the southeast, to Shan-tai-ko, on Ying-cheng-zu Bay,[11] to the northwest. Forward of the main ridge was the commanding height of Kuen-san, from which flanking fire could be brought to bear along the whole of the range and its forward slopes.

Nogi had been able to bring no more than limited pressure to bear on the Russian defence line, since, until May 31, when the 11th Division was landed at Kerr Bay, his strength was some 10,000 less than that of his opponents, who, moreover, were falling back on partially prepared positions. Furthermore, even with strengthened forces, the general's immediate prospects were gravely handicapped by the loss of the siege train intended to support the Port Arthur offensive. For eighteen 28-cm howitzers had been sunk when the Vladivostok squadron, once more eluding Admiral Kamamura's detached force, had encountered the transports *Izami Maru*, *Hitachi Maru*, and *Sado Maru*. The two first-named had been sent to the bottom with all the pieces of ordnance stowed in their holds, the troops aboard, 1,100 men of the Guard *Kobi* (or Reserve) brigade being either shot, drowned, or taken captive. The *Sado Maru* narrowly escaped a similar fate. "The loss of the guns to General Nogi cannot be too much dwelt upon, for they were part of the pre-arranged plan to capture the town by assault after a terrific bombardment; and three batteries of the heaviest guns ever employed at any time by an army assuming the offensive, would materially have altered the scheme of escalade."[12]

Nonetheless, with General Nogi's headquarters established at Pei-pao-tze-ai and ten transports a day landing everything other than heavy artillery for the army of investment, Japanese patrols probed steadily forward into the Green Hills.

It was General Fock's oft-reiterated view that it would only be wasting time, men, and ammunition to try and stand on the Green Hills line; that it would be far better to withdraw behind Port Arthur's permanent fortifications without delay, the better to man the stronghold with the maximum number of troops. Smirnoff was equally insistent that the outlying positions should be held as long as possible, so that unfinished work on the fortifications could be carried to completion. He further pointed out that with the Japanese in possession of Kuen-san and the two eminences of Ta-ku-shan and Sia-gu-shan, farther to the rear, they could bring indirect fire to bear on both the inner and outer harbours, rendering them quite untenable by shipping.

Smirnoff's lucid exposition eventually persuaded the Council of War to try and hold the Green Hills line firmly, and belated attempts were made by the entire sapper complement of the garrison—a mere 800 men—to increase the natural strength of the position by field works along its length. Fock's 4th East Siberian Division was made responsible for the left flank, and the right was entrusted to four reserve battalions and a couple of companies of Frontier Guards.

In retrospect, it is clear that had the outer line of field works been built up as strongly as the inner line of fortifications, it might well have been possible for the garrison to keep the besiegers at arm's length. The harbour would have been out of range of observed fire, and in proper hands Port Arthur would indeed have qualified as a virtually impregnable stronghold. But as things stood, the outer defensive positions were never more than makeshift, and the Russians were further handicapped by complete ignorance of the Japanese plans. For the Intelligence service in Port Arthur, as elsewhere, "was extremely badly run, the only source of information being the local Chinese, who, working both for the Muscovites and their enemies, naturally favoured the latter, as the District Staff paid a starvation wage."[13] Nogi, on the other hand, despite the field gendarmery especially recruited by Smirnoff for counterespionage work, was fully informed of all that transpired within the enemy camp down to the very last detail of the governor's most recent quarrel with the commandant of the fortress. When it comes to spying the West will always find itself outmatched by the East.

Shtakelberg's preparations to carry out his orders for an advance to Port Arthur's relief had scarcely passed the preliminary stage when they were arrested by a sudden demand for troops to reinforce Kuropatkin's newly threatened left wing. For Kuroki's First Army was on the march and had advanced along the Mukden road as far as Ai-yang-cheng. By this route the Japanese could strike directly at the Russian communications, either at Liao-yang, or between that centre and Mukden, or at Mukden itself. Kuropatkin always had his head half turned over his shoulder to keep an eye on the railway—for whose guardianship 55,000 men were allocated between the Urals and Mukden, with an additional 25,000 in Manchuria itself—and any threat to it brought immediate reaction.[14] Rather than tap his general reserve, the army commander preferred to strengthen his seemingly menaced left wing at the expense of his right.

Under cover of this move on the part of Kuroki's First Army, General Oku pushed forward his cavalry, which came upon some Russian reconnoitering squadrons just south of Te-li-ssu. A skirmish ensued in which the Japanese—never anything but indifferent horsemen—were pretty roughly handled, being charged in front and flank by Cossacks, who used their lances as quarterstaves to tumble their opponents from the saddle. But however indifferent they might be in shock action, throughout the entire campaign the Japanese mounted troops so skilfully screened the movements of their infantry that the Russians could never ascertain in what locality they were massing.

Despite the thinning of his ranks, the impetuous Shtakelberg, believing that he had to deal with no more than a thinly spread covering force, secured the army commander's somewhat tempered sanction for a bold thrust to recapture Nanshan and reopen the way to the beleaguered fortress.

Actually, Oku had under his command the 3rd and 5th Divisions, with the 4th Division marching to join him. Thus he was in a reasonably confident mood when, on the morning of June 14, his patrols made contact with their opponents posted in a defensive position astride the railway below Te-li-ssu. Instead of the 20,000 effectives Shtakelberg believed him to possess, Oku had a force totalling 37,000 with 216 guns, whereas the most the Russians could put into the field was 28,000 rifles and 96 guns. Shtakelberg, finding himself confronted by so formidable an array, abandoned all idea of an advance and took up a position south of Te-li-ssu to await attack.

At the outset the Russians had two things in their favour: their left was strongly posted in broken hilly country, with a good field of fire, while on their right, to the west of the railway, any artillery support for an enemy assault would be committed to open country. But with considerable cunning, the guns of a single Japanese division succeeded in teasing the Russians into exposing virtually all their artillery positions, and fire began to beat upon them mercilessly. Oshima's 3rd Division thereupon launched an assault against the enemy left and centre. Although somewhat cramped for the development of an effective counterattack, the Russian position was well sited for defence, and the struggle swayed to and fro with little gain on either side, although Shtakelberg undoubtedly let himself be persuaded that this attack directed against his centre and left constituted the Japanese main effort.

During the night of June 14–15 both sides received reinforcements; but the Russians' subsequent attempt to overwhelm Oshima's troops was so ill co-ordinated that it failed miserably in its purpose, although the Japanese had difficulty in places in holding their ground.

With the 3rd Division hanging on grimly, Yamaguchi's 5th Division, supported by troops of the 4th Division, began to move up from the southwest in a wide flanking movement to turn Shtakelberg's right. At the same time the two regiments of the cavalry brigade, with six machine guns and a mountain battery, were told off to make a separate turning movement around the Russian left, in the hope of cutting their line of retreat.

Shtakelberg hurried to the scene of the mounting danger

on his right, and in his endeavour to organize the necessary measures to oppose it had two horses shot under him. A man of frail health but fiery temper, he was a conspicuous target in his white linen jacket and mounted on a white charger, and he always drew fire if he rode within range of the enemy marksmen.

In the early afternoon, fighting in the centre gained a new intensity as the 3rd Division sought to pin down as many enemy troops as possible. "Again and again the Russians, who had brought up to their front line three regiments of the 1st East Siberian Rifle Division, flung themselves against their opponents with the utmost intrepidity; and at one point the hostile lines approached so close to each other that, when ammunition gave out, stones were freely thrown by both sides."[15] With only two battalions left in his general reserve, Oku unhesitantly hurried one of them forward to the support of the hard-pressed Oshima.

West of the railway, however, the Russians were already wavering, and following the loss of the key position of Ta-fang-shan, with no reinforcements to bolster it up, the front began rapidly to dissolve. Without waiting for orders, some of the reserves—who had not fired a shot—scuttled to the rightabouts to lead a scrambling withdrawal. This was the moment for Oshima's indomitable troops to pass briskly over to the attack; and as their assault carried the gap which gave exit to the railroad, one position after another buckled and retreat became general all along the line, the rear guard being harried by artillery fire and the horsemen of Akiyama's First Cavalry Brigade. With the congestion on the road from Wu-Chia-tun and in the defile at Te-li-ssu, defeat might easily have been turned into rout had not a blinding rainstorm effectually prevented the Japanese artillerymen from laying their pieces with any accuracy. In the prevailing murk, and with the victors exhausted and running out of ammunition, pursuit was out of the question.

From the Russian point of view, the whole sorry business was succinctly summed up by the junior officer who observed, "The smash-up occurred, as at Chiu-lien-cheng, because we didn't notice in time that we were being outflanked."[16]

Once some sort of control had been imposed upon it, however, the retreat was most efficiently covered by Samsonov with six squadrons of dragoons and six *sotnias* of Siberian Cossacks. They were usefully supplemented by three *sotnias* of Frontier Guards and the Mounted Scouts of the 13th Siberian Light Infantry, supported by the Third Battery of Trans-Baikal Cossacks. "The duties of this force were exceptionally trying. Day and night in touch with the enemy, rest was impossible,"[17] for the likelihood of an attempted surprise could never be disregarded. In twenty-three days this cavalry rear guard retreated no more than 33½ miles, always hanging onto the enemy and observing his movements. At times the whole formation was on duty for seventy-two hours at a stretch, without offsaddling; but behind their impenetrable screen Shtakelberg's slow-plodding columns were enabled to make good their escape.

Having regard for the ferocity of the fighting at Te-li-ssu, especially in the centre, the Japanese were fortunate to have suffered no more than 1,064 casualties; those of their opponents numbered three times as many.

Viewed objectively, it seems irrefutable that the unfortunate Shtakelberg had been the victim of contradictory orders, which cancelled themselves out. Urged to act with energy and rapidity to ensure a breakthrough, at the same time he was directed not to become so seriously embroiled as to commit his reserves. Indeed, throughout the whole of the campaign Kuropatkin's curious tendency to hoard his reserves rather than employ them in the counterattack or to exploit a promising situation crippled Russian efforts as the chainshot dragging at his leg hampered the movements of a Botany Bay convict. Furthermore, "at Te-li-ssu the Japanese derived an immense advantage from the superiority of their artillery; their shells exploding over the Russian trenches, blowing the infantrymen to ribbons and annihilating whole companies."[18]

On June 22 Witgeft suddenly decided to take the Pacific Ocean Squadron to sea; and in the preliminary sweeping operations the gunboats *Vsadnik* and *Gaidamac* received superficial injury. On the day following the fleet put out in line ahead, the *Tzesarevitch* just managing to escape a mine that had broken free from its moorings. When the mine sweepers in the lead came under fire from the Japanese destroyers, the *Novik* hastened to their support. Warned by wireless telegraph, the Japanese main armament hurriedly set out from its Elliot Islands base. But Witgeft was not prepared to accept battle, and putting about, headed for home. Because of an unfavourable tide, the Russian vessels found they could not make harbour until the morning; and Togo's destroyers promptly concentrated on the four rearmost vessels. Sheering to port to avoid a collision, the *Sevastopol* failed to avoid a mine, and the explosion flooded one of her compartments. Moving slowly to the shelter of White Wolf Bay, she dropped anchor and swung out her torpedo nets. All through the night the Japanese small craft kept up their attack; but the shore batteries maintained so hot a fire that the enemy could achieve nothing decisive and withdrew with daylight, having sustained a certain amount of injury.

With morning, the South Pacific Squadron could return once more to its moorings. But under cover of this somewhat abortive activity the First *Kobi* Brigade had been safely put ashore.[19]

Port Arthur had learned, with somewhat mixed feelings, of the sinking of the Japanese transports by Admiral Essen and his Vladivostok flotilla. In the light of this dashing exploit the reluctance of Witgeft's vessels to try and impede the flow of enemy troops and stores into Hon-to-shih and Dalny seemed almost inexplicable. The answer lay, of course, in the stultifying influence exerted by the "Great Edict of Renunciation," whose effect on both officers and men had been progressively demoralizing. "Of discipline," Semenoff ruefully noted, "there only remained the outer forms. Its real basis, belief in the superiors, was gone. But it was this belief alone which could guarantee obedience, self-denial, self-sacrifice—in a word, success."

Patrols were still sent out, but fortune seldom favoured them. Indeed, on the night of July 24 the Japanese, creeping into Takhe Bay, succeeded in getting between the Russians and the shore, and from this unexpected angle brought their fire to bear with considerable effect. "The *Grosevoy* was not hurt, but the *Boveboy* was much damaged, her foreward stokehold being blown up. But the worst was the *Lieutenant Burakoff*, our only fast boat, which was blown nearly in two. With her we lost the only half-way reliable means of getting into communication with the Commander-in-Chief *via* Niuchuang."[20]

Save for a rare wireless from Chefu and the messages brought in, at great risk, by secret agents, Port Arthur was cut off from all contact with the outer world.

Napoleon held that a besieging force should be four times stronger than the defenders of a fortress. At no period did General Nogi enjoy anything like this numerical superiority. There was never a time when he could dispose of more than 90,000 men and 474 siege and field guns, as against a defence force totalling 41,800 troops, and 500 pieces of artillery of one sort and another, and the shore parties from the naval vessels in the harbour and such weapons as they brought with them. But in General Baron Nogi the Russians had a singularly intrepid and determined antagonist. A brigade commander in the war of 1894, this short, slim, smiling little man, in his spruce tunic and shining thigh boots, had more than a touch of that dogged persistence for which Ulysses S. Grant was famed— and something of that hardheaded leader's recognition of the fact that you cannot make omelettes without breaking eggs.

Having got his troops deployed on their main positions, and reinforced by the First *Kobi* Brigade, brought up from Dalny, the Baron lost no time in probing hard into the outer Russian defences. On June 23 a strong patrol pushed out from Shao-ping-tau, along the hills overlooking the foreshore toward Lun-wan-tun Bay. Shelled by Russian gunboats that had ventured out into Takhe Bay, the Japanese were turned back by five companies of Frontier Guards. But their movement was no more than a probe, the purpose of which was to ascertain in what strength the right flank was held. After endless wrangling and in the teeth of both Smirnoff's and Kondratenko's objections, Fock had insisted on strengthening the left wing of the outer defences at the heavy expense of the right, despite the extreme importance to the whole line of resistance of the steep hills of Ta-ku-shan ("The Great Orphan") and Sia-gu-shan, and the lonely but commanding eminence forward of them known as Kuen-san. The Great Orphan towered 600 feet above sea level, on one face as sheer as the Rock of Gibraltar. From its summit a comprehensive view was obtainable of the outer defence system all the way to Louisa Bay in the west. So long as it remained in Russian hands, artillery on its summit could enfilade any hostile advance over the Green Hills across the river Tai to the outer fortifications. But it was obvious that before The Great Orphan could be tackled Kuen-san would have to be nipped out and firmly held.

There was no longer any need for Nogi to look over his shoulder. On June 11 Ying-kou had been blockaded by the Japanese, its status as a Treaty Port having been invalidated by its military employment by the Russians. The retreat of Shtakelberg's forces from Te-li-ssu had been the signal for the Muscovites to scuttle out of Niu-chuang and Ying-kou with all possible speed. The former had been taken over by five Japanese cavalry scouts, but not before the Russian quarter had been thoroughly looted by the local Chinese. Such military stragglers and government officials as were still in the town made haste to tear off their shoulder straps and exchange their uniform caps for any sort of civilian headgear they could acquire. At the same time a positive rash of "neutral" bunting—kept carefully in reserve for just such an occasion—had made its hopeful appearance throughout the commercial and residential quarters.

On June 25, therefore, General Nogi, aware that he was shortly to be further strengthened by the 9th Division, opened a heavy bombardment of the Green Hills position. This was followed by a general attack all along the line; and by midday the emphasis of the assault was clearly on the enemy centre and right.

The assault was supported on both flanks by Japanese cruisers and small craft. The *Askold*, *Pallada*, *Bayan*, and several other vessels of the Pacific Ocean Squadron sallied out to tackle the hostile ships in Takhe Bay, and the *Bayan* got in an 8-inch shell on the *Itsukushima*. It was only a little later, however, that the *Bayan* herself struck a mine. But despite a flooded forward stokehold, she contrived to creep back to port.

Kuen-san was held by a single company of the Fourteenth Regiment; and although its capture was an objective for which the Japanese were obviously prepared to make heavy sacrifice, demands for its reinforcement went entirely unheeded by both Fock and Stössel. The forward post of Waitu-shan had early fallen into Nogi's hands, and thereafter this 368-metre hill was the focus of a fully supported infantry assault that even some carefully placed land mines could do no more than delay. The ascent of the hill was sufficiently exhausting in itself, but "a small company of men at the head of the line would clamber up the rocks and precipices, ready for annihilation; encouraged by their example, larger forces would break in upon the enemy like a flood. The Russians resisted desperately; this heaven protected steep Kuen-san was too important for them to give up."[21] But the sheer weight of the onslaught was more than the remnants of a single company could hope to repel. With three-fourths of their number fallen, the men of the Fourteenth slowly withdrew down the reverse slopes of the hill to rally in the valley of Lun-wan-tun. Kuen-san had fallen; in many places the Green Hills defence line had been pierced; and with the capture of the island of Shao-ping-tau the effective intervention of the Russian destroyer and gunboat flotilla on the left flank was rendered far more difficult.

Stössel had already received one signal from General Kuropatkin, demanding to know when he would be handing over command in Port Arthur to General Smirnoff. In the act of ordering an immediate counterattack to restore the situation on Kuan-shan, the Baron received a second enquiry from his army commander, couched in terms similar to the first; and to this he replied in characteristically bombastic strain. "Your despatch of July 2nd," he wrote grandiloquently, "was handed to me on the positions as I was repelling an attack in force by the enemy. I was anxious to leave Port Arthur, but as things are at present I consider my presence here essential for the good of the Fatherland and our troops. Everyone here knows me, Chinese as well as Russians, and they trust me, knowing that the Japanese will never get into the place save over my dead body. Neither Fock nor Nikitin believes in General Smirnoff, who is unknown to the Officers and men, and who calls the latter cowards. He may be all right in his way, but he is a professor, not a fighting General. If you are determined that I should come to Liao-yang, I will do so on receipt of fresh instructions to that effect from you."

With the Russian counterattack in preparation, an illuminating glimpse of Stössel in his role as the Hector of Port Arthur's defence is furnished in a note by the ubiquitous Nojine.

"On July 1st," he records, "I met a young Officer in the street.

" 'Would you care to come with me to the Green Hills?' he said casually. 'A night attack has been fixed for tonight on Kuen-san; but it is a great secret.'

"As I had already heard the news discussed by Chinese shop assistants, I went at once to the District Staff and told the senior *aide de camp*, for, as the whole town seemed to know the 'secret,' it must, of course, be known to the enemy. 'Yes, the General let it out, so we have telephoned to cancel the move. In any case it wouldn't have succeeded, as the General was dead against it. The attack will take place another day, and Kondratenko is going to command the right flank. Fock will now only nominally be the senior.' "

Purely local attacks had restored the Russians to some of the positions from which they had been driven in the Green Hills line, but the gains were of no permanent significance. It was the navy that next took up the running. Early in the morning of July 3 the destroyer and gunboat flotilla steamed out toward Shao-ping-tau, seeking without much success to harry the enemy lines of communication. At the same time the Thirteenth Regiment made a gallant attempt to recapture Kuen-san, swinging into action to the stirring strains of their band. "When the distance between the two sides became only seven or eight hundred metres, they deployed, shouted 'Woola!' very loud, and rushed on us bravely, encouraged by the sound of fife and drum. We met them with violent rapid fire, killing both those that advanced and those that retreated."[22] Reduced to a mere cadre, on the night of July 5 the remnant of the Thirteenth Regiment sullenly withdrew, having lost 500 men in an enterprise that had yielded little or nothing in return for the heavy cost involved.

For over three weeks conditions remained at a virtual standstill. Throughout the course of this temporary lull Ta-lien Bay was entirely cleared of mines, and access to Dalny became unrestricted. Opportunity was also taken to bring the 9th Division into the line, while two independent infantry brigades were landed, together with the Second Independent Artillery Brigade and a number of siege howitzers and naval guns.

If Stössel had been brooding on any comprehensive plan for a sortie in force, he was anticipated by Nogi, who on July 26 launched a strong assault against the Russian left, between Nytonsu and the eminence of Ho-shan. A major effort would be worth its cost, since occupation of any one of the chain of hills between Nytonsu and the railway would impel the Russians to abandon their entire line and force them back to the protection of their forts.

The first attack was drowned out in mist and teeming rain. Nogi went in again on the following day, and by 3 P.M. the assailants "had forced the Russians to retire from the lower trenches. These were at once occupied by the Japanese, and then began one of the most remarkable fights in modern history. The upper parts of the hills were so steep that it was a marvel that any man could climb them, but the Japanese went to work undauntedly. The very steepness of the hillsides was in a way an advantage to them, as everywhere there was 'dead' ground. Little by little they succeeded in creeping up close to the upper trenches, though with very considerable loss. In some places they reduced the distance between themselves and the trenches held by the enemy to five or six yards, but this distance must be reckoned vertically, and not horizontally. Short as it was, this space was insurmountable without the aid of scaling ladders. The Japanese had to stand with their backs to the rocks and fire up into the air, and the Russians had to lean over the precipice and fire vertically on the heads of the assailants."[23] In a few places the attackers succeeded in reaching their opponents, and while some of them kept the enemy in play others hauled up their comrades to join in the fray. Slowly the whole defence began to crumple until the entire range of outer works from Nytonsu to the railway was in Nogi's hands. But on his left flank towered the steep slopes of The Great Orphan, notoriously difficult to scale except from the south, and with its stony peak bristling with six field pieces and several machine guns.

It is possible that the Baron entertained hopes that the Russians would voluntarily abandon Ta-ku-shan and the neighbouring Sia-gu-shan as forming too dangerous a salient. But it was not a poltroon such as Fock that the Japanese confronted on the Russian right flank, but the dogged, tenacious Kondratenko; and thus until the early days of August the situation remained unchanged.

On Aug. 7, as Port Arthur's churches filled with congregations gathered together for a special service of prayer for the town's safety, a preparatory bombardment opened, which was sustained without pause throughout the day. For the Japanese had concealed their heavy guns with such skill that they could not be located, and accurate counterbattery work was therefore out of the question. Both from front and flank heavy fire was concentrated on Ta-ku-shan and its neighbour, which Smirnoff had never succeeded in fortifying to his satisfaction. Without casemates or splinter-proofs, they were little less than death traps; but the Russian gunners and riflemen of the 13th East Siberians stuck to their posts with stolid courage, hoping vainly for relief.

At 7 P.M. the Japanese infantry attacked in full strength, the Twelfth Regiment advancing on the south slopes of Ta-ku-shan while the Forty-third assailed the eastern face of Sia-gu-shan. But the heavy rainfall was positively blinding, and for the time being the assailants could do little more than establish themselves on the lower spurs of their objectives. "The powder

smoke covering the whole scene was like surging waves, and
the dark showers of rain may be likened to angry lions. Above,
the steep mountain stood high, kissing the heavens—even mon-
keys could hardly climb it."[24] Steadily, remorselessly the rain
poured down, immobilizing both the attack and the defence,
many of the Russians being driven out of their waterlogged
trenches to shiver in the open.

At eleven thirty on the morning of Aug. 8th the men of
the Twelfth and Forty-third Regiments came under heavy fire
from seven warships that sallied out from Port Arthur to shell
the exposed left flank of Tsuchiya's 11th Division. Casualties
were heavy, as there was little cover on the bare mountain
slopes, and for a time the positions won on the lower crags of
Ta-ku-shan had to be relinquished. By a little after noon a concentrated shoot by the Japanese 9-cm howitzers had driven the
warships back to shelter behind Golden Hill. But it was not
until 7 P.M. that the Japanese infantry again received the order
to advance. While the 12th Division once more drove in from
the southeast, part of the Twenty-second Regiment endeavoured to scale the fissured slopes and broken spurs on the northeast, an ascent that at any time would have been a considerable
feat of mountaineering. In the face of opposition by a stubborn, well-armed foe, it is almost incredible that any of the
assailants should have survived to reach the top. But the first
to scale the crest were speedily joined by those who came
panting hard on their heels, and a stupendous tussle ensued for
the possession of the mountaintop, which was fought out with
the utmost fury. "The shriek and yell of men, the boom and
roar of guns, the gleam of bayonets and swords, the flowing
blood, the smashing of brains and bowels—a grand confusion
and a tremendous hand-to-hand fight! The enemy rolled down
huge stones from the top, and many an unfortunate was thrown
into the deep valley and crushed against the rocks. Shrieks of
pain and yells of anger made the whole scene more like hell
than like this world. But presently a great shout of *Banzai!*
shook the whole mountain, rising from the top and foot simultaneously. What had happened?—Behold, a flag is waving in
the dark clouds of smoke! Is it our dear Rising Sun?—Our

assault has succeeded! Our standard is already unfurled on the top of the hill! We saw this and we cried for joy."[25]

Ta-ku-shan was in Japanese hands by 8 P.M., and by 4.30 the following morning the last of its defenders had been hurled from Sia-gu-shan. All attempts at recovering the lost positions were confidently swept away.

For a cost to the Japanese of 36 officers and 973 men killed, and 173 officers and 4,536 men wounded, Port Arthur's garrison had been driven back within the narrow confines of its fixed defences. Blockaded from the sea, the girdle of investment was completed by an army fanatically determined that, long before help could be sent from distant Europe, Russian resistance in the Far East should be ground to nothing between the upper and lower millstones of Togo's fleet and the armies now under the direct command of Field Marshal the Marquis Iwao Oyama.

TIGER AT THE GATES

"IT IS USELESS TO TRY AND KEEP A TIGER OFF THE FRONT GATE IF THE WOLF IS ALREADY AT THE BACK DOOR."

—JAPANESE PROVERB

5   IT IS OF SMALL VALUE to gain a victory unless its advantages can also be secured. How best to exploit his success was the question which confronted General Oku the day after Te-li-ssu. One thing was clear: before any further move could be made, it was necessary to replenish his sorely depleted stores of food and ammunition and thus regain mobility. In this particular, he was singularly handicapped by persistently unhelpful weather. For although the annual rainy season had yet, theoretically, to set in, torrents continued to pour from the skies, turning the indifferent roads into quagmires. Even in good weather the movement of matériel would have posed a sufficiently knotty problem. For although some three hundred freight cars were available in Dalny, the Russians had cannily removed all the locomotives; and although the Russian wide-gauge was eventually narrowed to take rolling stock brought from Japan, the process of conversion had only just begun. Transport by Chinese carts proved a vexatiously sluggard way of satisfying the demands of a force increased in number by the arrival of the 6th Division under General Okubo, and an ingenious staff officer hit upon the device of loading up the railway cars and having them manhandled along the rails by gangs of Chinese coolies—thirty to a flatcar. The method was sure but irksomely

slow. Consequently, it was not until the first week in July that the Second Army was in a position to make any advance, its movements being carefully synchronized with those of the Fourth and First Armies, farther east. Neither of these formations had been without its troubles over transportation. For despite the shorter overland haul, the even flow of supplies had been greatly hindered by the indifferent landing facilities prevailing at the entry port—if such it could be termed—of Hon-tu-shih. Kuropatkin's preoccupation with operations in the direction of Te-li-ssu had given Kuroki's First Army an excellent opportunity to push forward. But the difficulties of the terrain that had to be traversed slowed down an advance which, if it could have been energetically pressed, might well have taken the Japanese straight into Liao-yang, so jumbled and disordered at this stage were the Russian forces on their sensitive left flank.

With Shtakelberg's detachment thrown into retreat, the last hope of Port Arthur's speedy relief by the Russian land forces had vanished.

With the victor's shouts of *Banzai!* still ringing in his ears, Shtakelberg had withdrawn his troops in the general direction of Kai-ping, where a byroad branched from the main highway to Niu-chuang and its port of Ying-kou; a rear guard was left to delay any advance in the direction of Tung-chia-tun. Movement in this direction would threaten the junction of Ta-shih-chiao, where the main railroad was joined by the branch line from Ying-kou; possession of this junction would greatly simplify Oku's supply problem.

Kuropatkin's general line of resistance was some twenty-seven miles forward of Liao-yang; with General Mishchenko in touch with Kawamura's Fourth Army[1] and General Count Keller confronting Kuroki's First Army in the region of Mo-tien-ling. At Keller's disposal were 42 battalions. On his right, on the line Fen-shui-ling–Hai-cheng, Mishchenko could call on 28 battalions to oppose Kawamura's two divisions and one *Kobi* brigade. The most powerful Russian concentration was on the right, where Shtakelberg could bring 48 battalions to deal with Oku's Second Army, plus one division detached to him from the Fourth Army. In addition to the garrison of 6 battalions, 8 squadrons, and 32 guns quartered in Liao-yang, Kuropatkin retained 15 battalions in general reserve. Many of these battalions, however, were under strength. Exclusive of Nogi's army of investment in front of Port Arthur, at this time some 80,000 strong, the Japanese had approximately 118,000 effectives in the field. In all, the Japanese were to mobilize some 1,200,000 men, the Russians approximately 1,365,000. Of these totals 650,000 Japanese were to be actually employed in the theatre of operations, as against 699,000 Russians.

It was Count Keller's firm belief, in which Kuropatkin finally concurred, that the First and Fourth Japanese Armies would march westward to concentrate with the more numerous Second Army, lest one of their corps should find itself exposed to overwhelming attack before the others could come to its aid. With this link-up completed, the Japanese would be in a position to move on Hai-cheng.

It was not long before Keller, demonstrating on the Russian left, discovered that the Japanese had hoodwinked him and retained a far stronger array with the right wing of their First Army than had been supposed. Alarmed at the strength of the forces brought against him, the Count hastily withdrew, leaving the Japanese to seize the Mo-tien-ling passes without firing a shot. Particularly vile weather chose this moment to intervene and bring operations to a temporary halt. But the rhythm of the forward movement was restored on July 6 when Oku, with some assistance from the Fourth Army, advanced to capture Kai-ping as the first step in an advance on the railway junction of Ta-shih-chiao; the Russians retreated to positions in the hills about Hsi-mu-cheng. Threatening movements by the Fourth Army in support of Oku successfully deterred Mishchenko from attempting any return blow, a stroke he considered far too hazardous while Kuropatkin's forces were separated into three groups barely in touch with one another. To bring about greater cohesion, the army commander had to reconcile himself to leaving Ying-kou and the railway junction at Ta-shih-chiao in enemy hands. At all costs Liao-yang—"the key to the strategic position"—must be defended until the arrival of the whole of the XVII Corps rendered it possible to stage a powerful counterstroke. But Alexieff was pressing for immediate action, and "General Kuropatkin, in order to satisfy the Viceroy, decided to assume a partial offensive with Count Keller's forces, giving instructions to the troops on the railway to retire if attacked."[2]

Employing only twenty-four of the forty battalions left to him, Keller attacked at Mo-tien-ling on July 17 and was vigorously repulsed, while the Japanese 12th Division's capture of Chiao-tou, on the highway to Liao-yang and Mukden, brought it level with the remainder of the First Army. Kuroki was now in a position to threaten the railway directly by way of Pen-hai-hu, a mere twenty-two miles across country from the branch-line station serving the Yen-tai coal and tin mines.

Oku next took up the running with an assault on the reinforced position in the Ta-shih-chiao range of hills. Since the opposing forces were virtually equal in number, no attempt was made to secure a decisive victory, the object being to manoeuver the Russian troops eastward so that a concentric attack could be made upon them by Oku, Nodzu (back in command), and Kuroki in combination.

The assault on Ta-shih-chiao, although held initially, appeared sufficiently menacing to warrant retreat. Kuropatkin consoled himself with the thought that the sprawl of his extended front had been reduced by twenty miles. What he failed to appreciate fully was that, as the outcome of the action, Oku and Nodzu had been enabled firmly to join hands. The last chance of defeating the Second and Fourth Armies separately had been lost. Moreover, considerable booty, in the way of railway material and engineer's stores, was left in Japanese hands.

Kuropatkin, hurrying to his disrupted left, sent orders to General Sluchevski that, should Kuroki's First Army attempt to cross the Tai-tzu-ho River and move towards Mukden, he was to advance forthwith to strike at the Japanese communications.

Russian attempts politically to exploit the fact that the Japanese had infringed international rights by occupying the

Treaty Port of Ying-kou were checkmated by Tokio's ironic reminder that it had been necessary to turn the Muscovites out of the said haven at the point of a gun before the Mikado's forces could take it over.

Having come to regard Chiao-tu as the most dangerous point of penetration in his line, Kuropatkin prepared to mount a weighty attack, under Sluchevski, for its recovery. But the Japanese forestalled him by launching a surprise assault whose initial emphasis was on the thrust against Count Keller—a forward move whose prosperity soon spread to envelop Sluchevski's forces. Once again the failure to co-ordinate activities and to employ reserves at the crucial point at the decisive moment led to the breakdown of what had started as a resolute resistance. By nightfall on July 31 the Russian centre was in a state of complete turmoil, while the eastern group was on the verge of retreat. The Japanese were through the mountain passes, and Kuropatkin was left with no option but to abandon all thought of recovering Hai-cheng and retire behind his prepared positions at An-shan-chan (on the railway), Lang-tzu-shan, and An-ping-ling, the cornerstones of the Liao-yang defences.

The Russian troops had fought resolutely and well whenever competent leadership had afforded them the opportunity to put forth their best. The responsibility for failure lay with those senior officers whose ideas of command had fallen behind the quickening pace of war. Nonplused by the dilemmas their outmoded pedantries had precipitated, they lacked the confident spirit of aggression; even Kuropatkin was more prone to react than to initiate. Men such as Sluchevski and Count Keller, like the Bourbons, had "learned nothing and forgotten nothing," and their creaking methods of procedure were more often harmful than constructive.[3]

The Japanese, on the other hand, had been learning all the time. Their battle drill had improved immeasurably; they no longer exhibited so fatal a tendency to "bunch," and their short, sharp alternating rushes in the advance were carried out at such a pace as to commit the sections to the minimum of exposure to hostile fire. Moreover, the general adoption of

khaki uniform had rendered them far less conspicuous targets.
With the training they had undergone in their own craggy
country, at anything like mountain warfare they outclassed the
Russians in every respect, while their mountain artillery had
demonstrated its worth time and time again.

Each war has to be learned while it is being fought; and it
is upon the side which absorbs its lessons the more readily that
victory bestows her laurels.

In February it had occurred to no one that the day might
come when the Pacific Ocean Squadron would need bolstering
up by the considerable naval strength concentrated in the
Baltic. But as blow after blow had been dealt at the Port Arthur
vessels without any commensurate injury being inflicted on
Togo's fleet, the need to strengthen Russian sea power in Far
Eastern waters could no longer be denied. At Kronstadt, Libau,
and Reval the Tsarists had over a hundred naval craft of one
sort and another, including four new battleships fitting out that
were the equal, it was claimed, of anything afloat.

When, in mid-June, the decision was taken to send an additional armament to the Yellow Sea, its command was vested in
Admiral Zinovy Petrovitch Rozhestvensky. With experience
in action on the Black Sea and in Far Eastern waters, Rozhestvensky was recognized as a man of courage and determination,
a good organizer, a strict disciplinarian, and the best gunnery
officer in the service. He also enjoyed the advantage of having
won the confidence of his Imperial master. Unhappily, his
energy and boundless capacity for work—he thought nothing
of toiling a solid eighteen hours a day—were not characteristics
shared by the majority of his associates. So although the admiral somewhat rashly informed the St. Petersburg correspondent of the *Petit Parisien* that "We shall sail on July 15th," week
after week went by with even more still to be done than had
already been accomplished. "Final *directives* have not been
issued," the admiral had added, "but of course it is a long
voyage taking many weeks, and there will be nothing for us
to do in the Far East by September. The Japanese will have
capitulated long before then"!

As against the very considerable resources at Russia's disposal, the Japanese had fifteen destroyers and forty torpedo boats under construction in their yards. But there could be no hope of replacing any capital ships that might fall victim to the enemy. It followed that the existence and potentialities of the Baltic or Second Pacific Squadron constituted a factor that on no account could be left out of Admiral Togo's consideration.

Time is neutral with a bias in favour of the side that exhibits the more intelligent initiative. Six battleships, with a strong cruiser and destroyer force, remained in Port Arthur. Several of them were damaged, but none beyond repair. Their presence confronted General Nogi with a problem in which the time factor was of paramount importance. If the Second Pacific Squadron were to make its way to Far Eastern waters and were joined by the vessels in Vladivostok and the survivors of the Pacific Ocean Squadron in Port Arthur, the combined naval might at the Russians' disposal would be more than Admiral Togo could be confident of defeating. In any case the maritime lines of communication would be under gravely increased menace, to the jeopardy of the field armies that relied upon their untrammelled use for their support. Since the vessels in Port Arthur were virtually unassailable from the sea, they must be put out of action from the landward side. To ensure this necessitated the capture of the northwestern heights, on the Russian left flank, and particularly of 203 Metre Hill. For from this eminence the harbour was plainly visible, and fire could be concentrated on the warships by direct observation.

There were subsidiary works well forward of 203 Metre Hill—the irregular range known as Pan-lun-shan, with lonely Angle Hill (174 Metre Hill) to the northwest, Namako-Yama and Akasaka-Yama closer to hand, and Divisional Hill behind the eastern hump of Pan-lun-shan. Although not strengthened with permanent fortifications, there were fieldworks defending these positions on which the Russians were still frantically labouring. But wood for the splinterproof works was in almost as short supply as barbed wire. The soil was stony and resistant, so that the men were speedily exhausted through combining night duty in the trenches with continued backbreaking toil on them by day. For "the enemy were at close quarters and could attack at any moment, and a night attack might always be crowned with success, so that our men did not get much sleep," recorded Colonel Tretyakov, whose East Siberians were responsible for this sector of the front. "Throughout the siege," he continues, "a third of the regiment was always on the alert. This would not have been necessary if we had had a better line of defence and obstacles, or at least twice as many forts as we did have. . . . We began to work seriously on the fortifications only from the time of the general retreat into Port Arthur." And by this time the scale of subsistence was beginning starkly to reveal Stössel's imbecile want of foresight in failing to build up his stores while still in touch with reliable sources of supply. In mid-July, for a garrison of some 42,000 men and 4,500 horses, Chief Commissary Vershinin estimated that he had flour for 180 days, oatmeal for 37, meat for 18 days (13 days salt and 5 days "on the hoof"), sugar for 190, tea for 320, and forage for 150 days.[4] At best this meant a hygienically unbalanced scale of subsistence, with a totally inadequate meat ration, while the absence of any antiscorbutic element in the diet speedily led to an outbreak of scurvy. This soon found a malign companion in that form of "camp dysentery" which has haunted warfare since first men were forced to herd together under disease-breeding, unsanitary conditions.

The first shell from the Japanese landward batteries had fallen into the town on Sunday, Aug. 7, and from then on the civilian population shared the perils as well as the privations of the siege with their military defenders. With the residential quarter under fire, "the people, especially those with families, began to build themselves bomb-proofs; but, owing to lack of the necessary materials, labour and knowledge, most of them were made in a primitive fashion, and would have given absolutely no protection against shells, or even splinters; but, ostrich-like, the builders obtained a sense of security from the concealment afforded."[5] Stössel, while cynically deriding these amateur efforts, was careful to have a substantial bombproof built for himself, in which he was never slow to take cover.

When fire was particularly heavy, "the town became untenable, and the inhabitants had to seek shelter in cellars, in specially excavated shell-proof caves under the face of the gravel pit, and in the stone quarries."[6] In the circumstances, it was as well that, through evacuation to Chefu and elsewhere, Port Arthur's civilian population, other than the Chinese coolie element, had been reduced to a little over a thousand, nearly half of which, however, was made up of women and children.

Supplies were as short with the townsfolk as with the men in the trenches. The raids on the shops by officers from Liao-yang, which had been such a marked feature of the early days of the war, had never been made good; and such food supplies as were brought in by blockade runners did little to fill the provision-merchants' gaping shelves. In any case, all but one or two staple commodities commanded starvation prices quite beyond the means of all but the fortunate few with well-lined purses. For them there was always a trickle of incoming "extras." Although Louisa Bay was no longer safe, by hugging the eastern coast and taking full advantage of the frequent mists, shipmasters of all description tried their utmost to land their cargoes and reap the rich reward that recompensed them for the risks incurred in dodging the ubiquitous Japanese destroyer patrols. These had been sharply stepped up and brought off many a fruitful haul—as when the *Osiva* captured the German-owned *Blume*, crammed with corn and forage. This treasure-trove immediately went to swell the main reserve of supplies at Dalny; which had been cleaned up and opened up as a flourish-ing base, with Japanese and Chinese tradesmen setting up shop to furnish many of the small comforts and little luxuries that the expeditionary force had hitherto been obliged to forego. Looted Russian goods were sold at knockdown prices; while under the impression that they were peddling soda water, some of the Chinese hucksters were gladly parting with superb champagne at ten cents a bottle![7] The arrival of a large number of Chinese emigrants with their families, to settle in the town, was a sure sign which way the wind was blowing.

In the Sino-Japanese War, Port Arthur had been won in a single day, and General Nogi was rashly optimistic enough to believe that, in the face of modern artillery, machine guns, and magazine rifle fire, the feat could in essence be repeated. Confronted by a fifteen-mile defence line, the Baron's first probing attacks were directed against the isolated Angle Hill and the Pan-lun-shan ridge in front of Divisional Hill, as a balloon sent up on Aug. 13 had subjected this sector to particularly careful scrutiny. But the first night attack delivered against the eastern flank of Divisional Hill was held up by barbed wire, and the Japanese suffered heavy casualties. "There were piles of dead heaped up around the entanglements," Tretyakov recorded. As the war of 1914–18 was so painfully to demonstrate, there are few things better calculated to break up an assault than a belt of uncut wire. Throughout the day following it was left to the artillery to carry on the fight, the Russians losing a lot of men from the shells of the 5-inch siege guns they had left in enemy hands at Nan-shan. Morale was further impaired when Russian guns on Golden Hill started firing "shorts" that fell on the supports behind the line of resistance. On the night of Aug. 14–15 the Japanese put in two separate assaults; but their gains were purely local and trifling, and the Russians remained in firm possession of Angle and Divisional Hills.

On the morning of Aug. 16, as a concession to the "customary usages of war," General Nogi sent in a flag of truce bearing a letter for the governor which read:

> The Russians have given signal proof of their gallantry, but Port Arthur will be taken all the same. Therefore, to avoid useless loss of life and any possible violence, murder or looting by Japanese troops fighting their way into the town, which it will be difficult at once to prevent, His Highness the Emperor of Japan suggests a discussion of negotiations for the surrender of the Fortress.

Obviously, if Stössel was not prepared to throw in his hand, continued resistance, once overcome, could anticipate little mercy. But the governor was so infuriated by the summons that it was with difficulty that he was persuaded to couch his rejection of the proposal in suitably dignified terms. With the refusal to consider *pourparlers*, Nogi promptly intensified the weight and volume of his attack against the northern and northeastern face of the defences. On Aug. 19 artillery fire opened at 5 A.M. and roared in a swift crescendo that clearly heralded a full-scale onslaught. At this stage the besiegers could bring ordnance to bear that included one hundred and eight field guns, forty-four 4.7 or 6-inch field howitzers, seventy-two mountain guns, twenty-six 4.7 or 12-pounder naval guns, four 4.2-inch Krupp guns, thirty 4.7 bronze guns, and ninety-six mortars.

The opening phase of the attack took the form of a demonstration by the 1st Division against the Russian left, to distract attention from the real attack by the 9th and 11th Divisions against the two buttresses of Ehr-lung-shan (Fort No. 3) and Chi-kuan-shan (Fort No. 2). There were no helpful saps running across the Shui-shih-ying valley, which had to be crossed in face of the concentrated cross fire of the defence. Every advantage had to be taken of the smallest hummock or fold in the ground if the assembly positions in the shelter of the foothills were to be reached unscathed. It was stiflingly hot, and the yearning ache of thirst soon came to torment the survivors of the death-haunted dash across the open. Many had fallen under the searching sleet of bullets from the Russian machine gunners and marksmen, but a sufficient number reached the ravines crisscrossing the foot of the glacis to constitute a formidable striking force.

At 4 P.M. the attack went in, no longer in column but in "large groups." In the main it failed to reach its objective save in one or two places where the opponents were so close that they started to stone each other.

As dusk fell, a *ketshitai*, or "suicide squad," crept out to cut the barbed-wire entanglements or loop a stout rope round the strands and haul them away bodily; in the lull the Russian wounded were borne away by stretcher parties made up of bandsmen, orderly room clerks, sailors, and civilian militiamen. With nightfall the attacks were renewed again and again, and Angle Hill became impossible to hold. Kondratenko and

Tretyakov had already stopped one panic rush to the rear by men who only needed courageous leadership to return resolutely to the fray. But the Japanese grip on the positions they had won was not to be loosened, and to Smirnoff's bitter fury all further plans to retake Angle Hill had to be abandoned, together with those to recapture two other positions in the forward zone. The Russians were back in their fieldworks behind the village of Shui-shih-ying, and by the time they had completed their withdrawal, the defenders of the outpost line had lost half their number.

"But the vigilance of the garrison and the havoc wrought by the machine guns defeated the attempts of the Japanese to gain the ground necessary for developing the assault. At eight o'clock in the morning a small force rushed and carried a small fortification at the point of the bayonet, but were quickly shelled out and forced to retire with the other troops. The attacks on 'Q' fortification [just southeast of Fort No. 2] were easily checked, and the infantry operating in this work were unmercifully handled in the morning before the Japanese artillery could smother the Russian fire and cover their retirement. The lines of stretchers, with their burdens of torn flesh, passing through the shady *kao-liang* fields all morning, were conclusive evidence of the hard night's work."[8]

The balance of the day was spent by the Japanese in preparation, the infantry infiltrating steadily across the open to the shelter of the dongas and broken ground below the works. "Lines of khaki-coloured men pressed forward across the valley, through the tall stalks of maize and corn that were being cut and scattered by the terrible concentrated fire of the Russians. . . . From the shadow of the donga a flag waves, the red centre standing out clearly as the sun catches it for a moment."[9] With darkness the Japanese launched the first of a series of attacks mainly directed against Chi-kuan-san—where a powder magazine had received a direct hit—and Erh-lung-shan. As in most night attacks the confusion was almost indescribable. To add to their difficulties, the attackers were confronted with a new weapon of defence. "The searchlights went round so fast as to dazzle our assaulting detachment," recorded Tadayoshi Sakurai; "their star-lights burned over our heads and made us an easy target for their shooting. . . . White blades flashed in the dark, like reeds in the wind, but the flash gradually ceased, the loud yell of a few minutes before stopped. We heard only the shouting of the enemy behind their ramparts. They came up and danced for joy on the breastwork, while we had been killed to create a hill of corpses and a stream of blood."

While the struggle swayed to and fro on the northern face of the defences, the 11th Division made repeated attacks on Forts 3 and 2 and on the Kuropatkin Lunette, to the flank of Chi-kuan-shan. "Rifles cracked, machine guns spluttered, guns boomed and boomed again and the air was turned into an inferno of shrieking missiles. The rays of the searchlights flashed up and down, rockets shot up into the sky like enormous fiery snakes, and burst, and hundreds of brilliant balls filled the air, eclipsing the light of the eternal stars and blinding the heroic little infantrymen who were attacking. They ran forward, fell, jumped up again and pressed on, in groups together. In the shimmering rays of the searchlights, the flashes of the bursting shells seemed almost blood-red."[10] A second assault, put in at 2 A.M. was also thrown back, but still the Japanese came on with undiminished valour. From Fort No. 3 "the devilish searchlights slowly sweep the valley below, and when one rests its rays on any particular spot, red spurts from the black void behind it belch forth shells which tear ghastly gaps in the Japanese lines wading through the millet and cornfields below. In spite of the terrible carnage *en route* a few remnants of these brave battalions under Ichinobe reach the base of Ban-u-san[11] and clamber up the *glacis* with faint shouts of *Banzai!* which are echoed by their comrades across the valley. But they can go no further; they halt, press forward a few yards, then in the face of all these superhuman difficulties they break, and hurry down to the friendly shelter of the donga below."[12] For a short while part of Ehr-lung-shan fell under assault, when a *ketshitai* crept forward to thrust through the casemates 10-foot bamboo poles to which grenades had been bound with their time fuses spluttering. There was savage fighting with bayonet, sword, and rifle butt before the handful of intruders were overthrown and trampled down in death or mortal injury.

A Japanese attempt to force a way into the heart of the defences and capture Yi-tzu-shan (Fortification No. 4, to the west of Quail Hill) was made on the night of Aug. 23–24. But the troops were tiring, and the assault, not being driven home, was repulsed at no great cost to the defence. "The positions reached by the Japanese in this attempt were plainly marked by their dead, who remained unburied until the capitulation of the fortress. The slopes of the fortification, the ground between them and the Chinese Wall, and the slopes of Wan-tai knoll were liberally sprinkled with skeletons in khaki uniforms, many of whose skulls, following the lines of least resistance, had rolled down the slopes and gathered here and there in clusters of four and five."[13]

On the night of Aug. 25–26—a night of howling wind and torrential rain—the besiegers made one more effort to gain possession of Namako-Yama. But they failed to effect any sort of surprise and were driven off the slopes they had scaled so valiantly, with very heavy losses.

With the dawn the Japanese were in possession of the outlying ridge of Pan-lun-shan and the even more isolated Angle Hill. On the eastern face, below Erh-lung-shan, Redoubts Nos. 1 and 2 also remained in their hands; and they were prompt to drive communication trenches to link these forward posts with their support works in the rear. All the other positions remained in Russian grip. Their defence had cost the garrison 3,000 in killed and wounded, as against a butcher's bill of 15,000 for General Baron Nogi. In addition, he had a sick list of 8,000, and 16,000 of his men were suffering more or less acutely from beriberi, an affliction brought about by the fermentation of the rice ration, so much of which had been transported on open decks under skies that wept with constant rain. The flow of reinforcements through Dalny, however, soon made good the worst gaps in his ranks.

It was obvious that to repeat the *coup de main* of 1894 was out of the question. As both combatants were to demonstrate on an even larger scale in the war of 1914–18, when defensive positions are stoutly defended and there is no chance of turning a flank, sapping and mining and all the elaborate ritual of siege operations constitute the only alternative to trying to *create* a flank by driving a costly dent in consolidated defences that in turn are found to be backed by yet another system of elaborately constructed fieldworks. "A fortress must be breached," declared Vauban, "before it is assailed." But siege operations aimed at breaching fixed defences demand time for their steady prosecution; and the expenditure of time was the one thing that Nogi was most anxious to avoid.

Not the least of Kuropatkin's worries was the increasing pessimism characterizing the governor's despatches from the fortress. All the boastful confidence had evaporated, to give place to a gloomy defeatism no less extreme. With the Japanese closing in on the outer ring of the port's fixed defences, the only hope for a spirited resistance was to replace the sagging, incapable Stössel with someone who could be relied upon to fight it out to the last round and the last man. In the circumstances, the army commander had little hesitation in sending off a signal directing Stössel to hand over his command to Smirnoff and make his way out of Port Arthur by cruiser or destroyer.

The arrival of this uncompromising directive involved its recipient in a very real dilemma. To obey the order would be to incur public disgrace such as a man of the governor's self-esteem refused to contemplate. On the other hand, to continue in the command in defiance of orders would be a deliberate act of insubordination which only an outstandingly brilliant victory might serve to vindicate. With the desperate hardihood that only sorely pricked vanity can inspire, Stössel pocketed both the order directing him to hand over to Smirnoff and the confirmatory telegram addressed to the fortress commander himself. A bold and successful defence of Port Arthur until Kuropatkin could arrive would assure his reinstatement. Success is its own justification, and "insubordination in the higher ranks was not uncommon, but the culprits were often advanced afterwards to higher posts."[14] Of this Stössel was fully aware.

Entirely ignorant of the governor's duplicity, Smirnoff

went steadily about his exacting task of strengthening the defences in every possible way that experience and ingenuity could suggest.

With the Russians driven out of all their forward positions, that hardheaded sailor, Commander Semenoff, grimly noted down in his journal, "The real siege of Port Arthur can be counted as commencing." It was probably a reluctant realization of this hard fact, plus the prodding he received from his Imperial master, which prompted the viceroy to send Admiral Witgeft a signal to "Keep before your eyes that the Squadron can only remain in Port Arthur as long as it is safe there. In the other eventuality, go to sea in good time and proceed, without engaging in battle, if that can be possible, to Vladivostok." Once concentrated in the northern port, the Pacific Ocean Squadron could await the arrival of the reinforcements from the Baltic that were already under orders to hasten preparations for their 18,000-mile passage to the Far East. It was a directive that Alexeieff had phrased with such exquisite care that, whatever the outcome, he personally would be in a position to cover himself.

The deliberate imprecision of the order was such that for several days Witgeft hesitated as to which course to pursue. A broad hint of what lay ahead of him, should he continue to hug the harbour, was embodied in the activities of a Japanese battery of 4.7-inch naval guns, firing from a concealed position in the hills. "The Japanese fire was not continuous, but in a series of seven or eight rounds. Between these they paused. The first series fell altogether in the main street, near the Port Hospital; the second fell more to the westward, that is, on the quay of the commercial port. It destroyed the coal which was stacked there. The third series fell on the open place in front of the Admiral's landing steps, a little to the west of the place where the *Tzesarevitch* lay alongside. Luckily, only one of the shells was well placed. It destroyed the wireless office on board. The operator, a torpedo-machinist, was killed as he was sending a message. The Admiral Commanding, Rear-Admiral Witgeft, was slightly wounded in the leg by a splinter. About 1 P.M. the fire was directed towards the entrance. As before, the

Japanese fired a series of seven or eight guns. These series were apparently laid for successive points from south to north."[15]

The cannonade was continued throughout the following two days; and although at the outset the Japanese fuses were obviously defective—thirty-two out of seventy-six missiles failing to explode—this fault was soon remedied, and the shooting showed a marked improvement.

The growing menace to his vessels embodied in this persistent and increasingly accurate bombardment furnished the determining factor which persuaded Witgeft to interpret his ambiguous orders as a definite command to put to sea. After due deliberation he resolved to leave port on the turn of the tide at daybreak on Aug. 9, although there were still those to protest that in any sally the two slowest vessels, the *Poltava* and the *Sevastopol*, should be left behind to "strengthen the defences." Alternatively, Rear Admiral Gregorovitch proposed that while the more powerful and speedy vessels fought their way toward Vladivostok, the two veterans, supported by four gunboats and ten destroyers, should take advantage of the temporary absence of the Japanese fleet in pursuit of its prey to bombard Dalny, with the object of disrupting what had become the enemy's principal entry port and base for supplies. If it turned out that this detached squadron fell in with Togo's main fleet, then taking advantage of the mine defences and supported by the coast batteries, Gregorovitch could occupy the enemy while Witgeft and the more serviceable vessels under his command made good their escape.

Had Gregorovitch's self-sacrificing proposal been agreed to, it is very possible that Togo, by yielding to the temptation to divide his fleet, would have lost the balance of advantage— and maybe some irreplaceable major craft. But Witgeft refused to entertain the suggestion. "My orders," he pronounced, "are to go to Vladivostok with the whole squadron, and that I shall do."

On the eve of putting to sea an air of depression overhung the whole squadron like a paralyzing miasma. Everyone realized that with much of their armament dispersed among the shore defences, the ships' striking power had been gravely diminished, while the presence of the *Poltava* and the *Sevastopol* in their midst would slow down the speed of the other vessels to the veterans' 12 to 14 knots maximum. Moreover, the hope that Witgeft's injury would persuade him to hand over the command to one of his more experienced seagoing subordinates had not been realized.

At the hour appointed to weigh anchor, although the *Tzesarevitch*, the *Pallada*, and the patched-up *Retvisan* were prepared to set forth, the *Pobieda* was still unready to sail, her captain pleading a sudden indisposition. It was not until 4.21 the next morning, therefore, that the *Novik* led the six battleships, with their attendant cruisers and destroyers, out through the narrows. Four of the craft were in the hands of men new to command, but on this occasion the squadron got to sea without mishap.

It is extremely unlikely that Admiral Togo experienced any surprise at the re-emergence of the three reconstituted battleships; Japanese Intelligence would have kept him fully informed as to the progress made in their repair. If, in the ensuing engagement, he avoided close action in favour of a protracted duel at long range, it was because his aim was to keep the Russian fleet in play so that it would be compelled to re-enter harbour after dark, when the mine field laid the previous night, plus a concentrated destroyer attack, should ensure serious losses among his antagonists' main fleet elements. Moreover, this particular plan relieved him of the need to risk capital ships he knew it would be impossible to replace.

Following a course parallel to the eastern shore of Liao-tieh-shan, the *Novik* and the first destroyer flotilla preceded the battleships, sailing in single line ahead, with the *Tzesarevitch*, wearing the flag of the admiral commanding, well in the van. The *Retvisan* put to sea with a crudely repaired gash below her waterline, and with 400 tons of water still aboard that she had shipped at the time of her injury.[16]

The waiting Japanese fleet was drawn up in inverse order, with the smaller craft well to the fore, the six torpedo divisions forming the arc of a circle at a distance of eleven miles from the shore. In the intervals, and five miles beyond the destroyers, were the armoured and protected cruisers. Three miles farther to the south loomed the surviving battleships, blocking the escape route to the neutral ports of Wei-hai-wei and Chefu as decisively as they menaced the course that would take the Russian armada in the direction of Vladivostok. The day was fine and calm, with a low-lying mist.

At 11.15 Witgeft altered course to S50°E. At 11.50 the flagship gave the 'K' signal, intimating that she was not under control. The whole squadron slowed while the mechanical defect was more or less put right, whereafter speed was increased to 15 knots. Then the *Pobieda* ran up the "K" signal, and there was another delay. Indeed, the squadron had not picked up speed again when firing broke out at 12.22. More by good luck than good management the *Tzesarevitch*, showing the way to the rest of the squadron, contrived to evade a floating mine field by turning sharply 4 points to starboard, the flagship opening fire with what was left of her heavy armament. As the duel gained in volume, the destroyers manoeuvred to work their way between the bigger craft, Togo's four battleships coming up at half speed. The weight of metal was clearly with the Japanese guns, which pounded the *Retvisan* and *Tzesarevitch* with such accuracy and persistence that they were set temporarily on fire. As the shells rained about the wallowing veterans, their speed fell away. The Japanese destroyers immediately dashed in to discharge their torpedoes, while the armoured and protected cruisers thrust themselves like so many wedges between Witgeft's divisions, seeking to separate them, the better to hammer them in detail. Witgeft had been killed at his post in the conning tower of the *Tzesarevitch*, and with his death virtually all control of the scattered Russian craft dissolved.

At 12.50 Togo made a 16-point turn and by so doing sought to concentrate his fire on the three cruisers. The sea all about the *Diana* and her consorts was fairly aboil with plunging shell, to which the Russians sought to reply with equal vigour. "The rear ship—the *Diana*—got no direct hits," Commander Semenoff carefully noted, "but our sides, boats, superstructures, ventilators, funnels and masts were riddled by small splinters;

yet we had only two men wounded." "True," he adds, "I had seen the *Askold*'s foremost funnel and the *Pallada*'s starboard cutter each struck by a shell. But these ships suffered no losses in men, and had no serious damage. The final encounter had ended in our favour. When they crossed our tail the Japanese turned again to southward. They steamed along on our starboard quarter and kept up a slow fire at long range, which only our battleships could reply to."

Soon after three o'clock firing ceased altogether, but at 4.45 the exchange of shot reopened, the Russians being careful to keep their distance, since they had been denuded of much of their secondary armament for the benefit of the shore defences. So far, the damage sustained by the squadron had not been too crippling. The conning tower of the *Tzesarevitch* had been destroyed, with the loss of everyone in it. The main topmast of the *Peresviet* had been cut in half, and she was therefore without means of hoisting signals, while the plates of the *Poltava* and the *Diana* had been dangerously pierced.

Then, suddenly, something went wrong with the flagship's steering, and she proceeded to turn a complete circle. It was impossible to guess where she might plunge next; and such formation as the squadron had hitherto been observing broke up into bewildered confusion. With the flagship reduced to steering precariously on her engines, Witgeft's flag captain despairingly signalled, "The Admiral hands over command." But since Prince Uktomsky in the *Peresviet* was without the means of making signals that anyone could pick up, it was impossible to ascertain into whose hands the command had passed. In the *Askold* Rear Admiral von Reitzenstein notified his charges that he was "steering N.W.," and it was from this implied command that the cruisers took their cue.

By this time the battleships' evolutions resembled nothing so much as a demented maritime circus. "Their firing was so wild that some of their projectiles fell very close to the cruisers."[17] In the nightmare confusion some vessels recalled their original orders and sought to head for Vladivostok, pressing on northeastward. Others ran blindly from the scene of action, heading back where they had come from; and a signal from the Japanese flagship sent the *Osiva* and her fellow destroyers racing to get between the fleeing vessels and the sanctuary for which they were heading. A flutter of bunting from the *Tzesarevitch* hurled the Russian destroyers and torpedo boats in savage attack on the enemy mosquito craft, to clear a passage for the battleships lumbering back to the relative safety of Port Arthur. Hotly pursued by the *Iwate, Yakumo, Azuma, Asama,* and six of the protected cruisers, the Russians fought back with everything they could bring to bear. At one stage the exchange of shot became so close that the *Hiroya* turned her lesser armament onto the *Retvisan*, killing a number of her crew at short range. In reply, a blast from the battleship's 32-cm tore into the *Hiroya*'s bows, to start a leaping fire. Although struck by at least one torpedo, the *Retvisan* contrived to make her way slowly back to harbour, as did the equally battered *Peresviet*. Even in the last stages of their retreat, ill fortune continued to dog the Russians and their crank and unwieldy vessels. Within hailing distance of the shore the *Sevastopol* struck a mine, but was just able to reach shallow water and drop anchor. All through the night Togo's destroyers dashed in, in the glow of the defenders' searchlights, seeking to strike a mortal blow at the helpless leviathan. But the torrent of fire from the shore batteries kept the Japanese craft from discharging their torpedoes at effective range. Yet it was not until dawn was paling the searchlight beams that the last enemy ship put about and made for the open sea, shot-torn and limping like many of her sister ships.

In all, five battleships, one cruiser, and three destroyers regained the harbour, most of the other survivors having dispersed to seek safety in internment. Gashed and crippled, the *Tzesarevitch* limped into sanctuary in the German Treaty Port of Kiao-chau; the *Askold* reached Shanghai. Blundering along in helpless flight, the *Diana* found refuge as far afield as Saigon. With a rare combination of resolution and good fortune, the *Novik* fought her way through her enemies and eluded their pursuit to steam northward toward Vladivostok. But her run of good fortune was not destined to endure. On Aug. 18, in an engagement between the Vladivostok cruisers and the detached force under Admiral Kamamura, the *Rurik* was sunk and the *Gromoboy* and the *Rossia* so badly damaged that it was clear that their repair would take a matter of months. The gallant *Novik*, putting in to coal and water at Sakhalin's Korsakosk Bay, was cornered by the Japanese cruisers *Tsushima* and *Chitose*. For an hour she fought back valiantly, but the odds against her were obviously too great to be overcome. Bringing his ship's company ashore, the *Novik*'s commander determined to sink his vessel in shallow water, with the hope of one day refloating her. This was done, but the *Chitose* returned to shell the craft where she lay half submerged, and any immediate hope of retrieving her had to be abandoned.

Of the eight destroyers that left Port Arthur bound for Vladivostok three returned, while the remainder scattered to various Chinese ports. The *Grozevoy* joined the *Askold* in Shanghai. The *Burni*, chased by Japanese small craft, ran ashore on the northern coast of Shan-tung, ten miles from the eastern limit of the British territory of Wei-hai-wei. Her captain destroyed his vessel and then sullenly marched his men into internment. If Togo's over-all design had attained no more than limited success, he had the satisfaction of knowing that, penned in in its harbour, the Pacific Squadron would soon find itself the helpless target of the heavier pieces of ordnance with which it was planned to strengthen Nogi's hand.

With the Russian vessels once again at their moorings in the inner harbour, querulous voices were not long in demanding what value was to be attached to a fleet that always turned tail. In their rancorous chagrin at the navy's failure to raise the blockade, the snarling critics spared no one, however humble or exalted his rank. "Everywhere on shore—in the streets, in the restaurants—there was nothing but abuse and curses for the Naval Officers, from the highest to the lowest."[18] A sense of proportion is one of the rarest of human attributes. With the Japanese already swarming on their doorstep, the best that the Russians could do was to bandy diatribes.

Except for the frustrated escapists of the Pacific Ocean Squadron, licking their wounds under the protection of the fortress guns, General Nogi's perfunctory proposal for surrender must have had about it a peculiarly corroding quality of contempt.

THE TROUGH OF
THE WAVE

"HE WHO TRIES TO ACCOMPLISH TOO MUCH OFTEN ENDS
BY ACCOMPLISHING NOTHING."
—SIR JOHN CHANDOS (A.D. 1360)

6   A CHAIN is as strong as its weakest link; and the weakest link in General Kuropatkin's chain of command was the Trans-Siberian railway, by which he was kept so precariously in touch with his base. With a single-line track, trains were run in what was known as "pairs," one travelling east and one west; and it was a rare occurrence for the schedule of five pairs of thirty-five-car trains per day to be attained. The line had undergone little change since the day when a traveller journeying eastward had recorded: "On this occasion we had a broken rail which made us nine hours late at Irkutsk; another in Trans-Baikalia, which delayed us hours before reaching the Manchurian frontier; and on the East Chinese line, a military train ahead of us ran off the rails, blocked the line all day, and caused us to be twelve hours behind time at Harbin."[1]

To try and improve running conditions, so that the movement of troops and supplies could be accelerated, would only have had the effect of choking the line with cars bearing sleepers, rails, ties, and other railway material at a time when reinforcements and ammunition were most urgently needed. Winter, which set in early, would appreciably worsen conditions with which it was always difficult to cope. For the steel-fingered Siberian cold hampered smooth running to a degree that was positively fantastic. To bypass the Lake Baikal obstacle, Prince Khilkoff, the Minister of Ways and Communications, was tirelessly urging the construction of a loop-line round the water's southern shore; but there was little hope of the task being completed before the spring of 1905.

Yet according to Kuropatkin's estimate, a steady flow of at least fourteen pairs a day was required to furnish him with the field force and matériel he required. An attempt to ease the burden on the railway by endeavouring to transport men and supplies by way of the Arctic Ocean and the Yenissi River having proved a costly failure, all efforts were concentrated on seeking to improve running conditions on the line. But although a certain amount of progress was made, it took five months from the declaration of war to concentrate *one-half* the troops earmarked for the Manchurian theatre; and it was not until Kuropatkin had taken up position in the Liao-yang defence line that he could count on possessing numerical superiority over his opponents—150,000 men to Japan's 125,000. Even so, the army commander was short of the strength he had asked for by 350 officers and some 14,800 men.

The flow of Japanese reinforcements, on the other hand, had been steadily maintained from the outset. Field Marshal the Marquis Oyama, arriving at Dalny in early July to assume supreme command, had been accompanied by twenty troop transports, and "most of the soldiers were landed at Pitsewo (Pi-tzu-wo) and only 12,000 men are left to reinforce General Nogi."[2] Moreover, the newcomers brought with them many of the light, portable machine guns that were beginning to increase the Japanese volume of fire so potently.[3] A further draft of 17,000 men was due to leave Japan early in September, and recruiting in the homeland was still proceeding briskly. The fact had to be recognized, however, that with the heavier ratio of casualties suffered by the Japanese field armies, the age limit for reservists and volunteers would have to be raised and the conscripts in the 1905 class called up prematurely. Nonetheless, a sharp-eyed observer could record, "They have still as many soldiers waiting to come to Manchuria as they have already brought there; money they will raise at need."[4]

Liao-yang's defences consisted firstly of an indifferently entrenched outpost line ten miles south of the city, and some fifty-five miles in length. Another system of fieldworks had been sited seven miles farther back. Soundly built up on the right, they degenerated into a very sketchy network of trenches on the left, in which considerable reliance was placed on the *trous-de-loup*, or rifle pits, so favoured in the Crimea. An inner, strongly fortified nine-mile defensive position ran just south and west of the town limits.

To crack the triple line of defences was the first task that confronted Oyama upon his assumption of over-all command. A swart, leathery, globular, rather slow-thinking individual, he was singularly calm and levelheaded, although he was capable, on rare occasions, of a terrifying rage. A veteran of the war against China, he was thoroughly familiar with the terrain; and he not only enjoyed the confidence of the men under his command, but of the whole nation. Solid and dependable, he was exactly the man to stabilize the venturesome Oku, lend support to the thrusting Kuroki, and encourage the frank and genial Nodzu to put forth his best effort. At Oyama's elbow was always to be found his chief of staff, Major General Fukushima. A close student of the writings of Helmuth von Moltke, he was the real strategist of the campaign, and was very well aware of the fact. Restrained and reticent though he was, there was an air about him that was singularly suggestive of a schoolboy who is fully alive to the fact that he is something of a prodigy.

With the Japanese closing in, Kuropatkin initially took his stand on the outpost line, determined to go over to the offensive should the opportunity offer. The battle opened on Aug. 25, with the Japanese striving impetuously to overrun the forward positions. It was characteristic of each commander that Kuropatkin kept one-third (two divisions) of his force in general reserve while Kuroki was content to hold back a single formation, the Twenty-ninth *Kobi* Regiment, which had arrived on the scene during the night of Aug. 24–25 in a thoroughly exhausted condition.

The first Japanese attempt to envelop the enemy right

flank was driven back in some confusion; but General Bilderling, in command in this sector, made no attempt to exploit
the situation by following up with a counterattack while his
opponents were off balance. On the Russian left the Japanese
assault was pressed with a furious energy that swiftly used up
all local reserves, but succeeded in throwing the enemy out of
a very strong natural position, which almost certainly could
have been held had more Russian troops been committed to
the fray in time. By the night of Aug. 28 Kuropatkin's formations were all back on their second line; and Aug. 29 was
devoted by both sides to the reorganization of their forces.

On Aug. 30 the Japanese left, at some sacrifice, pinned
down their opponents so that Kuroki could put in motion a
daring advance across the Tai-tzu-Ho, a move he achieved
without encountering serious opposition.

"I have today seen the most stupendous spectacle it is
possible for the mortal brain to conceive," recorded the senior
British military observer; "Asia advancing; Europe falling back;
the wall of mist and the writing thereon."[5]

On the day following there was desperate fighting in the
west; the Japanese suffering something of a reverse owing to
the need to hoard their scanty reserves to deal with an expected
turning movement on their left. On the Russian left General
Vasilier, observing a Japanese move to the northeast, eagerly
proposed a slashing stroke to catch them in the flank. He was
coldly instructed that any extra troops he might have should
be sent to the reserve; and the best opportunity with which
the Russians had been presented to achieve a scarifying riposte
was sacrificed on the altar of an outmoded piece of textbook
pedantry.

Having permitted Kuroki to get across the Tai-tzu-Ho
practically unchallenged, Kuropatkin decided to withdraw to
the inner, strongly fortified Liao-yang line and man it with
so reduced a garrison that he would be able to concentrate the
bulk of his troops against the Japanese forces over the river.
On this eastern sector of the line Sept. 1 witnessed a dogged
and costly struggle to win and retain possession of the Manju-
Yama mountain. "Till midnight confused and passionate fight-

ing took place backward and forward over the shell-scarred features of this little Rice-cake hill, about which hour the last handful of Russians holding on round a small tumulus on the summit were fairly forced back into the surrounding *kao-liang*."[6]

Elsewhere, the bulk of both forces was marching to assembly positions on the north bank of the stream. Kuropatkin was resolved to hold on around Liao-yang and concentrate all his energies on countering the threat to his communications by driving his opponents into the Tai-tzu-Ho—not to be recrossed save at one or two fords which could be kept under concentrated fire. In the ensuing battle the Japanese fought with no sign of weariness or diminished ardour. In and about Liao-yang they could make little impression on their strongly entrenched antagonists; while on the eastern flank, the Russians, in great strength and with their second attempt, succeeded in regaining the crest of Manju-Yama.

Throughout the whole of the fighting the Russians never forgot Suvorov's famous dictum, that "the bullet is a mad thing; the bayonet only knows what it is about." Japanese losses attributable to this weapon, Soloviev recorded, "were almost as large as those caused by artillery, in spite of the enormous development of the latter."[7] Not that Oyama's men were any less ready to resort to the bayonet than their opponents. When at close quarters both sides would frequently leave off firing simultaneously and have at each other with the cold steel.

Early in the forenoon of Sept. 3, as Kuropatkin was in the act of issuing orders for the continuation of the battle, news was brought to him that, without orders, the left of the line had retired 2½ miles, abandoning the position in the region of the Manju-Yama without further fight. At the same time Zarubaeff, commanding the Liao-yang defences, reported that he was nearly out of ammunition and desperately in need of reinforcement. In the army commander's eyes, Kuroki's turning movement had gained such impetus that, rather than attack it in flank or seek to sterilize it by a vigorous assault on the static Japanese left, he decided to pull out and retire on Mukden—and this with an untapped reserve of over 60,000 troops.[8] Had the 80,000 men pinned down in front of Port Arthur been available to Marshal Oyama, another Sedan could have been enacted between the spurs of Manju-Yama and the walls of Liao-yang. As events had transpired, it had been touch and go with the Japanese on more than one occasion. "Each reinforcement appeared on the scene in the very nick of time,"[9] and it had been only by exerting every ounce of energy and fighting ability that Oyama's men had won through so handsomely. But as the United States military representative justly commented: "This campaign has proved that a frontal attack against an entrenched position can be made. But it seems equally proven," he went on, "that the attack must be made by not only brave but by thoroughly trained soldiers. I do not believe that half-trained soldiers could do it, except at a cost that would be practically prohibitive."[10]

With 23,615 casualties as against Russian losses in killed and wounded of 17,900, Oyama's troops were too exhausted to organize a vigorous pursuit over impassable country swimming in glutinous mud; and the Russians slipped away from Liao-yang virtually unimpeded.

The Japanese commander had undoubtedly displayed great courage in sanctioning Kuroki's audacious crossing of the Tai-tzu-Ho while his centre was barely holding together; but "what at first sight may appear to be rashness on Marshal Oyama's part may in fact be termed a brilliant example of judicious opportunism."[11] Unquestionably, Kuropatkin had been outfought; "he fell back because he was beaten."[12] Many of his troops had stood their ground manfully. But by this time "most of the men were reservists who had forgotten a good deal,"[13] and many of them had small stomach for the fight. Helping a wounded comrade to the Regimental Aid Post presented the shirker with an admirable opportunity to leave the field, of which far too many took advantage; while so large was the number of men detailed to perform non-combatant duties in the depots that front-line units never had more than 75 per cent of their bayonet strength actually with them. Throughout, there was a dearth of howitzers firing high explosive shell, while the salient effect of the belated appearance of quick-firing guns among the artillery was a wild expenditure of ammunition, 100,000 reserve rounds being blazed away on the last two days of August. In general, the staff was woefully inefficient. Orders were rarely circulated or received at the proper time, and were invariably prolix and clogged with superfluous detail. In effect, there were far too many officers serving on the staff who had secured their appointments by favour rather than merit. "The explanation is that in Russia influential family connections or friends were almost paramount, and Officers, pushed on to high posts, had been brought up to think nothing of duty."[14] This applied equally to the senior formation leaders, of whom Kuropatkin himself mournfully recorded that, "Unfortunately some commanders even of large forces have confessed themselves unable to carry out the operations entrusted to them, at a moment when they still had in hand big reserves who had not fired a shot." True as it may be, as a comment this is not without irony, since Kuropatkin reproaching a subordinate for failure to make timely use of his reserves is tantamount to Satan sternly rebuking sin.

After the costly repulse of all their August attempts to rush the Port Arthur defences out of hand, the Japanese required a little time in which to reorganize. Between the first of the month and the twenty-fourth their losses had amounted to 190 officers and 5,284 men killed, and 470 officers and 14,179 other ranks wounded. Decimated battalions had to assimilate the drafts sent up from Dalny; there was urgent need to replenish the depleted reserves of ammunition and field stores, to evacuate the field hospitals and bury the fallen. Moreover, there was the narrow-gauge Decauville field railway to complete—it eventually ran to a length of fifty kilometres—and the spider's web of telephone and telegraph wires to run out, to link headquarters with all subordinate formations. The one thing that gave no cause for anxiety was the morale of the survivors of the recent ordeal by fire. Stoked with the self-renewing fuel of patriotism, they remained unfaltering in their confidence in ultimate victory. And no troops could have been more cheerful than these men in wrinkled khaki, gathered about their camp kettles to eat their simple meal of meat, biscuits, and rice, with a relish in the form of cucumber, dried radish, edible ferns, or dried sweet potato, and an occasional issue of saki on the scale of half a pint per head—a veritable feast to the former coolies among the ranks, whose daily diet had rarely gone beyond a handful of boiled millet seed. Sometimes the officers in the forward positions, under close observation by the enemy, indulged in a good-humoured grumble when called upon to "swallow hard biscuit without water or to welcome as a great treat one or two salted pickled plums."¹⁵ But in bivouac or in billets, in one of the innumerable hamlets that dotted the countryside, there was nothing but cheerfulness as the men paraded for the physical exercises that formed part of the day's routine training and helped so tremendously to maintain the troops' unflagging vigour. This was followed by arms drill and musketry instruction, with the N.C.O.s gently but firmly exhorting the new arrivals from Japan to "Pull the trigger as carefully and gently as the frost falls on a cold night."

With the Japanese soldier drawing a mere 6 yen (3 cents) a day, there was not much chance to profiteer out of him. Nonetheless, "here and there," a British war correspondent noted, "a sutler's shanty is surrounded by groups of men buying little luxuries. Some of these are different from what you would find in most European camps—long, horn-handled tooth brushes and little packets of tooth-powder, sweetmeats, canned fruits, and Nestlés' milk. . . . The tooth-brush is an essential part of the Japanese campaigning kit. The first thing a Jap apparently does when he gets up in the morning is to stick a tooth-brush in his mouth. You can see hundreds of men rubbing away at their teeth and gums, walking about chatting with each other during the operation."¹⁶

The training programme was rigorous, and when the day's work was over, the troops were glad enough to gather quietly about the campfire that the nipping chill of early autumn made so welcome. Relaxed and silent, they would sit and listen as one of their number produced his *yesivan*—the stringed instrument used by the geishas—and played and sang the nostalgic ditties so popular in the Yoshiwara:

Madunagta nika kura
Otovara masiné.

And more often than not, just visible in the glow from the fire, a spruce, grey-bearded figure might be seen making his way from one group to another, with a smile and a friendly word that warmed the heart of both veteran and raw recruit. For like Henry of Monmouth hobnobbing with his bowmen on the eve of Agincourt, Gen. Kiten Nogi was rich in that human quality that inspires the common soldier.

It was a far different spirit that prevailed behind the girdle of Port Arthur's shell-swept defences. Perpetual hammering by the Japanese batteries and the need to restrengthen and extend the fieldworks kept the men toiling in the forward zone all through the hours of darkness, with little chance of rest. So rock-pitted and stubborn was the soil that nothing short of blasting served to deepen the trenches on 203 Metre Hill. But after the repulse of the last of their August attacks "the Japanese were so listless," Tretyakov thankfully records, "that we began to work on the defences by day." But as the work became more and more arduous, so the scale of rations steadily declined. Mule and horseflesh were the only form of fresh meat available, and there was little more of this than of preserved meat. "Fortunately," Tretyakov philosophically observes, "there was plenty of horse-radish, and with what zest did we devour that bitter root!" A typical dinner consisted of rice soup, roast horseflesh with rice, garnished with rancid butter or tallow. Occasionally a few "goltsies"—small dark fish—would be caught in the horseponds, and these were regarded as far superior to the rockfish sometimes obtainable from Pigeon Bay. Small birds and nighthawks were shot or snared and, roasted on a wooden spit, were considered a most succulent luxury. "There was plenty of vodka and wine to be had," Tretyakov noted, "but I hardly saw anyone drunk," which, considering the normally bibulous habits of both officers and men, indicates an uncommon spirit of self-discipline. Saratov's restaurant remained open but could offer nothing substantial in the way of a meal; and the wild drinking parties that had characterized the early days of the siege no longer filled the dusty, wind-scoured, rutty streets of the town with a crowd of tipsy officers weaving a serpentine way home to barracks. But if wine and vodka were indulged in with exemplary moderation, tea was consumed in prodigious quantity. Fortunately, it was one of the few things of which the commissary was not desperately short.

All this was in striking contrast to the liberal scale of subsistence of the field armies. "The supply of provisions for the troops was well organized. There was never any lack of meat; the cattle were large and fleshy; there was always a great variety and abundance of fruit and vegetables; fresh bread was always served, and biscuit was used but rarely. Hot food was served every day; the field kitchens being of great advantage. Each company had a wheeled field kitchen, where the food was cooked on the march."[17] Kuropatkin's forces were, of course, in the fortunate position of operating in a theatre of war in which stockbreeding was only second in importance to the cultivation of grain. "From the end of April the Cossacks had commenced to denude the country of cattle, going out in troops of fifty each, accompanied by a Chinese interpreter. Each troop considered it an unlucky day when a bullock apiece had not been captured."[18] The despoiled villagers promptly appealed for help to the Hunhuses, and there were raids and counterraids, and savage border warfare. Considering that these banditti and accomplished cattle rustlers were made up of some 80,000 crafty warlike hillmen, they constituted a standing menace to the Russian lines of communication. Their menace increased when they yielded to Japanese persuasion and agreed to follow guerrilla leaders selected by the general staff—obliging individuals who placated local susceptibilities by sewing a pigtail in their caps. The Hunhuses, in short, constituted a threat to Kuropatkin's western and northwestern flank that time was materially to enhance.

Rozhestvensky's boast that he would set out for Far Eastern waters on July 15 had, of course, not been redeemed. Work on fitting out the flagship *Kniaz Suvoroff* and her sister

battleships *Borodino, Oryol,* and *Alexander III* was still proceeding, as was the task of trying to knock a little discipline
and sense of seamanship into crews made up very largely of
disgruntled reservists, merchant seamen entirely devoid of
service experience, and bucolic conscripts who regarded the
navy as an unfathomable mystery surrounded by seasickness.
Since there was a strong contingent of embittered revolutionaries distributed throughout all the ships' companies, the
spirit of subversive insubordination was hard to check and
virtually impossible to extirpate.

It was not until August that the admiral succeeded in
mustering his vessels for a training exercise in the Baltic. As
it turned out, the experiment was more notable for the dis-
closure of innumerable defects of tactics, gunnery, torpedo
firing, and mine laying than for the display of any enthusiasm
for the task that lay ahead. Since engine-room breakdowns
had been a notable feature throughout the whole exercise, at
its conclusion the fleet returned to harbour to have its mechanical defects looked into and some of the grosser abnormalities
in its fittings and armament subjected to drastic overhaul.

But the fact that the Second Pacific Squadron had really
put to sea, and was presumably nearing the point when it
would actually set out upon its odyssey, was something the
Japanese had to take very seriously into their calculations.

Mid-August had witnessed a brisk encounter between
Kamimura's detached force and the Vladivostok squadron,
steaming hopefully southward under the erroneous impression
that Witgeft had won his fight and was heading northward.
Both the *Rossia* and the *Gromoboy* had suffered considerable
damage, while the *Rurik* had been sent to the bottom with 170
of her ship's company still aboard. With the news of the Pacific
Ocean Squadron's failure to break out of Port Arthur, Essen
again took refuge under the lee of Vladivostok's shore defences.

Despite the temporary suspension of infantry attacks
throughout the last few days of August, the Japanese guns
kept up a steady rain of missiles not only on Port Arthur's

defences, but also on the residential quarters. "It was by no means pleasant in the town. Shells fell not only on the houses, but on the hospital. It became dangerous to walk about."[19] Although the abuse of the Red Cross flag was not deliberate, the damage done to the buildings was considerable, and "the hospitals were full, although men scarcely able to walk were sent back into the trenches and forts."[20] The whole system of defences was under constant fire, but Forts Nos. 2 and 3 in particular were the targets of a constant stream of shells, and Sung-su-shan also came in for an exceptional share of attention.

The redoubts captured under the lee of Fort Erh-lung-shan had been neutralized by the gunfire that both sides poured into them. But Smirnoff's urgent desire to get them firmly into Russian hands once more, even at heavy cost, was peremptorily vetoed by Stössel. On Tretyakov's front the Japanese may have appeared somewhat "listless." But they were busy enough burrowing toward Fort Kuropatkin and the Waterworks and Temple Redoubts; and by Sept. 13 some of the sapheads were within 80 yards of their objective.

At 7 A.M. on Sept. 19 the Russian works were brought under the fire of the 15-cm and 12-cm guns hidden away a mile behind Shui-shih-ying village. Field howitzers and some of the divisional artillery, deployed behind one of the spurs of Mount Ho-shan, also joined in the shoot. The bombardment continued at a steady rate until 4 P.M., when a hurricane of rapid fire was directed against all the defences.

The wire entanglements in front of Fort Kuropatkin (or Waterworks Redoubt), the foremost work, had been cut by a *ketshitai*, who had set about their dangerous work under cover of the darkness, while a thorough search had been made for the mines sown throughout the whole area. A lucky find had been the contact box by which all the mines were connected. This had been removed after the ground had been filled in so carefully that the Russians entertained no suspicion that their mine field had surreptitiously been put out of order. The electrified strands of telephone wire were dealt with by men working in gloves made out of old bicycle tyres.

By the late afternoon of Sept. 19 three battalions of the Japanese Thirty-sixth Regiment and one of the Nineteenth Regiment were all in their assembly positions. Their first two rushes were stopped by furious rifle fire, but an assault put in after darkness had fallen reached the moat. At one point the struggle worked its way over to a miniature gorge behind the work, where a number of Russians had taken refuge. A fierce fight with grenades ensued, with the Japanese gradually reinforcing their forward line until they had obtained a lodgment in their objective. The Russians rallied, however, and put in a sharp counterattack which won back all the ground they had lost.

No further move was made until 4 A.M. on Sept. 20, when a determined onslaught in strength delivered Fort Kuropatkin and the adjacent broken country into Japanese hands. The fort itself immediately became the target of the Russian counterbatteries and soon became untenable. But the Japanese were pushing forward to secure the positions adjacent to the Waterworks. These were carried at about the same time as the fieldwork known as Temple Redoubt, the Russians retreating to their entrenchments in the neighbourhood of the railway embankment. With the Waterworks in their hands, the Japanese immediately set about cutting the pipes supplying both the Old and New Towns, reducing the garrison and the unfortunate civilians to reliance on such few wells as were in operation, or distilled water from the horseponds and the lake behind Golden Hill.

Naval co-operation in the preliminary bombardment had cost the Japanese the gunboat *Heiyen*, which struck a mine off Pigeon Bay. Subsequently, Admiral Togo ordered his vessels to withdraw until the local waters had been swept.

The attack on Fort Kuropatkin and the adjacent works had cost over 1,000 casualties. Even so, the stroke was subsidiary to the 1st Division's assault on Namako-Yama and the coveted 203 Metre Hill. For Nogi had redesigned his tactics. It was his aim to advance on a narrow front, very largely ignoring the forts while he thrust a wedge between them. Surprise, shock, and concentrated force were the keys upon which he relied to prise the fortress portals open. The plan had the obvious disadvantage, however, of permitting the defence to concentrate against a single point of attack.

The approaches to both western objectives were extremely steep, the grassy glacis of Namako-Yama being broken halfway up its northern slope by rocky ground that offered some hope of protection. Covering fire for the assault could be brought to bear from Angle (174 Metre) Hill, some thousand metres across the valley to the westward, as from a small knoll just to the north of the objective.

The 1st Division's commander, General Matsamura, could dispose of the First and Fifteenth Regiments, each of three battalions, together with one *Kobi* brigade—fifteen battalions in all. In support, sixty carefully concealed guns were deployed to concentrate their fire on the two objectives. But the most formidable pieces available were the field howitzers, throwing a 45-pound shell; the heavy 11-inch howitzers which Nogi had requested had not yet put in an appearance.

As the hostile fire on Namako-Yama and 203 Metre Hill intensified, the sector commander, Colonel Irman, and Colonel Tretyakov, responsible for local defence, proceeded to their observation post. "We received a report," the latter notes, "that the Japanese were moving in force against these hills, so we expected an attack on both of them simultaneously. I therefore moved my reserves to the hollow behind Akasaka-Yama, so that they should be under my hand and easily despatched to either 203 Metre Hill or Namako-Yama. The situation was unchanged, but our men were suffering severely from the artillery fire. Hence we came to the conclusion that the Japanese intended to leave things as they were, and compel us to evacuate the Hill without making an attack."

As it turned out, this was an accurate enough short-term appreciation of the situation. But as the day lengthened, the intensity of the cannonade ominously increased in volume, reaching its zenith about midday. An inspection of the forward trenches revealed that while those on 203 Metre Hill had stood up well to their battering, those on Namako-Yama were virtually obliterated. Yet, as Tretyakov had forecast, no immediate infantry assault developed. The guns slammed away in full-throated chorus, their greatest fury being reserved for the right flank of Namako-Yama; and return fire from a 10-inch piece in the Pai-yu-shan fortification, on Quail Hill, searched diligently for the hostile batteries. The deafening bark of the guns and the querulous screech of their missiles never ceased hammering at men's nerves until even the most stout of heart winced at their relentless clamour. The summit of Namako-Yama and the double row of entrenchments on its slopes "presented the appearance of an active volcano, the smoke from the bursting shells and the earth thrown up after each explosion enveloping the trenches and completely hiding them from view."[21]

At 6.30 P.M., with the guns on Namako-Yama completely out of action, the first trickle of Japanese infantry broke shelter and dashed for the cover offered by the rocky ground halfway up the hill. So effectually was the shrapnel keeping the Russians huddled in their splinterproof cover that the first thin wave crossed the open stretch almost unchallenged. But as the supporting guns fell silent lest they should pepper their own men, the Russians sprang to their battered breastworks and poured down a steady blast of musketry. But the light was failing, greatly impairing the defenders' aim, and by threes and fours the Japanese sank to cover behind the rocky outcrop until quite a sizable force was concentrated in the "dead" ground below the first trench, only awaiting the signal to advance.

There was no questing searchlight on Namako-Yama; only the glare of the star shells and the flare of exploding missiles intermittently lit the darkness that enshrouded the hillock's crowded slopes and its sinister, brooding peak. To sharpen the chill of autumn, a searching wind blew in from the sea to numb the rank and file of the First Regiment, crouching on the hillside in their thin khaki, without overcoats or blankets, and carrying nothing but their rifles and ammunition.

It was five o'clock in the afternoon on the twentieth when the final assault went in, after a thorough bombardment of the whole position by the artillery. "The trenches were reached and the nearest part carried in a very short time; but the Russians still put up a good fight. Silhouetted on top of the trenches as the combatants were, we could easily follow the hard-contested, hand-to-hand fight. We could plainly see every thrust parried, every blow that struck home. We could see how with bayonets and swords, stones and clubbed rifles, both sides strove furiously for the mastery, until the garrison was overpowered and the hill was in the hands of the Japanese."[22]

Flung out of their trenches as they might be, the Russians still clung to Namako-Yama's peak, from which they sniped at any khaki-clad figure who as much as shifted his position to ease his cramped and shivering limbs. It was an assault with hand grenades charged with pyroxylin[23] that finally won the crest. The Russians left unhurt "rushing headlong down the hill. . . . After the men on the right flank had run, the others from the battery and the enemy appeared simultaneously on the crest. A few minutes later, from the left of the battery, appeared a group of our men, who opened fire on the Japanese and drove them off the top. Unfortunately, our men did not remain where they were but also ran back down the hill. It all happened in a very few minutes. We immediately sent all the Officers and orderlies near us with orders to the retreating companies to stop on Akasaka-Yama and occupy the trenches there."[24] Namako-Yama was firmly in the Japanese grip at last, and it was essential for them to hold it, despite the harassing fire from the flanks, since the attack developing against 203 Metre Hill would be certain to demand support.

The first rush at this most vital of all objectives swung in from the west at a run. But the troops had 300 yards of open ground to cross and were in far too close order. So, like the Napoleonic columns in the face of Wellington's extended line of marksmen, they were swept out of existence by a combination of rifle fire from their front and from Saddle Hill on their flank, aided by some well-placed bursts of shrapnel. "Out of all who started, only two or three ever reached their destination. As for the rest, their bodies remained on the hillside, a gruesome monument to their wasted gallantry."[25]

"The assault increased; column after column rushed forward on to 203 Metre Hill, covering all its fore-hills and slopes with heaps of dead; but at 8.45 they were repulsed. This assault was distinguished by particular obstinacy. I myself saw how, when their attack was repulsed, instead of retreating, the enemy began to build parapets of their dead and wounded comrades on the granite slopes of the hill, for they had no sandbags."[26]

From 9 P.M. till 11 P.M. the assault was maintained with unexampled vigour. "Several desperate attacks were successfully repulsed, in spite of the fact that the first of them was made before the completion of the [newly dug] trenches, when our men had to stand up in them without any cover, under a perfect storm of shells. They *had* to stand up, as they could not fire down the steep slope of the hill in a sitting position."[27] With scant regard for their own assault force, the Japanese gunners were still pounding away at the crest of the hill, and many a man in khaki fell victim to shells fired by his own side. But the execution among the defenders was infinitely greater. "The situation was critical. We were losing men so fast under the terrific fire that the companies were literally melting away minute by minute. In view of this Colonel Irman sent for reinforcements from the general reserve, all our local reserves having been used up. Danger threatened 203 Metre Hill's other neighbours, especially the left flank of Akasaka-Yama, where there was some dead ground right up under the trenches."[28]

But with daylight it was seen that the Japanese gains amounted to no more than possession of a battered earthwork on the forward slope of the Hill. Yet it was not to be ignored that out of the five companies engaged in its defence 371 men had already fallen.

The day was spent in striving to restore and strengthen the defences on the hilltop; and the suggestion was put forward to roll mines down onto the Japanese-held trench on the face of the northern slope. Nothing of immediate value came of the proposal, however, as the mines brought forward proved far too heavy. But a later attempt with mines of much lighter weight wrought considerable havoc, and contributed materially to the Hill's defence. Encouraged by this successful stroke, the Russians refused to be budged from their battered works on the northeast peak, although the Japanese remained obstinately in possession of the complementary high ground to the west.

"The General [Smirnoff] was disturbed about the position on 203 Metre Hill, though for that front, as a whole, he had no fear. He thought that the enemy would storm the hill that night, and that they must therefore have large masses of reserves collected somewhere close by; he wanted to find those reserves. His theory was justified, for at 1 P.M. a report was received from an observation post at Pigeon Bay that, from a small peak half a mile away, a good view could be had of a deep ravine running to the foot of 203 Metre Hill, and that in it the enemy's reserve of almost two regiments was hiding, waiting apparently till dark to make a fresh attack on the hill.

"Smirnoff at once telephoned to Colonel Khvostoff to send a section of quick-firers to Liao-tieh-shan or Fort No. 6 to shell them, and at the same time told him to warn all guns on the western front to be ready to sweep the south-west foot of 203 Metre Hill, where the enemy were bound first to show themselves on leaving the ravine. The section of quick-firers moved cautiously towards the ravine without being seen from the enemy's siege batteries. It then suddenly opened rapid fire on the crowd of reserves massed in the ravine, and caused great loss. They were surprised, and, as had been foreseen, bolted out into the slopes of the west front, where they came under fire of the guns of the west front and scattered in panic, leaving great numbers of dead behind. . . . On the morning of the 23rd another Japanese battalion, which was in this same ravine, came under the fire of our guns, took to the slopes, and in about ten minutes was almost wiped out of existence."[29]

By Sept. 24 the Japanese clinging to their shattered eyrie on 203 Metre Hill had been subjected to such a whirlwind of 10-inch shells that General Mutsumara reported that he was no longer able to maintain the position, although Namako-Yama could be securely held. With that Nogi had to rest temporarily content.

The Japanese had taken care that the news of the Russian defeat at Liao-yang should find its way into Port Arthur; and the erratic shooting of the Electric Cliff batteries on Golden Hill inspired a sardonic anonymous note suggesting that if the gunners did not fire more carefully they might hit Kuropatkin! The garrison's confidence was further shaken by "letters from the Japanese saying: 'Why do you hold on? Port Arthur has been sold to us. We have it here on paper.' "[30]

On Sept. 28 the besiegers concentrated most of their fire on the Erh-lung-shan and Chi-kuan-shan Forts and the Kuropatkin Lunette, just southeast of the last-named, toward which they had been burrowing from the outer works already in their hands. Sorties by the Russians to disrupt this tunnelling activity led to savage fighting, but their only outcome was to add to the defenders' losses; the Japanese continued with their sapping operations regardless of interruption.

The twenty-eighth also witnessed a steady bombardment of the anchored fleet by the Japanese naval batteries from their position behind Sui-shih-ying village, the *Peresviet* and *Pobieda* being hit a dozen times or more and set on fire.

Yet, all in all, the September operations had once again lent emphasis to the folly of seeking to apply the technique of field operations to the peculiar circumstances of a siege. Namako-Yama had been won, but it was no more than a consolation prize so long as 203 Metre Hill remained in Russian hands; and the bludgeoning head-on attacks on the western front had cost over 4,500 casualties.[31]

Reorganization and a good deal of hardheaded rethinking were obviously essential. The 28-cm (11-inch) howitzers were due at Dalny any day; with the mole warfare of sapping and mining to burrow into and disrupt those defences that could not be pulverized by heavy siege artillery, the triumph so long withheld must at last be achieved, and then Port Arthur and the fleet it sheltered would have no recourse but to beseech the conquerors' mercy.

THE HORNS OF
DILEMMA

7   EARLY IN OCTOBER a letter was smuggled out of Port Arthur which revealed that "Our principal forts are uninjured, but the houses in the town are badly damaged. Most of them are in ruins, and the harbour works are in sad plight. Some of our ships have been badly injured by falling shells, and it is impossible with our scant resources to repair them. We have not a single bottle of anaesthetics. The food is of the coarsest, and even that is beginning to be scarce; while there is much disease."

Casualties were mounting steadily and, unlike those suffered by the Japanese, they could not be replaced. Scurvy in its most debilitating form was rampant, with dysentery vying with it for predominance. The scarcity of the necessary medicines made it almost impossible to restore the sufferers to health. For "the Japanese blockade appears to have been very effective. According to a statement of the inhabitants, but three small steamers managed to elude the Japanese fleet, each bringing in a cargo of flour. Intercourse with Chefu by Chinese junks, landing in Pigeon Bay, was so precarious and uncertain as to have been an almost negligible factor."[1] As it turned out, October was to prove a particularly unlucky month for the blockade runners, the capture of the German steamer *Rundschau*, crammed with grain and other foodstuffs, being followed by the roundup of no less than ten Chinese junks in one swoop. It was a coup that impounded cargoes valued at 200,000 roubles.[2]

As September gave way to October, the first of the Japanese 11-inch shells thundered into the works, to be followed very shortly by another which fell on Fort No. 2 and "destroyed the masonry and killed and wounded several men. A pillar of smoke, sand and stones rose up out of Chi-kuan-shan Fort, as if a gigantic tree had sprouted up and been thrown down. Then, with clock-work regularity, fantastic trees grew up every few minutes in different directions all along the north-east front, and we heard the roars of dreadful explosions. Eight of them occurred in Erh-lung-shan and Chi-kuan-shan Forts this day and did great damage."[3] Supplementing the siege howitzers were the new Japanese mortars, 11 inches in diameter and weighing 110 tons apiece. The Russians returned the fire with an improvised and somewhat erratic grenade-mortar, projecting a 4.2 cm artillery shell on the end of a "stalk." But as the Japanese were well dug in and sandbagged, their practice was only occasionally rewarding. In conjunction with the besiegers' steadily maintained cannonade, sapping and mining were carried forward on a progressively extensive scale.

For the early days of October found General Nogi in something of a quandary. Hitherto, attempts to storm the fortress had been attended by casualties altogether out of proportion to the modesty of the gains achieved. Undiminished as the ardour of his troops might be, it was obviously out of the question to continue their expenditure at the rate that had earlier prevailed. Port Arthur must be taken at the smallest possible cost. For unless Nogi's troops, in good number, could be sent north to reinforce the field army, the slow but steady build-up of the Russian forces would presently endow Kuropatkin with a numerical superiority it would be impossible to overtake. In the long run Russia could call upon legions that were virtually illimitable: in Japan the military authorities were left with only the 7th and 8th Divisions for home defence and internal security.

On the other hand, the news that Rozhestvensky's Second Pacific Squadron was almost ready to put to sea gave added urgency to the need for Port Arthur's capture. Moreover, it was impossible for Nogi to ignore the longing throughout the whole of Japan that the port should not just be worn down into negotiated surrender, but should be carried triumphantly in a daring, spectacular feat of arms that would earn the Western nations' unqualified respect and admiration. Fort Arthur had been transformed from an important military objective into a veritable talisman.

Nonetheless, it was essential for caution to play counterpoint to daring, for the spade to share pride of place with the rifle and the bayonet.[4] And so, by day and by night, the mole warfare of trench and sap and mine gallery went steadily forward. An unbroken line of entrenchments speedily linked Saddle Hill to Namako-Yama, with saps thrust forward to the fieldworks—two strongly enclosed keeps—on 203 Metre Hill, which was now encircled by a complete belt of wire, reinforced by a tough abatis. On the eastern face of the defences mining operations had brought the besiegers, in some places, to within 40 yards of their opponents. The volume of gunfire directed against the fortress had been increased enormously. The American military representative with Nogi's forces reported on Oct. 17: "Colonel Satow, Chief of Staff to the commander of the siege artillery, stated that the following additional siege armament had been brought up during the preceding month; twelve 28-cm howitzers, two 15-cm naval guns, and four 15-cm howitzers. The total artillery armament on this date before Port Arthur comprised 240 siege and 180 field and mountain guns." Sorties did little more than momentarily hinder the Japanese in the prosecution of their subterranean activities; although of all things the besiegers least relished grenade attacks, and the wonder is that the Russians did not employ this form of assault more frequently. For there was no lack of the necessary missiles. The three grenade factories in the town could turn out between them a steady 1,000 of these hand bombs per diem; if day and night shifts were worked this total could be increased to 2,500.

At no point were the Japanese nearer to the defences than below Fort No. 2 (Chi-kuan-shan). It was to this danger spot that the sapper colonel, Rashevski, together with a subordinate and Col. Nikolai Tretyakov—who had gone to the Constantine Military School and Engineer Academy—made their way early in the month. "We ordered everyone out of the countermine," Tretyakov subsequently recorded, "and climbed in to listen; but our movements and breathing prevented our hearing well, so my two companions went out and I was left alone. Putting my ear close to the wall nearest the enemy, I held my breath and listened intently, but not a sound broke the dead silence. I acknowledge that when my companions cleared out of the mine, which dropped down sharply in the enemy's direction, I felt none too happy. Suppose the enemy had laid his charge and was just about to explode it? There would not be much of me left! In my imagination I conjured up some very disquieting pictures; and all the time not a sound from the enemy. . . . Long and intently I listened, several times changing my position, as my legs got stiff and cramped owing to my not being able to stretch them out. I strained my ears . . . not a sound. Suddenly, . . . a blow, a very careful one; then another and another. I tried to guess the enemy's direction and how far off he was. Though the formation was somewhat of the nature of sandstone, still one should have been able to judge fairly accurately. The man was working very cautiously with a pick, and I could hear it on all sides of the mine. As if it were now, I remember that the blows sounded near the left side of the passage and a little above it. The scraping sound was plainly audible through the intervening rock, but it was thought, very probably, that an enemy on the other side could not hear it."

With little skilled labour to set to work countermining, the best the Russians could do in most instances was to block the galleries toward which the Japanese were working with large rocks and heavy stones cemented together. Undeterred, Nogi's men continued doggedly with their labours, their activities extending toward Fort No. 3 and Fortification 3, farther to the west. But it was not until Oct. 9 that the Japanese succeeded in expelling the Russians from the positions they had dug in the railway embankment running at the foot of the two buttresses of Sung-su-shan and Erh-lung-shan. But once the embankment was in their possession they were in admirable position to drive their saps right forward under the works themselves.

The Japanese patrols off the Liao-tung peninsula had been strengthened early in October by the arrival of eleven new destroyers from the Osaka and Shimonoseki yards. Despite this lengthening of the odds against them, on Oct. 8 the *Pallada* and the two destroyers *Batrackzi* and *Borinsky* made a sudden dash for the open sea, intent on finding sanctuary in Vladivostok. The torpedo boats *Kioto* and *Oswa*, supported by the cruiser *Akagi*, immediately engaged the fugitives, bringing so brisk and well-aimed a fire to bear that the *Batrackzi* was speedily sunk and the battered *Borinsky* forced to haul down her flag. Both the captain and lieutenant had been killed, together with thirty-four out of her crew of sixty-two. Badly hammered, the *Pallada* managed to hobble back into port, to resume her demoralizing role as a target for the Japanese long-range guns.

Kuropatkin's retirement on Mukden had been stubbornly covered by the 1st Siberians, and behind this screen he had been able to pull clear with inconsiderable loss in guns and baggage.

In their new position the Russian forces fell into two groups. On the right, Bilderling, with the XVII Corps and ten battalions of the 5th Siberians, occupied the main position on the left bank of the Hun-Ho.[5] The left flank, from Fushun westward, was under the command of Ivanoff, who disposed of the Second and Third Brigades of the 4th and some elements of the 5th Siberians.[6] Linking these two groups were the 1st Siberians under Shtakelberg, guarding that portion of the Hun-Ho running from Chiu-tien to Pu-ling.[7] A general reserve was also divided into groups, and in this way Kuropatkin retained no less than 56 battalions, 12 squadrons, 192 guns, 12 mortars, and 2 sapper formations immediately under his hand.

But the Russian position was not without its defects. Owing to the configuration of the river, the left was thrown back too far; almost immediately behind the operational zone ran the Hun-Ho, unfordable at this time of the year and lacking in sufficient bridges; while forward of the lines lay the Fu-shun coalpits, whose retention was essential if there was to be no breakdown in the supply of railway fuel. Moreover, drafts to replace the casualties suffered at Liao-yang were arriving in little more than driblets.

Nonetheless, with the knowledge that the mobilization of the II Manchurian Army Corps had virtually been completed, Kuropatkin decided to assume the offensive, the better to ensure that none of the Japanese field army formations should be detached to reinforce Port Arthur's besiegers.

Oyama's troops occupied a line on the right bank of the Tai-tzu-Ho, running from Pen-hsi-hu in the east, through Yentai, across the railway, and on to Sha-tai-tzu in the west; with ten divisions in the forward zone, backed by brigades in reserve. It was the Russian aim, by a frontal attack, to hurl their antagonists back from their hastily contrived fieldworks onto the left bank of the Tai-tzu-Ho, dislodging them from their hill positions by a turning movement against their right. Bilderling's group was assigned the task of assailing the Japanese left and centre, while Shtakelberg, with eighty-five battalions, supported by 174 guns, was given the responsibility of rolling up their right.

At the outset, the brunt of the attack fell on the Umezawa Brigade, rather precariously perched in a tangle of mountainous country about Ping-tai-tzu, and it was soon sorely beset. "He and his Brigade would probably have been past praying for had the Russians come down like the wolf on the fold; had they developed even a touch of audacious, headlong hunger for a fight which has so often been associated with successful military enterprise."[8] But although forced to give ground against a numerical superiority of something like six to one, the Japanese commander hung on grimly to the range running from Tu-men-ling pass, on the west, to Pen-chi-Ho, on the east, thus continuing to safeguard Kuroki's line of communications running eastward to the coast.

In the centre the Russians undoubtedly got the better of the preliminary artillery exchange. But the infantry attack was ill co-ordinated and badly wanting in vigour; and Shi-shan, an important *point d'appui*, was snatched by the Japanese under cover of the morning mist early on Oct. 10. At the same time a useful reinforcement was sent to bolster up Umezawa's harassed right flank. The coup at Shi-shan sparked off a weighty counterstroke against Bilderling's strangely hesitant legions of the centre. It was led, on the extreme left, by the dashing, intrepid Okasaki, across a flat plain offering little in the way of cover for an advance, and with a formidable backstop in the form of the arrow-shaped Tera-Yama eminence, strongly held by the Russians. But the assault, well supported by artillery, went in "Hell for leather! Bullets fell thick amongst those who ran for life or death across the plain and the yellow dust of their impact on the plough rose in a cloud almost to the men's knees. . . . The formation was not solid but exceedingly flexible and loose, offering no very vulnerable target even to a machine gun. The speed was marvellous, and the men got across the plain more like charging cavalry than ordinary infantry; and as their leading files reached the sunken road they dashed unhesitatingly into it, right on top of the crouching Russians. Next second the Russians and their assailants were rushing up Tera-Yama slopes in one confused mob, the whole mass convulsively working bayonet and bullet and clubbed rifle as they ran. The hill was carried."[9] Although it was yet to gather momentum, the movement toward general retreat had been set in train.

By Oct. 12 Bilderling's troops had been forced back on their main position on the Sha-Ho. The centre thus becoming exposed, Shtakelberg fought hard to retain the ridge running eastward from the Yen-tai coal mines. A height named One Tree Peak[10] constituted the key to the battlefield, and fighting for its possession was fierce and long-sustained. But with a desperate effort the Russians succeeded in driving their enemy from its crest and upper slopes, the Japanese stumbling away to leave eleven guns, a machine gun, and a number of limbers in their enemies' hands. But there was no Russian attempt to exploit the situation. Indeed, by midnight on Oct. 13 Kuropatkin's forces were in the process of retiring behind the Sha-Ho, to occupy defensive positions they had been careful to prepare in advance. If Oyama's plan had fallen short of his aim to drive the Russians eastward into the tangle of mountains and away from Mukden and their line of communications, the balance of the fight had unquestionably gone in his favour.

With the end of the Sha-Ho battle, major operations ground to a standstill, having cost the Japanese 3,951 killed and 16,394 wounded and missing and the Russians 5,084 killed and 39,267 wounded and missing. Thereafter both sides settled down to spend the worst of the winter in their respective positions.

While the men of the Umezawa Brigade struggled with their opponents on the bleak heights of Ping-tai-tzu, their comrades of Nogi's besieging forces were no less strenuously engaged in front of Port Arthur. The trenches on the slopes below Erh-lung-shan changed hands more than once, but in the outcome they remained in Japanese possession. Grimly Nojine recorded in his diary: "The enemy approaches are getting closer up. With wonderful energy and perseverance they are digging them towards Chi-kuan-shan Fort, Open Caponier No. 2, and B Battery. Early this morning two additional approaches were made towards Kuropatkin Lunette, and parallels were begun. Our artillery fire is not continuous enough to stop them. We are all alarmed for the condition of the caponier on the main face of Chi-kuan-shan. They have mined behind the counterscarp, and evidently mean to blow it up. In anticipation of this we are making two counter-mine galleries from the corners of the caponier, which, running for twelve yards, ought to hit their main gallery; but as the soil here is almost rocky, progress is slow, and we may be late in intersecting the enemy's gallery."

In order to ascertain the lie and general position of the Japanese shaft with greater accuracy, a sortie was organized, headed by a contingent of trained sappers. But, like so many of its predecessors, it was so clumsily carried out that the Japanese were fully alerted, and the attempt to destroy their work was without result.

This Japanese mole warfare was not confined to the eastern face of the fortress. Slowly but steadily they were worming their way into the slopes of Akasaka-Yama and 203 Metre Hill, as fixed as ever in their resolve to possess the heights from which they could dominate the harbour and the shell-dented remnant of the fleet, where it lay helpless at its moorings.

For on Oct. 15 the Second Pacific Squadron had actually set out—though not entirely without mishap, the battleship *Oryol* having promptly gone aground on a sand bar upon leaving Kronstadt harbour. Encountering the *Gamecock* fishing fleet on its North Sea trawling grounds, the squadron opened fire on the harmless smacks under the incredible illusion that behind them lurked a force of Japanese destroyers! Leaving the *Crane*, with its dead and wounded, to founder, the maritime juggernaut had thrashed its way blindly down channel, the next fishing fleet it encountered being fortunate to lose no more than its trawling gear.

Naturally, this was scarcely the end of the matter. But if echoes of the international hullabaloo reached Rozhestvensky at his next port of call, they meant little or nothing to a man oppressed by the fearsone task of coaling and keeping together a fleet as badly wanting in seamanship, gunnery skill, and discipline as it was prone to mechanical breakdown. As he sweated his way around the west coast of Africa the admiral was less concerned with the minor contretemps of the past than with an uneasy foreboding as to what might lie in store for him in the future.

The fact that the Second Pacific Squadron, however remote at the moment, was actually heading eastward undoubtedly spurred General Nogi to intensify his efforts to break into the fortress's inner ring of defences. On Oct. 16 the advanced trench at Erh-lung-shan passed finally into the besiegers' hands. On the seventeenth the observation post on Namako-Yama reported a number of hits on the warships in the roads and harbour, the *Poltava* receiving four, the *Bayan* five, the *Retvisan* six, and the *Peresviet* seventeen. On the twenty-second the town and fortress were lashed from both sea and land, the cannonade continuing until the target was obscured by a heavy sea mist. To prevent any attempt at escape under cover of the murk, the Japanese light craft closed the harbour entrance in a tight cordon.

In front of Chi-kuan-shan, Nogi's engineers had tunnelled almost as far as the caponier chamber guarding the northeast angle of the fort ditch. On Oct. 23 Russian sappers, listening in their own gallery, estimated that the enemy could not be more than 20 to 25 yards distant and were advancing rapidly. At 4 A.M. on the twenty-sixth the muffled thud of tools seemed much nearer and more distinct. By 9 A.M. it was judged that the work was proceeding 5 feet to the left of the Russian gallery and a little above it. This obviously called for counter-measures to be taken, and without delay. With every encouragement from the indefatigable Kondratenko, Colonel Rashevsky got to work on the fabrication of a camouflet,[11] charged with 320 pounds of powder, to destroy the enemy tunnel; and work on a chamber for its reception and on materials with which to tamp[12] it was hastily begun. "After listening most carefully," Rashevsky noted in his diary, "we all came to the conclusion that the enemy were sinking a shaft from the surface of the *glacis* with the object of destroying our left gallery." On the matter's being reported to General Smirnoff, the commandant expressed his eager wish to fire the camouflet himself.

It was a calm, moon-drenched, frosty night when the general appeared at Chi-kuan-shan and announced his determination to descend into the mine gallery personally to inspect the work. "Everyone looked at each other in astonishment; this daring act of Smirnoff surprised us. Amongst the men the word was passed in an instant: 'The Commandant himself has crawled into the gallery!' Some believed it, some did not, but it made a great impression."[13]

Smirnoff's inspection left him in no doubt that the state of affairs was extremely serious—any moment an explosion might tumble the fort into ruins. It was a question of who could detonate their charge first.

It was not until 11 A.M. on Oct. 27, however, that Rashevsky could report the camouflet ready for firing. After a careful inspection of the tamping, Smirnoff gave orders for the electric leads to be run out from the casemate to the outer parapet. Then, with an unhurried air, he grasped the firing key and pressed it home.

"Above the caponier rose a cloud of dust and smoke, out of which projected stones, planks and bodies. We had succeeded, and the garrison breathed again. The awful weary hours of waiting had passed. Congratulating everyone, the General went down into the inner courtyard. His presence as Head of the Fortress at the most dangerous place in the defences soon became known, and inspired everyone to further efforts."[14]

Unfortunately, although the explosion had accounted for some twenty-eight men labouring in the work, its ultimate effect was greatly to simplify the Japanese engineers' task, since it had blown a small hole in the roof of the caponier chamber itself. Once this narrow tunnel had been gained, the Russians were driven from it by the simple expedient of hurling in hand grenades until the occupants were forced to retire. On the other hand, from the gallery where they had withdrawn the defenders could pick off anyone who sought to pass through the hole in the roof. The Japanese then proceeded to drop down sandbags until the fort entrance to the gallery was blocked; whereupon they took possession of the whole chamber. But beyond it they were quite unable to penetrate.

On Oct. 26 the advanced trench in front of Erh-lung-shan was firmly secured and sandbagged, and on the same day possession was taken of the trench right under the lee of Sung-su. Among the booty were two machine guns and one of the powerful searchlights which had caused the assailants so much trouble during the earlier operations, when its rays could be brought to bear on every foot of the escarpment. At Chi-kuan the Japanese tried the effect of hurling over cartridges filled with pyroxylin or melinite, to which they had attached wadding soaked in kerosene. The wadding, being set alight, acted as a time fuse to explode the cartridges, the aim being to set fire to the sandbags, planks, and beams incorporated in the defences. But there was very little upon which these incendiaries could get to work, Chi-kuan's upper structure being almost completely wrecked by the heavy shells from the 11-inch howitzers.

On Oct. 27 reinforcements of 8,000 were landed at Dalny; and with his ranks once more brought up to strength, Nogi resolved to risk another attempt to carry the fortress's eastern defences by direct assault. After four days of continuous bombardment, at 4.30 A.M. on the thirtieth a mine was sprung under Fort Erh-lung; and at 9 A.M. a concentrated shoot was opened on all the works from Chi-kuan battery to Fort Sung-su. "By 10 A.M. the whole eastern front was enveloped in dense smoke; the hills were literally reeking. The entire destructive energy of hundreds of guns was thrown on the portion of the works from B Battery to Fortification No. 3. It seemed as if everything there must be destroyed—every living thing killed, that no one could be left to defend, and that at any moment the enemy would dash in to fight in the very streets."[15]

Oshima's 9th and Tsuchiya's 11th Divisions had been assigned to the attack; and with the whine of the Russian missiles and the snarl of their own heavy shells overhead, they quietly mustered in their assembly trenches. Passing among them, a veteran war correspondent noted: "The weather is cold and gloomy, and the troops, to show less of their dark winter uniforms, have ripped up their khaki jackets, back, front, or sides, and have laced them over the dark blue. They are free of blankets and all other impedimenta, with the exception of an iron ration, a waterbottle, and the full complement of ammunition, 200 rounds, in their waist-belt pouches. They are stripped for the fight and trudge forward with faces full of expectancy and cheerfulness, determined to win or die."[16]

It was well after high noon before the word was given

and the troops leaped from their assembly trenches and started to climb the slopes toward their objectives, Open Caponier 2, Chi-kuan-shan, the Kuropatkin Lunette, and Fortification 2. The open caponier was the first to fall into Japanese hands; but progress on the left was less assured. "Looking again at that hill," one onlooker recorded, "I saw that the column had passed through the wire entanglement and was just entering the trench half-way up, which was deserted, the artillery fire having driven out the Russians. Many men had fallen in the trail of the column, and were lying scattered about in all directions, some among the wire, some on the hillside, but by far the larger number close to the trench, where they had gone down by scores."[17]

Continuous fire from the east and from machine guns and musketry behind the shelter of the Chinese Wall and the covered ways of the works ahead, took them in front and flank and reaped a speedy and bloody harvest. A few survivors reached the steep escarpment, and some of them succeeded in clambering over the top. But almost immediately their dead bodies were flung out onto the sward, where they lay spread-eagled like dead flies on flypaper.

Reinforcements were flung in, scurrying forward into the pelting sleet of fire. But they got no farther than the vacated Russian trench, which soon became too hot for them to hold. The approach to the Kuropatkin Lunette was up a more concave slope, offering a certain measure of protection. But no sooner was it breasted than the Russian riflemen on the flanks and those posted behind the Chinese Wall brought a blast of fire to bear which, supplemented by shrapnel bursts over the supports crowding in the hollow ground below the crest, wrought such havoc that the assault dissolved into tangled heaps of dead and wounded. A second wave was launched up the slope, but this was no more than reinforcing the dead. A third attempt simply added more and more to the tally of the injured and the slain.

It was not until the fighting farther south had died away that any move was made against Chi-kuan-shan, where the Japanese had run out saps both to the northeast and northwest corners of the ditch. But their grip on the work itself only extended to the caponier chamber in the northeast corner, whose wall had been breached during the night to offer a readier access than was afforded by the hole blown in its roof.

The escarpment in front of the fort was nearly 50 feet high, but the 1st Battalion of the Twelfth Regiment poured onto the *glacis* undaunted, sweeping past the last trench to be evacuated by the Russians. "It was all easy going till the Japs were about half-way up to the fort's parapet, when a hail of shrapnel seemed to crumple up half the contingent. Dead, wounded, and the living seemed suddenly to sink into the earth, and no one moved. The cover of the enormous shell holes once more befriended the gallant little men, and for many minutes there was no sign of life among them. Presently one of the black dots moved forward. Could he be going alone? No one followed. On went the plucky little fellow up to the fort ditch; passing down and up, he hung onto the counter-scarp. Two more dots from the shell-holes came to life again, and followed, and then others were resurrected from the shell-pits, and hurried up the ditch. The man on the counterscarp, looking back, saw his supporting comrades, sprawled over the parapet, and disappeared into the fort."[18]

After a lengthy pause, about fifty men, out of all those crouching in precarious shelter, scrambled up the counterscarp and sought to heave themselves over the parapet. But they formed no more than a forlorn hope, for even in the act of levering themselves up they were shot down by defenders who had only to thrust their rifles through the loopholes against the bodies of their opponents and press the triggers. In the event, they were very largely saved even that expenditure of energy, since the Russians in the galleries and the uncaptured caponier chamber at the other end of the ditch picked off their assailants one after another as they came into view at the top of the slope. Of those who had contrived to force a way into the fort, only a few were able to scramble back over the parapet and bolt down the glacis to join their comrades crouching in the shell holes. Suddenly "the sky-line of the Fort was broken by tall and stalwart figures; touching to the left—a squad of Russians—as if on parade. An Officer stood forward with flashing sword; he looked down the *glacis*. Not a movement was to be seen of the black dots on the slope. His work was not required there. He quickly pointed to the P. fort below. The Japs had passed round it and over it, and were pressing against the Chinese Wall. The Officer turned his men half-left, . . . and in rhythmical order the men, standing grandly upright, took cartridges from pouch, moving each with the other like clockwork. They load and present, eject empty case, reload and fire."[19]

Eventually, the squad on the parapet sloped arms and withdrew to the interior of the fort; the fighting had ended. In front of Chi-kuan-shan, as elsewhere, the attack had been swept out of existence; while the few men still hanging on in the open caponier, taken in the early stages of the fight, were in too isolated a position to maintain themselves with any feeling of assurance, realizing as they did that they could always be thrown out by a counterattack launched from the fieldworks at the foot of Eagle's Nest. With more than $150,-000 expended in ammunition and a casualty list of over 1,200, Nogi had to accept the fact that once again Port Arthur's defences had survived assault. "The attacks were short, but most determined and bloody," Nojine recorded the day after the fight. "As regards their success, it was but slight. The enemy has gained some dozens of yards—no more. Our total loss was Open Caponier No. 2, already quite destroyed by the bombardment. The Japanese had fired over 150,000 shells." By way of postscript, on Oct. 31 Nogi's gunners concentrated their attention on the shipping in the harbour. The *Giliak* sustained several hits, and two merchant vessels were sunk.

For the second time, Nogi had gravely underrated the power of resistance embodied in a series of interlocking defence works, while at the same time overestimating the degree to which they had been weakened by his engineers. Moreover, he had made the mistake of assaulting the permanent forts without first destroying the guardian defences on their flanks. In any case, if there had been any serious intent to essay anything more than a reconnaissance in force, an elaborate tryout, then considerably more than the 5,000 infantry actually employed should have been committed to the venture, while the costly method of advancing in close order should sternly have been forbidden, as it had been in the field army after the battle of Te-li-ssu.

A military commander does not employ a sledgehammer to crack a walnut. But at the other end of the scale, neither can he expect a dollar's worth of victory for the expenditure of a single dime. The successful general is the man who can hit the happy mean between miserliness and extravagance. Nevertheless, it is only fair to suggest that Nogi would have devised a far better plan had his judgment not been influenced by his preoccupation with the element of time.

THE SPIRIT OF
YAMATO DAMASHII

"IT IS NOT THE BEGINNING, BUT THE CONTINUING THE
SAME UNTO THE END, UNTIL IT BE THOROUGHLY FINISHED,
THAT YIELDS THE TRUE GLORY."

—SIR FRANCIS DRAKE

8 AFTER EIGHT MONTHS of costly fighting, reappraisals,
either by Russia or Japan, were not entirely free from an
undercurrent of anxiety. It was impossible for the Tsarists
to ignore the fact that, although their army was still intact, they
had allowed themselves to be driven from the natural strategic
centre of Manchuria. Their Pacific Ocean Squadron had suffered serious loss and was still divided, with its major elements
mewed up behind their harbour defences, and Port Arthur was
in increasing jeopardy. The Japanese, having demonstrated
that an insular power could confidently penetrate into the
territory of a vastly stronger continental power and impose
defeat upon it in two major battles and many minor actions,
nonetheless had been forced to acknowledge their inability to
muster the numbers requisite to bring about another Sedan
either at Liao-yang or Sha-Ho. Furthermore, Japan had failed
to secure such an overwhelming naval victory that her complete control of local waters would be ensured. Should the
rump of the Pacific Ocean Squadron succeed in uniting with
Rozhestvensky's reinforcements and the vessels based on Vladivostok, Togo, with two irreplaceable battleships lost, would be
confronted with a challenge it would not be easy to meet. On
paper, at least, Rozhestvensky's armada enjoyed a 50 per cent
superiority in 12-inch guns over any force the Japanese could

put to sea. And there were persistent rumours of yet another squadron in process of formation under Admiral Nebogatoff, with which Rozhestvensky was scheduled to be reinforced before reaching Far Eastern waters.

Japan, which perforce looked to Europe and the United States for the loans which subsidized her war expenditure, was only too conscious of the fact that while the Russian war loan stood at a steady 89, her own 4 per cent bonds were quoted on the open market at no higher than 79. Obviously the Mikado's forces must strengthen international confidence by achieving at least one outstanding success. With the withdrawal of the Russian field army, either Port Arthur must be forced into swift surrender or the combined Russian fleet must be brought to action and decisively defeated.

One thing was overwhelmingly clear: with the Second Pacific Squadron ploughing steadily eastward it was imperative that the Japanese warships, after eight months at sea, should be brought back to maximum efficiency. Even if they worked at highest pressure, barely sufficient time was available for the dockyards at Sasebo and Shimonoseki to restore the vessels to full fighting trim. In these circumstances the task of destroying what remained of the Pacific Ocean Squadron within Port Arthur became the urgent duty of the besieging army. There were still four battleships, three cruisers, destroyers, gunboats, and auxiliary vessels secured at their moorings in the Basin. Penetrating as the Japanese Intelligence might be, it was impossible to determine to what degree of fighting efficiency the First Pacific Squadron could be restored.

The Mikado's birthday was Nov. 3. It was obvious that General Nogi would not be in a position to hand him Port Arthur as a birthday present, but the pressing need to hasten the reduction of the fortress was given additional emphasis by the arrival of Marshal Oyama's chief of staff at the army commander's headquarters "for consultations." He was greeted with the news that on Nov. 1 the Japanese artillery, "firing by the map," had sunk two steamers of approximately 3,500 tons, and another vessel, of 3,000 tons, on the day following. Violent explosions in the north of the New Town justified the assumption that a lucky hit had been registered on one of the powder magazines. But the Japanese were still without direct observation over the target area, and the warships were hidden from view by Pai-ju-shan hill, behind which they had prudently taken shelter.

In some respects random fire is more to be dreaded—at the receiving end—than a shoot controlled by direct observation. Something of the harrowing conditions under which Port Arthur's residents and the men of the garrison eked out a miserable and danger-haunted existence was reflected in a letter, which its writer contrived to smuggle across to neutral territory. "The time will come," he wrote, "when there will be no bearing the inconvenience of the siege, due to the sickness, scarcity of food and cramped quarters; no enduring the unceasing hell of bursting shells—shattering houses, killing unfortunate friends, and tearing huge holes in the ground—to say nothing of the miasma arising from a thousand corpses rotting on the hills and in the ravines round the forts. Lately the bombardments have increased in fury, and the fiery messengers of hate and destruction greet us every minute."

Rank with scurvy and suffering from progressive debilitation owing to unsuitable and insufficient food, the garrison, as Nojine glumly recorded, "was already demoralised; it was tired, it was morally and physically worn out." The vile weather, with blinding snow, bitter winds, and a clammy, impenetrable mist regularly creeping in from the sea to obscure the battered streets and jumble of defences in a grey shroud of opacity, only added to the apathetic feeling of hopelessness in which the majority were sunk. Only a very few were still confident and stout of heart—men such as Smirnoff, Kondratenko, the stalwart Rashevsky, and the indomitable Tretyakov and his handful of Siberian riflemen clinging to the defences on 203 Metre Hill.

It was a small company of the elect which certainly did not include Stössel's toady, the egregious General Fock. In a lengthy, rambling memorandum, dated Nov. 3, he had expressly affirmed that "A besieged fortress can be compared with a man suffering from gangrene. In the same way that he must sooner or later succumb so, too, must a fortress fall." That privately Stössel was of similar recreant opinion must be inferred from the fact that the memorandum could not have been circulated without his sanction and implicit approval. Furthermore, Smirnoff's unflagging attempts to strengthen the second and third lines of defence were obstructed at every turn by the very man who should have given him support.

On Nov. 9 the defences, the town, and the harbour were subjected to a particularly violent cannonade by Japanese heavy mortars, a hammering which sent the engineers to the hurried repair of Fort No. 2 (Chi-kuan-shan), which was generally in a most precarious condition. All through the night wood fires were kept burning in the ditch of the caponier in order to prevent the Japanese from breaking through unseen. Elsewhere, Nogi's guns had succeeded in blowing up the magazine in the Zarebout Battery—under the lee of Eagle's Nest (or Wan-tai) —and penetrating two casemates in B Battery, which, like Kuropatkin Lunette and Chi-kuan-shan, had suffered some of the heaviest punishment inflicted on the northeastern face of the defences. In the main, however, the bombardment had been concentrated on the town and harbour. For the Japanese had changed their technique. Having realized how easy it was to overestimate the effect of their cannonade on the forts and bombproof trenches, they bent most of their energies to a sustained effort to sink the ships and destroy the town and its arsenals, stores, and magazines. The Basin had been so showered with mortar shells that one destroyer made a dash for the open. Having boosted her fuel by dousing it in oil, she managed to show the lurking Japanese patrols a clean pair of heels, to find the sanctuary in the neutral haven of Chefu.

But there was no escape for the hungry, ragged scarecrows manning the defences. "All along the front men lived just like everyone else—they ate, slept, hoped and died. To the noise of bursting shells and firing they had long grown accustomed. A shell burst, a man—perhaps two or three—were killed. Up came others to separate the wounded from the dead; but there was no bustling, no excitement; it was nothing unusual—merely routine! Of course, in some parts of the front, where the enemy were within fifteen or twenty yards of our parapets, neither side dared show up to the other; each was always waiting for a shot. It was particularly so with Erh-lung-shan and Fortification No. 3. Here the merciless, dogged struggle never relaxed for a moment. It was the most vulnerable point, to which the enemy stuck like leeches, daily establishing themselves more firmly. They dug, dug, dug, and burrowed like moles, laid fougasses, exploded mines, pounded the works with shells and shrapnel bullets."[1]

It was a situation that was little affected by the news that Alexieff had been recalled to Moscow and that Kuropatkin had been invested with the full powers of commander-in-chief. The fact that his forces had been divided into three armies— the First under the cold, prideful, self-sufficient Linevitch, the Second under the gloomy, secretive Grippenberg, and the Third under the swaggering, rambunctious Kaulbars—would not have the effect of bringing a single battalion to Port Arthur's relief. The fortress must stand or fall by the efforts of those who still survived to man its riven battlements.

The lessons of the October failure to carry the fortress had not been lost on General Nogi and his advisers. There must be no more costly 300-yard advances over the open in broad daylight.[2] Parallel and sap must be pushed forward to bring the assailants within leaping distance of their objective. The attack must be made on a bigger scale and include the western sector of the defences, so that the Russians would be unable to concentrate anything like a really strong force at any of the points assailed.

Throughout the early days of November, therefore, the saps were carried much closer to the works, and were very widely extended, the approaches between the parallels being doubled in many places to facilitate the passage of supports, ammunition, and supplies. Especially in front of Fort No. 3 (Erh-lung-shan) a veritable spider's web of saps and communication trenches seamed the slopes, as deep and well sandbagged as the trench in front of Sung-su-shan, from which two strongly fortified approaches were carried right up to the top of the counterscarp. Similar burrowings were carried out against the works on the eastern face, in front of the Chinese Wall, while the parallels and sapheads were also pushed up closer to 203 Metre Hill and Akasaka-Yama.[3]

Where permanent defence works such as Sung-su-shan and Forts 2 and 3 were concerned, the only method of crossing the moat in anything like safety was to tunnel right to the back wall of the caponier, chisel holes in these walls, and fill them with dynamite. The detonation of the charges would not only destroy the caponiers and drive out the defenders, but the *débris* from the explosion would help to fill up the moat and facilitate the passage across it. These shafts were very narrow and at most a couple of men could work in them at a time, and the stubborn, rocky nature of the soil—a conglomerate of limestone, flint, and quartz—made their toil both difficult and exhausting. In most instances a winding stairway, cut out of the rock, led from the manhole down into the shafts. "The Russians, of course, did all in their power to impede the progress of the work. Not a night but they came out and made savage charges upon the sap-heads. In the beginning they succeeded in throwing some of their hand-grenades into the man-holes, doing much damage to the works and killing every man in the shafts. Later on, the Japanese erected solid breastworks around these places, enabling them generally to keep the Russians off, though the casualty list remained heavy."[4]

Deep in the bowels of the earth there was always the chance that a Russian countermine would obliterate both the shaft and its occupants in a rumbling subterranean explosion. In such of the caponiers as had passed wholly or partly into Japanese hands, many a bloody hand-to-hand struggle accompanied the defenders' attempts to regain possession.

By Nov. 15 tunnelling and sapping were well under way, but still uncompleted, at Forts 2 and 3 and at Sung-su-shan. There was still much to do; but the naval authorities were pressing even more pertinaciously for the fortress's reduction. For although the Second Pacific Squadron had not yet left Tangier, Admiral Togo was insistent that the vessels in Port Arthur harbour should be put out of action once and for all. Moreover, a demanding note of impatience had crept into the war-report-ing in the Japanese press—a note that only too clearly echoed the general public's restless dissatisfaction with the conflict's tardy progress. With whatever reluctance, Nogi could only yield to the pressure put upon him and bring forward the date of his third full-scale assault.

On Nov. 17 the mines in the back wall of Sung-su were exploded with no more than partial success, only about two-thirds of the moat being filled with débris. But the Japanese remained in possession of the front moat and proceeded to con-struct a bombproof passage by which it could be crossed. On Nov. 20 the mines in the counterscarp of Erh-lung were sprung. Once again the eastern part of the moat was filled with rubble, while the less successful explosion to the west persuaded the Japanese engineers to build a bombproof bridge over the gap, supported on heavy wooden trusses—a target which was speedily demolished by the fire from the Russians' 6-inch guns positioned behind Sung-su.

On the night of the twenty-third a preliminary attack was launched on the fieldworks below the southern face of Fort No. 2 (Chi-kuan-shan). "The Japanese saps were a bare thirty yards from the Russian trench, and at six o'clock, just at dusk, the 12th regiment assaulted. What followed was tragedy. A spurting line of fire and a furious volley, then another and an-other, and the air was sobbing with human cries and the thirty yard gap was strewn with wounded and dead."[5] With their files terribly thinned, the men of the Twelfth retired, beaten but not defeated. Re-forming their ranks, they charged again, the fury of their momentum carrying them right into the enemy trench and to handgrips with its defenders. On both sides men fought with the ferocity of animals, locked in a snarling, brutish struggle in which death was nothing but a madness in the blood and survival no more than the chance to deal out more destruction. Forced out of the trampled furrow at the point of the bayonet, the riflemen of the Twelfth stormed into it once more and for an hour remained its masters. Thrown out again, for the third time they battered their way back, only to be butchered in such swathes that the intervening 30 yards of ground was black with their sprawling bodies, their yellow faces blanched and contorted in the horrible, inhuman rictus of insufferable agony. To attempt to remove the wounded was to commit suicide, and very soon the barely living had joined the already dead. Once again an isolated attack had permitted reserves to be summoned from other, unthreatened points in the defences to smother the assault by sheer weight of numbers.

As reinforcements streamed in to replace the fallen, the Twenty-fifth, Twenty-sixth, Twenty-seventh, and Twenty-eighth Regiments of the 7th Division, together with a brigade of the 8th Division, swelled the numbers under Nogi's command to something approximating 100,000 men.

Undeterred by the losses suffered on the twenty-third, the home authorities continued to insist that the grand assault must be thrust home by every means available. At whatever cost, the interior defences of the forts must be attacked without waiting for the engineers to complete their work of preparation.

But it is not to be disguised that the repulse of Nov. 23 had exerted a profoundly depressive effect on the battle-weary veterans who had come through so much since the early days of the siege. They had hoped so fervently that victory in a straightforward fight in the open would put an end to the underground warfare they had come to detest so bitterly. General Nogi was fond of displaying a Russian pickaxe with the points so blunted as to be worn nearly to the "eye," and emphasizing the obvious moral. But the Japanese soldier had grown to distrust sapping and mining and all it entailed. "It was too slow for him, and it was taxing his tenacity and fortitude to a much higher degree than the most desperate attacks in the open. There, in the midst of his comrades, fired by the joy of battle, what mattered it to him if he were killed or wounded or if his brother or his best friend were struck down by his side? His blood was up, and his only wish or thought was to get to close quarters with the enemy in a square hand-to-hand fight. But in the sapping operations it was quite different. There was no excitement, it was daily, hard, prosaic work, digging his way through the stubborn soil, with only a couple of comrades toiling and sweating alongside of him, with bullets and shells flying about them, and with the Russian surprise parties continually making bayonet attacks or blowing them to pieces with hand-grenades; and always, all the time, the sight of the wounded being carried away, and the dead being sewn up in rice-bags, being taken to their last resting place. They did not like it, and they did not understand it, and the majority of the Officers shared their feelings."[6] The Old Hands were conscious, too, of a dangerous lack of experience in both the officers and the men who had come overseas piece-meal to fill the yawning gaps in the ranks. Doubtless they meant well, but what could troops fresh from the parade ground expect to know about real fighting? The best hope for the success of future operations lay with the men of the 7th Division. Not only had it been recruited in the notoriously martial Hokkaido District, but, after months of frustrating delay in the homeland, it had arrived on the scene as a fully integrated, homogeneous formation, complete in itself and with its own proud traditions, burning with ardour and only too ready and eager for the fray.

The outcome of the preliminary clearing operation of Nov. 23–24 had been sharply disappointing. But General Nogi was in no position to permit this minor failure to defer prosecution of his general plan of attack. Thus by dawn on Nov. 26 every gun on the northeastern front was in action. The whole line from Tumulus Hill in the north to B Battery on the east was wreathed in smoke from the hundreds of shells that beat upon it. "The assault began. Living waves of infantry rolled forward against the ruined front, and the moments of the Fortress seemed numbered. Time after time the Japanese threw themselves with extraordinary gallantry and persistence on Forts Erh-lung-shan and Chi-kuan-shan, and B Battery. Thousands were mown down, but the living surged onwards. But it could not go on for ever, and at 3.30 the infantry attack slackened and ceased. We had lost nothing but Open Caponier No. 2; but the enemy kept pounding us with their guns, and we awaited a fresh attack."[7]

It came with nightfall, when the searchlights picked out

dense columns surging up beyond the railway near Tumulus Hill. It was a *ketshitai* of 2,000 volunteers from four divisions, led by Major General Nakamura in person; and his orders had sternly warned his followers that, "The object of our detachment is to cut Port Arthur Fortress in two. No man must hope to return alive." Brought to a pitch of frenzied determination, the assault waves drove forward steadily. "All went well until a small bridge was crossed. Here a track led off south-west. Owing to the darkness the column had opened out considerably, and when the rear detachment, composed of men of the 7th Division, who were ignorant of the country, arrived at the bridge, it left the proper road and followed the track. Here the commander perceived that he had mistaken the road, and started across country to rejoin the main body, which he even eventually did. Some eighty men who had considerably straggled in rear, however, followed the track until they collided with four hundred Russians. Most of these men were either killed or captured";[3] but the alarm had been raised; the searchlights flashed out, and a withering fire was opened upon the advancing *ketshitai*. Despite numbing losses, the survivors were almost on the gun positions before they were halted and thrown back by a counterstroke which sucked into the firing line the whole of the naval detachment and its reserve company. Nogi's well-conceived attempt to establish his troops behind the Russian defences, where they could bring fire to bear in reverse on the Sung-su and Erh-lung forts, had been vigorously thwarted.

At Sung-su and Erh-lung the fighting was at close quarters, and the struggle was carried on with a bitter venom that was not exhausted even with the fall of darkness. If sheer weariness of mind and body imposed a brief interlude of inactivity in the earlier night hours, at ten o'clock the attacks were renewed with almost hysterical energy. In Erh-lung the defenders were driven headlong from the lower levels of the fort, but a tremendous effort to carry the upper battery was met by machine-gun fire that swept the assailants from the snow-powdered parapet almost as they set foot upon it. "Supports after supports were sent up, only to be mown down in their turn, and when at last the fighting slackened in the small hours of the morning, the Japanese had been forced back to their improvised trenches in the front part of the works, leaving the whole *terre plein* between the upper and lower batteries strewn with dead bodies, in some places piled six or eight high."[9]

Before Open Caponier 2, the men of the much-tried Twelfth Regiment poured from the sapheads and raced across the intervening 30 yards of bare ground toward their objective. But the Russians, by concentrating their fire upon them, so choked the points of exit with fallen bodies that the flow of necessary supports was dammed. The centre and east of the ditch was seized by assailants fighting with all their former gallantry. But the Russians, rallying behind their bombproofs and sandbagged breastworks at the western end, held doggedly to their ground amid the heaps of earth and rubble. To make a way through the mound of débris to get at the defenders was well-nigh impossible; to climb over it was to court instant death from sharpshooters perched on innumerable coigns of vantage in the neighbouring works. For with unlimited practice, the Russian soldiers' marksmanship had improved to such a degree that, seven times out of ten, it was deadly. "Reinforcements advanced in gallant fashion from the Japanese sap-heads; the regimental flag was carried forward over the fire-swept zone of thirty yards. Before it was half-way across the Ensign was killed, and another took his place, seizing the standard before it could fall. For about a minute the flag remained upright between the two lines, waving lazily in the breeze, and then it slowly sank to earth as the second bearer was shot."[10] Steadily, remorselessly, the supports were cut down, although the fight was boldly maintained throughout the ensuing hours by individual soldiers, long after all chance of success had vanished. Every officer who had taken part in the attack had been killed or wounded; the few survivors were scattered and without leaders. There was nothing more they could do save crouch in some abscure corner and await an opportunity to make good their escape.

At Chi-kuan-shan the Japanese, having possession of the counterscarp galleries and the ditch on the north face of the fort, placed scaling ladders against the steep face of the escarpment in order to reach its summit. With the parapet banquette wrecked by shellfire, as they believed, it was their aim to force their way into the fort and drive out its defenders. But much of the damage had been cunningly repaired and the summit of the escarpment divided by sandbags into numerous little compartments, which had the effect of severely localizing the mischief done by each shellburst. Snuggled down behind these sandbag defences, the Russian riflemen simply awaited the appearance of their assailants on the skyline of the parapet, to blast them out of existence.

It was the Redan and the Malakoff of the Crimean campaign all over again, but this time with the defenders armed with quick-firing weapons. As the Japanese swarmed into sight, they were shot down in droves, while those still on the ladders, unable to see the state of affairs ahead and above them, and bent only on pressing forward, thrust those who had not been laid low over the crest again by sheer weight of numbers. In scattered groups, the Japanese hung on grimly, while reinforcements sought to claw their way up to them from the ditch. In one or two places fascines made of cut cornstalks had been used to help form a causeway, and over these the defenders poured drums of oil, which they set alight by hurling down hand grenades to explode among them. Scores of the wounded perished in the flames leaping in the moat.

Grimly the fight went on, into the morning of the twenty-seventh. No permanent foothold was gained in any of the works despite the gallantry of the Japanese, which was matched by the stoic valour of the defenders.

With 12,000 casualties, including Nakamura,[11] the leader of the "forlorn hope," and Tsuchiya, the valiant commander of the 11th Division, General Nogi had only one card left to play, a concerted attempt to gain possession of the height that commanded a clear view of the warships in the harbour—203 Metre Hill, or Royusan, as the Japanese had learned to call it. After all, second only in importance to the capture of the fortress was the destruction of these elements of the Pacific Ocean Squadron still moored in its harbour. To accomplish that would go far toward redeeming the failures of the past.

Sapping operations at 203 Metre Hill were very far from completion; but time was speeding. So it was resolved that the attack should begin without delay. The main thrust was entrusted to the veteran First and Fifteenth Regiments, with the Thirty-eighth Regiment of the reserve in support. To the untried battalions of the 7th (Hokkaido) Division was assigned the responsibility of capturing Akasaka-Yama, to prevent enfilading fire which could sweep any Japanese on the plateau of Royusan out of existence.[12]

On Nov. 27, after a day-long bombardment, the first attack got off to a well-ordered start under cover of the gathering twilight. The Japanese poured out of the parallels that had been dug below the crest of 203 Metre Hill and its neighbouring height. Swinging in from the southwest, the Royusan assailants were masked from the crossfire from Akasaka-Yama by the intervening bulk of their objective. So impetuous was their rush that the Russians were routed out of their advanced trench and driven back to their fieldworks on the twin peaks. "The rear slopes were covered with men lying in different positions, wounded men who had died on their way back,"[13] men who had fled but who only awaited reorganization to carry the fight back to the captors swarming just below both "keeps." Warned by the day-long bombardment, Smirnoff and Kondratenko had concentrated ample reserves behind the position, and a contingent of these, led by Colonel Tretyakov, promptly put in a counterattack with hand grenades which exacted a heavy toll of the men in the captured parallel and sent the survivors scurrying back to the shelter of their lower trenches.

In the lengthy pause that ensued, the Russians toiled frantically to repair their tumbled defences, while a party of men from the fleet hurried up a fresh supply of grenades.

Throughout daylight on the twenty-eighth the Hill remained unassailed. But from dawn on the day following the artillery drenched the position with a continuous rain of shells. A second assault resolved itself into a duel with hand grenades, from which the Japanese retired discomfited. A third attack very nearly succeeded in winning the crest outright, many of the Russians fleeing down the reverse slope in something not far removed from panic. There were officers to rally them, however, and the Japanese onslaught was broken up by a bayonet charge, the mixed swarm of riflemen and sailors again being led by the amazing Tretyakov. But the fight for Akasaka-Yama was veering distinctly in the Japanese favour, and should they be able to win and retain the height, they would be in a position to bring cross fire to bear that would render the neighbouring peaks and their lines of communication quite untenable. With their laurels still to win, the men of the Hokkaido Division had surged up the hill in a series of short rushes, the sections alternately panting upward and then dropping down to cover their comrades' advance with their musketry. While the fire fight on the main position was gaining rapidly in intensity, a party of men from the Twenty-seventh Regiment spontaneously swung to the left and made for the rear of Redoubt No. 4, placed in echelon to the main trench line and held by the scout detachment of the 27th Siberians. Unexpected as the move might be, the Siberian riflemen were not to be flustered. While the even numbers kept up a steady fusillade on the enemy still coming up the slope, the odd numbers swung about to pick off the isolated detachment advancing on the rear of the Redoubt. A charge with the cold steel ended the business, the venturesome Hokkaido section being bayoneted to a man. With the failure of the attack on 203 Metre Hill, its garrison were enabled to reverse the process by which they had been threatened and break up the last wave of the assault on Akasaka-Yama with enfilade fire that was altogether too withering to be withstood.

After this severe rebuff the men of the right-wing attacking force busied themselves in thrusting forward their sap toward the extreme western corner of Royusan. "This was very serious for us," Tretyakov justly commented, "as it brought the Japanese up to a point on the hill from which they could observe the fall of their shell within the harbour area." It was obviously essential to turn the enemy out of this newly fashioned sap before they contrived to establish themselves firmly on the hillcrest. A night attack by three companies just enabled the Russians to eject their enemies from their new positions.

But the cost was heavy, and to it had to be added the constant loss of men under the flailing blows of a bombardment that neither paused nor weakened.

Later during the night hours two companies of reinforcements reported and a party of sappers brought up a fresh supply of sandbags to make good some of the damage done to the "keeps."

At daybreak on the thirtieth the gunfire again increased in volume, and the right face of the breastwork on the western "keep" was utterly destroyed by a well-placed salvo of 11-inch projectiles. "At 8 A.M. the Japanese suddenly attacked the left breastwork, captured the front portion, and raised their flag. The sight of the flag always aroused our men to fury. I knew this, and, pointing to it, shouted to the reserve, 'Go and take it down, my lads!' and like one man, our sailors rushed into the work. I led them for some distance, and a moment after there was no sign of the Japanese or their flag to be seen. Twice more the hostile flag made its appearance on top of the hill, but each time it was torn down by my handful of reserves."[14]

There were forays and scrimmages throughout all of Dec. 1, with some desperate hand-to-hand encounters on Royusan's western slopes. But on the morning of Dec. 2 the garrison could proudly reply to a message of enquiry: "All the assaults have been repulsed and the hill is completely in our hands."

It was not until Dec. 5 that the Japanese staged the attack that was to prove decisive. Throughout the previous days the engineers had slaved without pause to push their saps closer to the defences, which were kept under unremitting artillery fire. From first light on the fifth every gun that could be brought to bear concentrated its fire on Royusan and the neighbouring Akasaka-Yama. A little past noon Major General Saito led a full Brigade of the 7th Division up the communication trenches to the new sapheads in front of 203 Metre Hill, while a whole regiment made its way up the companion slopes of Akasaka-Yama. Officers and men had sworn to capture and retain the two hills or not to return alive.

As it happened, the leading files encountered little more than token resistance. The ceaseless rain of shells and the in-

THE SPIRIT OF YAMATO DAMASHII [147

cessant hand-to-hand fighting had worn away the 2,200 men
originally assigned to the defence until only a stunned and
weary handful was left to man the heaps of rubble and evis-
cerated sandbags that represented all that remained of the
elaborate defences.

In Royusan's western "keep" "only three Russians were
found alive among the battered earthworks, one of whom
was the commander of the troops on the mountain."[15] With
the undercrest of the western peak in their hands, 500 men, supported by the covering fire of their comrades, hastened to rush
the upper enemy trench line, some 40 yards to the east. They
entered the mauled and stinking jumble of thrown-up earth,
torn sandbags, and blasted timber without a shot being fired,
and pushed on immediately for the crest itself. "They encountered very little resistance, for the Russians had abandoned
the summit of Royusan, and almost before they could realise
what had happened, the Mikado's soldiers were in possession of
both peaks."[16] On Akasaka-Yama matters had gone in much
the same fashion. With saps pushed up to within thirty paces
of the defences, the Japanese had hurled themselves on the
garrison with such reckless fury that, of the East Siberians
holding on grimly in Stone-broken Redoubt, 60 per cent had
perished before the survivors turned to flee down the rearward
slope, which the Japanese immediately began to sweep with
rifle fire. Several officers sought to organize a counterattack,
but there was no Tretyakov to inspire it—he had been severely
wounded the previous day—and their forlorn attempt was
blasted out of existence before it could get under way. Half
the men who had started up the hill, including their leaders,
were laid low on the lower slopes; and with machine guns
brought up to the crest, all further attempts to wrest it from
its captors proved to no avail. Sullenly, the order was given
to withdraw into the inner line of defences.

The spectacle presented by Royusan's trampled slopes
must have chilled the heart of the most hardened of campaign-
ers. "There have probably never been so many dead crowded
into so small a space since the French stormed the great redoubt
at Borodino."[17]

The morning of Dec. 6 found a few stubborn riflemen clinging to the scattered remnants of earthworks on Akasaka-Yama. But as they came under heavy fire from Royusan and the batteries behind Shui-shih-ying, there was no choice but for them to evacuate the position and make their way into the the shelter of Fort Yi-tzu-shan.

The cost to the garrison of the twin hills' last desperate defence was 400 slain and nearly double that number incapacitated.[18] To take their objective, the Japanese had suffered casualties of close to 11,000 killed and wounded. But the dividend paid on this investment in death was direct observation of all that remained of the Pacific Ocean Squadron in the harbour. In addition, the Japanese could bring far more accurately aimed fire to bear on the inner ring of defence works. Moreover, the success of their arms bolstered Japanese morale, restoring a confidence in ultimate victory that the constant strain and frequent reverses of the previous four months had badly shaken. Taking into account the corresponding decline in the morale of the ill-fed and sickly garrison, the capture of 203 Metre Hill and its companion height may justly be regarded as the turning point of the siege—if not of the war itself.

THE SANDS RUN OUT

"IN WARFARE, PERSISTENCE IS EVERYTHING."

—NAPOLEON

9   As HE WAS approaching Madagascar, Admiral Rozhest-
vensky received the news that the Japanese had captured 203
Metre Hill. His only reaction was abstractedly to enquire:
   " 'And what is 203 Metre Hill?'
   " 'It overlooks the entire town and fortress of Port Arthur,'
he was informed.
   "The Admiral shrugged."[1]
   But there was no tendency to shrug off the importance of
the Japanese achievement on the part of the Pacific Ocean
Squadron's commander, Admiral Wiren, and his subordinates,
who realized only too acutely what the loss of Royusan meant
for them and their vessels; and in very short order their dismal
forebodings were fully realized. By the evening of Dec. 6 an
observation post had been established on 203 Metre Hill in
direct telephonic communication with the Japanese guns; and
naval officers admitted to hospital at this time "said that the
fleet was now doomed. It would soon be at the bottom of the
sea, and without it the Squadron coming from home would be
useless, in view of the enemy's strength."[2] Almost at once "the
enemy's siege batteries set to work to destroy the Squadron,
which perished under the eyes of the whole Fortress, and the
sailors now holding the land positions watched, helpless and
with sad hearts, as their ships were struck, and one after an-

other our great giants went to the bottom."[3] The slaughter, lasting three days, was deliberate and methodical. The Russians sought to protect the decks of their vessels with layers of bags filled with earth or ashes. But the fuses of the 11-inch shells required considerable resistance before they detonated. The result was that the projectiles went right through the sandbags and upper deck and exploded only on striking the stouter structure of the lower deck. Moreover, the angle of the ballistic curve was such that many of the missiles tore through the ships' hulls below the armour belt, which contributed materially to the vessels' foundering. "The only ship that was scuttled by the Russians themselves was the *Peresviet*, all the others . . . were sunk by the Japanese shells. The only ship that did not allow herself to be sent to the bottom without some show of resistance was the *Sevastopol*, commanded by the gallant Captain von Essen, of *Novik* fame. During the night of the 8th he took his ship, which had been lying in the dock, out of the harbour, and anchored her under the shelter of the Tiger's Tail peninsula. Here, out of reach of the enemy's guns she was later exposed to furious torpedo attacks for three days and nights, and after a splendid fight, . . . she was finally so badly hit that she ruled over, with a list of ten degrees, and sank in the shallow water. The attacks were then discontinued; but after some days Captain von Essen succeeded in getting her afloat and steamed out into deep water, where the vessel was scuttled."[4] The *Bayan* was sunk under Golden Hill; close to Quail Hill lay the listing *Retvisan*, with her bows clear out of the water; and beyond her were the *Pobieda* and *Poltava*, with turrets half awash and guns pointing dumbly to the sky; with the *Pallada* still oozing smoke from the fire that had raged between her decks, and the *Peresviet* almost entirely submerged.

With the main task accomplished, the howitzers turned their attention to battering the town; the destruction of the gunboats and destroyers being left to the Japanese 4.7 naval guns. Raising steam, the destroyers promptly took shelter under the Tiger's Tail promontory, returning to the harbour at night to escape torpedo attack under cover of the darkness. Eventually, all the destroyers stole out of Port Arthur and found refuge in internment.

A personal visit by Admiral Togo to 203 Metre Hill satisfied him that nothing more was to be apprehended from the wreck of a once-proud fleet, and he cabled to that effect to the Navy Department. "Of all the news that reached Tokio during the war, and with hardly an exception it was cheerful, there was none which caused such intense joy and gave rise to such a feeling of relief as the final destruction of the Port Arthur Squadron. To accomplish that result the Japanese had attacked the Fortress again and again. They had spent millions of money and sacrificed thousands of lives";[5] but with news of the Russian ships' destruction, they deemed the sacrifice to have been more than justified.

The Russians had got some of their guns away to add to the defences of Fort Yi-tzu-shan, across the valley from 203 Metre Hill, and the stronghold of An-tzu-shan farther south. But the Japanese were already probing along the Tai-yang-kou Valley toward Pigeon Bay, where they would be able to bring reverse fire to bear on the Old and New Towns and direct fire on Liao-tieh-shan. The net was steadily tightening.

On Dec. 8—in the absence of General Stössel—who had been very slightly wounded by a splinter, and was not averse to making the most of it—the Council of Defence met to consider the next steps to counter Japanese aggression. Smirnoff, stoutly supported by Kondratenko, insisted that there were food and ammunition to last out for at least another month, if not longer. It was true that among the poorer elements of the civilian population there were shortages, allied to prices that evidenced shameless profiteering on the part of traders whose stocks even yet had not been commandeered; $200 for a whole pig, pork at $2.50 a pound, eggs at $1.62 apiece, and 36 pounds of garlic commanding $320. But the garrison was not affected by these rapacious efforts to exploit calamity; far worse straits had been endured in Sevastopol during the Crimean campaign, as Smirnoff took occasion to remind his listeners.

Reduced to uneasy acquiescence by the fortress commander's inflexible determination to carry on the fight, Fock and the equally poor-spirited Colonel Reuss, the governor's chief of staff, could only hurry off to report proceedings and confer with Stössel as to the advisability of adopting a less uncompromising attitude, irrespective of the intransigent Smirnoff and those who supported him. For it was clear that the Japanese, enheartened by their recent victories, were resolved to carry the northeastern defences as soon as their battalions had filled up with drafts and undergone the necessary reorganization.

By Dec. 10 the besiegers were in the counterscarp gallery of Chi-kuan-shan; and there were even attempts by both sides to drive out the other by use of noxious fumes. The Japanese first tried burning kaoliang stalks, but the draft blew the acrid smoke back in their faces and they were forced into a hasty, if temporary, retirement. The next experiment was to burn rags soaked in arsenic; but since neither party could venture into the gallery until the suffocating smother had evaporated, and then both came hurrying back, attempts to stage an elementary gas attack were abandoned.[6]

Burrowing from the Chi-kuan moat deep under the fort, the Japanese bent all their energies to the completion of a double mine gallery, with extensions well forward under the parapet. In all, there were seven branches running from the two galleries, and at the end of each was placed a formidable charge of dynamite. The total weight of the explosive lodged beneath the fort came to a little over 2 tons.

Naturally enough, all this work could not be kept from the garrison's attention, and Kondratenko, with the indefatigable Rashevsky at his heels, was everywhere, personally supervising such countermeasures as could be taken. It was in a casemate of Fort No. 2 that he met his end, an 11-inch shell tearing into the shelter and burying Roman Isidorovitch Kondratenko, his faithful henchman, Rashevsky, and a number of other officers beneath a mound of smoking débris. Such a loss was irreparable, for "the death of General Kondratenko made a lasting impression on the garrison," as Tretyakov mournfully noted, and "everyone lost heart, since we knew there was no one to take his place." The soul of the defence had perished.

December 18 was the day chosen by General Nogi to spring the mines under Chi-kuan-shan. Immediately after the explosion the rush would be made, and the Japanese felt confident that during the first moments of alarm and confusion it would be possible to overwhelm the garrison. The *ketshitai* that volunteered for the first onslaught was divided into two squads, consisting of sixty men apiece, each section with distinguishing ribbons tied about the men's arms.

At a little after 2 P.M. on the day appointed, a terrific explosion burst with the shock of an earthquake beneath Chi-kuan-shan, and a huge column of black smoke towered a couple of hundred feet into the sky. A few seconds later a second roar sent another column of rubble and smoke and severed limbs hurtling into the air. Almost before the débris had fallen earthward, the ribbon-badged volunteers stormed forward on their perilous mission; while the batteries on both sides opened up a cross fire that speedily increased to maximum intensity.

Of the two explosions only that at the northeastern corner of the work had done what had been expected of it, blowing up the whole of the rampart and completely wrecking this angle of the fort. The mines elsewhere, having been insufficiently tamped, had "blown back," killing all the volunteers of the first squad and fatally delaying the second in their attempt to close with their opponents. While the Japanese were clearing the rubble sufficiently to launch themselves at their enemies, the Russians were given time in which to bring up reinforcements to help man the sandbagged entrenchments laid out in front of the barrack buildings at the rear of the fort. It was not until 5 P.M. that a battalion of the Thirty-eighth Regiment started to infiltrate into the interior of the work. Gradually, enough men were assembled under cover to warrant an attempt to engage the attention of the defenders while supports were sent up over the exposed jumble of the ramparts. Losses from the Russians' machine-gun fire were punishing, but the surviving assailants contrived to get to close quarters and engage the defenders hand-to-hand. Artillery fire on the communication trenches did much to prevent further reinforcement of the garrison. In any case, General Fock, Kondratenko's successor as commander of the northeast defences, "seems to have made up his mind at the first explosion that the fort must be abandoned. To be exact, a reinforcement of a company of sailors from the *Pobieda* and *Peresviet* were sent up by Smirnoff, but coming under a heavy fire on their way, few reached the fort and they were not numerous enough to render much assistance."[7] The dwindling garrison fought on grimly, and to silence their ever-chattering machine guns the Japanese brought up two of their handy mountain guns and got them into position on the battered parapet. One by one the Siberian riflemen were struck down at their posts, torn apart by hand grenades, or hunted into corners and spitted with the bayonet. "The Japanese troops had their blood up, and after the immense number of men they had lost before Chi-kuan-shan in the course of the siege, they were not to be denied taking a perfectly legitimate revenge on the garrison once they had gained the interior."[8]

At half past eleven, after nearly seven hours of continuous, savage fighting, the last remnants of the garrison—barely a score in number—fled into the darkness, blasting the bridge across the rear section of the moat by way of valedictory.

Out of a garrison of 300 only 25 succeeded in escaping, and there was one solitary Russian prisoner—preserved for interrogation purposes. Japanese losses amounted to between 700 and 800, but they deemed that a cheap price to pay for possession of the first permanent fort to fall into their hands; and the raging afterthirst of battle was duly slaked in quantities of sake and champagne.

Smirnoff, the officially appointed commandant of the fortress, learned of the intention to abandon Fort No. 2 only after it had become a *fait accompli*.

The Russians had, of course, mined Chi-kuan-shan, and the Japanese went very fearfully about the interior until their engineers had succeeded in—literally—running to earth the demolition charges placed beneath its foundations. The work itself had been reduced to a mound of formless rubble. "The destruction caused by the bombardments, and finally by the explosion, was so great that it was impossible to trace the original lines on which the fort had been constructed. The interior presented a scene of terrible confusion. Masses of concrete, rubbish, sand, earth, stones, old uniforms, broken guns, rifles, cooking utensils, empty shells, fragments of iron and steel, and *débris* of every description, covered the ground";[9] while to everything clung the charnel-house reek of death.

With Chi-kuan-shan in their hands at last, it was only to be expected that the Japanese would set about the reduction of the neighbouring forts. Erh-lung-shan was mined on similar lines to those taken at Fort No. 2, and at ten o'clock on the morning of Dec. 28 the charges were exploded. They had been better laid than on the previous occasion; the *débris* thrown up completely filled the moat, making the way easier for the assault waves, although they came under heavy fire from the batteries at Yi-tzu-shan, across the Lun-Ho Valley.

Some 500 men of the 26th East Siberian Sharpshooters formed the garrison of Fort No. 3, and about half this force had been drawn up in the lower battery. Many of them were instantly killed by the force of the explosion, and the remainder were so dazed by the shock of the stunning detonation as to be quite unable to make any serious resistance to the Japanese onslaught. The lower battery was speedily swept clear of all opposition, and the invaders proceeded to entrench themselves and erect sandbag breastworks, lest intensive mining operations to destroy the upper battery should impose a delay that would afford the enemy time to organize a counterstroke.

The staff decision, however, was in favour of carrying the upper works forthwith, and the Nineteenth and Thirty-sixth Regiments went at it with a rush, swarming in from all sides on the defenders. The Russians fought back with their usual stolid courage, disputing every inch of the ground with the utmost tenacity, in the barracks, at the gun epaulments, in the kitchens, and out in the open, now sheltering behind a sandbag breastwork, now firing from behind a broken wall—the sharp crack of rifle fire and the hollow belch of hand grenades blending in a crescendo of ear-splitting din. "The stairway leading from the centre of the fort underground to the barrack was the scene of a horrible struggle. The Japanese, cold, infuriated and determined to finish off their opponents, poured down it and encountered the equally determined Russians at the foot of the stairway. The Russians, shooting up the stairs, kept back the Japanese for a considerable time, but finally they were driven round the corner at the bottom into the barrack, followed by the victorious Japanese. Another desperate fight took place in the interior; many of the Russians climbed through the window in the barrack into the ditch of the fort, . . . the remainder, unable to escape, retreated from the barrack into the kitchen, and there made their final stand."[10]

Hour after hour the fight raged on, and had it been possible for reinforcements to reach the hard-pressed garrison, the day might well have ended in their favour. But no help was forthcoming; and, heedless of their losses, the Japanese fought on with undiminished vigour. In such circumstances the outcome could scarcely be in doubt. For all that, it was not until three o'clock in the morning, after seventeen hours of incessant, close-range fighting, that those few of the garrison who were left gave up the struggle, and retired, after setting fire to everything that would burn. Some 150 men got safely away, three prisoners fell into the invaders' hands, the rest were dead. Japanese losses had come to over 1,000 killed and wounded.

Just before dawn on the twenty-ninth the Russians made a final attempt to recapture the fort by an attack launched from the hills under the brow of Yi-tzu-shan. Two parties of East Siberians gained the ditch behind the work, and endeavoured to storm the barrack. But the effort was foredoomed to failure; it could have succeeded only by employing the element of surprise, and the Japanese were far too much on the alert for this to be feasible. Those of the assailants who were not killed were forced to retire to the shelter of the hills.

Of the northeastern works only Sung-su-shan remained in the defenders' hands. The fortification had, of course, been thoroughly mined, and the charges were sprung on the morning of Dec. 31. In this instance the explosion was particularly effective, as a large store of grenades within the fort was detonated, wrecking practically the whole of the interior. The greater part of the garrison, who had remained in their bomb-proofs, were buried alive under a deep layer of rubble. Appalled by the catastrophe, the remainder hoisted the white flag and surrendered. The Japanese at once set to work to free the men entombed, and soon succeeded in laying bare the entrance to what had threatened to be their grave; whereupon the 160 men left alive crawled out to yield themselves captive. With hardly a shot fired Sung-su-shan passed into Japanese possession.

It was New Year's Eve, Japan's one great festival of the year. But there was no thought for the traditional celebrations. Far sterner work demanded immediate attention. At 6 P.M., therefore, a mine was detonated under the Chinese Wall behind Redoubt No. 1 (East Pan-lun-shan), and through the breach thus made the assault waves advanced to attack the battery positions on the ridge behind. The fight speedily knotted about the narrow plateau of Wan-tai, where two 6-inch guns had been sited in bombproof and sandbagged emplacements. They were supported by infantry trenches that girdled the whole position, a little farther down the slope. Uplifted by their earlier successes, the Japanese went about their task with such a will that the infantry trenches were speedily overrun, leaving the small garrison in the gun sites completely isolated.

"The Russian artillery was almost silent, only a few guns to the west of Wan-tai, answering the Japanese artillery. The Japanese infantry, which had meantime been reinforced by about two companies from the Chinese Wall, commenced to advance up the slope, but by groups of about one-half *zug* [section] each. The leading group on the north-east slope soon crossed the Russian trench below the summit, showing that the latter must have been evacuated, and continued on to the little redoubt which crowns the top of the hill. No Russian fire could be detected coming from the work. A leading group of about twenty-five men soon reached the top parapet and one man was observed to look over cautiously into the redoubt. In a few moments the group commenced throwing into the fort hand-grenades that went off with loud reports, raising considerable smoke and dust. After about five minutes of grenade-throwing some ten Japanese jumped over the parapet into the redoubt, but in a few moments several returned hastily. Almost immediately a tremendous explosion occurred inside the redoubt. The Russians had fired their magazine. Immediately after the explosion a few Russian shells burst over the work, and after a few minutes the Japanese on the outside of the parapet again commenced to enter the redoubt. Presently the Japanese flag was waved from the summit to indicate that the position had been taken."[11]

Even if an attack on Signal Hill, near Takhe Bay, had been repulsed, there was no gainsaying the fact that the Japanese were steadily eating into all the northeastern defences. At the same time on the western flank strong forces were meeting with weakening resistance as they worked their way resolutely toward the port and the territory leading to the New Town from the south—from which a wedge could be driven to cut off Liao-tieh-shan from the Tiger peninsula. Success in war, if speedily and ruthlessly exploited, gathers a momentum that is as exhilarating to the victors as it is disheartening to the vanquished.

But although the Japanese, over the previous two weeks, had made enormous strides toward their ultimate goal, nobody, not even the best informed at General Nogi's headquarters, conceived that the end was so near. For if the inner line of defence in front of the Old Town was lamentably weak, the western and southern sectors, strongly garrisoned and armed, and supported by Liao-tieh-shan as a shelter for the reserves of men, munitions, and food supplies, could be turned into a formidable "keep," whose reduction would cost the besiegers dearly. But stubbornly as they had fought before, the riflemen of the Russian rank and file were yielding to a defeatism that expressed itself in endless bickering between the individuals who had "borne the heat and burden of the fray" and those whose service—or personal ingenuity—had kept out of the firing line. "Terrible scenes were enacted, men came to blows, were even killed—always arising out of the question, 'Where have you been hiding, you scoundrel?' "[12] In short, their recent setbacks and their gloomy prospects had so dispirited the general ruck of the Russian officers and men that only the clarion call of an inspired leader could have aroused them from their apathy. And in place of an inspired and inspiring leader they had General Baron Anatole Mikhailovitch Stössel.

At 6 P.M. on Dec. 29 a meeting of the Council of War had been held in which the general consensus of opinion had been stoutly in favour of continued resistance; even Admiral Wiren and Rear Admiral Loschinsky, whose vessels had been demolished before their eyes, insisting that "The place must be defended to the bitter end."

The die-hards had been solidly supported by the fortress artillery commander, General Biely, who gave assurance that "We have plenty of ammunition to repulse two more big attacks—102,000 shells of our own and 100,000 still available from the fleet, with 8,000,000 rounds of small-arm ammunition. From an artillery point of view, I do not consider that we are at all in a critical position. The defence ought to be continued."

Biely's attitude had been strongly endorsed by Khvostoff, Chief of the Fortress Staff, who reported that the supply depots still contained 1,422,000 pounds of flour, 132,000 pounds of wheat, 308,000 pounds of maize, 77,000 pounds of corned beef, 1,375,000 pounds of beans and fair stocks of rice, barley, and sugar; while some 1,920 horses still awaited slaughter to supplement the preserved-meat ration.

According to Major General Kostenko,[13] who kept a record of the proceedings. Stössel had abstained from arguing the matter further because he had already sent a message to the Tsar informing him that "We cannot hold out more than a few days; I am taking measures to prevent a street massacre."

Kostenko further affirms that Stössel had refrained from reading out this message to the members of the Council of War after the majority had so strongly declared against surrender, because of his comprehensible fear that his subordinates would combine to suspend him from command.

With the majority of the Council firm in their belief that defence of the fortress would be robustly maintained, the meeting had been adjourned; and for two days Smirnoff and his supporters had done everything in their power to rally the garrison to a last stand worthy of the rear guard of Smolensk and Borodino.

Then at half past four on the afternoon of New Year's Day the governor of the Kuan-tun District took the step for which he had already secretly paved the way. A *parlementaire* was secretly sent toward the Japanese lines under a flag of truce, bearing a missive written in English, which read:

> Sir,
>
> Taking into consideration the state of affairs in the seat of war in general, I find the further resistance of Port Arthur useless, and in view of the fruitless loss of men I would like to negotiate about the capitulation. If you agree to this, I beg you to appoint delegates for this purpose who would discuss about the conditions, and to choose a place where my delegates will meet them.
>
> I avail myself of the opportunity to express my senti-ments of esteem.
>
> [Signed] Stoessel

Shortly after the despatch of this portentous missive, Admiral Wiren was the recipient of a communication from the governor's chief of staff:

> A letter has just been sent by a *parlementaire* from General Stössel to General Baron Nogi proposing to begin negotia-tions for a capitulation; there is, therefore, only tonight for you to do what you consider necessary to your ships.

Admiral Wiren, conscientious and patriotic officer that he was, was thunderstruck at such tidings, and "immediately went off to Admiral Gregorovitch, to whom it was also news. Thence he went to General Biely, and even to the Commandant, who were both equally thunderstruck at what he told them. From them he went to Stössel, where the information of what had been done was confirmed."[14]

On Jan. 2, as the officers assembled at Tretyakov's local

headquarters, one of their comrades came galloping out of the town with the news that he had seen two emissaries riding out toward the enemy lines under a white flag. They were soon identified as the envoys from the district staff office sent to receive General Nogi's reply to the governor's communication of the previous day. "General indignation against General Fock was apparent, and every kind of accusation was heaped upon his head";[15] for Fock's pernicious influence over the weak-willed governor was notorious and universally deplored. A little before 10 A.M. the *parlementaires* were on their way back to district headquarters with the Japanese commander's reply:

Sir.—I have the honour to agree to your Excellency's proposal to negotiate for the conditions and order of capitulation.

I name Major General Kosuke Idichi, c/o Staff of the Besieging Army, for the purpose, and some Staff Officers and civil officers will accompany him. They are to meet your delegates at Sueishi[16] precisely at noon today, 2nd of January '05. The delegates are to be invested with full power to sign the capitulation, which shall take effect immediately after signing, without further approval. Full powers to be exchanged must be signed by the Officers in highest command on both sides. I avail myself of this opportunity of expressing to you my sentiments of esteem.

[Signed] General Nogi
Commander-in-Chief
Japanese Army Besieging Port Arthur

While these negotiations were proceeding, Admiral Wiren issued orders for such ships under his command as were still operable to be disabled by charges exploded in their most vital parts. But although the grim task was hastened in every pos-sible way, the last of the demolitions was only executed on the morning of Jan. 2. Soon after daylight the *Sevastopol* was tugged out by the *Silacha* to a depth of 30 fathoms, and her Kingston valves were opened so that, the sea water inlets flood-ing her hull, she heeled over to starboard and quietly foundered.

Biely, meanwhile, was unostentatiously putting out of action as many guns as possible and jettisoning as much ammunition as could be disposed of in the time still available.

It was too late to think of putting Fock and Stössel under restraint, terminating the *pourparlers*, and continuing the struggle. The troops had got wind of the fact that negotiations had been opened, and there was no fight left in them. "The conviction that the game was only kept up at the cost of the rank and file, that nothing mattered, that it was not worth while, took root and spread more and more."[17] The only action the rank and file were ripe for was mutiny.

An uncanny, almost frightening silence had replaced the noise of firing, the roar of explosions, and the whistling of bullets overhead. Dazed and bewildered, the garrison set about Fock's blunt order to abandon the third, and inner, line of defence. All of the northeastern and half of the eastern front was in Nogi's grip, and all the roads into the port were picketed by Japanese troops. The only sound to disturb the silence was the muffled thud of explosions from the direction of the harbour. As darkness fell, a fire broke out near the wharves and bathed the surrounding scene of desolation in a baleful crimson glare.

In a last gesture of protest against a course of action he had consistently opposed, Smirnoff sent Kuropatkin a telegram, which ran:

> General Stössel has entered into negotiations with the enemy for surrendering the Fortress without informing me, and in spite of my opinion and that of the majority of the Officers.

But no help could be looked for from the commander-in-chief. Even in mid-December he and his army commanders, meeting to discuss Port Arthur's parlous plight, had come to the conclusion that nothing could be done to relieve the garrison until the entire XVI Corps, the bulk which was still in transit, had been assembled in Mukden. In any case, Mukden was over 260 miles from Port Arthur, and winter paralyzed the Liao-tung peninsula.

At the hour appointed, the Russian and Japanese delegates assembled at Plumtree Cottage, one of the few places left comparatively undamaged in Shui-shih-ying village. Formalities were cut short, and the Russians were left with an hour in which to digest terms of a surrender which had, in fact, been drawn up two years previously by one of Japan's most astute and experienced lawyers.

Outside the house where history was in the making, "the sun shone with almost summer warmth on the proceedings, so unlike any which had taken place during the past five months. The house of peace was situated in the centre of the village, with a large open space before it, forming a sort of village-green. This square was thronged with a crowd of Japanese soldiers, who had come in from the surrounding camps to see their enemy armed with the olive branch in place of the rifle. In the centre of this throng, sitting on a little bank, were the Cossacks of the escort holding their horses. One of them held on high a long pole with a square of ordinary linen, the symbol of peace, and by his side sat a Japanese cavalry soldier who also held a similar pole with a similar square of canvas."[18]

The Russian delegation was headed by Reuss, and although it included Khvostoff, only Stössel's personal representative was endowed with plenary powers. Khvostoff's protest that the garrison should not be made captive but march out with the honours of war, was therefore not pressed. The surrender was, essentially, unconditional. The Japanese claimed all public and private property in Port Arthur, other than such small articles as the prisoners might require for their personal use. Officers who gave their parole not to serve again during the course of the war were to be repatriated to Russia. Those who refused their parole, together with the rank and file, were to be held. Facilities were to be provided for the evacuation of the 500 women and children in the town, together with such civilians as were in private business or employ. These totalled between 500 and 600. The control of hospital buildings was to remain unchanged; although the Japanese consented to lend additional surgical and medical aid to the inadequate and overworked Russian hospital staff charged with the care of the 13,613 sick—including civilians—and 3,387 wounded.

At 8.45 P.M. articles of capitulation were signed by which 878 officers, 23,251 of the rank and file, and 8,956 seamen surrendered their arms and passed into inactivity, either as individuals under oath to abstain from any further part in the conflict or as outright prisoners of war.

Four battleships, two cruisers, fourteen gunboats and destroyers, and twenty other vessels fell as spoil to the victors. Damaged as they might be, they were not beyond repair.

Russian losses in killed, wounded, and missing suffered during the course of the siege totalled 31,306. To set against this, the Japanese authorities admitted that the operations in front of Port Arthur had cost them, in killed, wounded and missing, 57,780. To this total must be added 33,769 sick, of whom no less than 21,023 had fallen victim to beriberi.

Under the inspiration of Kondratenko and such local commanders as Tetrakov, the Russians had fought with a sort of dogged stoicism which recognized that the only alternative to continued resistance was open mutiny. "But the news of the surrender being an accomplished fact soon spread among the garrison," Nojine recorded; "and our men seemed suddenly to change their natures, all discipline went to the winds and rioting commenced. Some, throwing their arms away, went straight down to the town, which became one vast scene of drunkenness and orgy. The shops and stores were looted, and wholesale robbery was the order of the day. The Officers, seeing that it was hopeless to try and cope with their men, hid from the maddened crowds."

In a panic for his own safety and that of his property, Stössel begged for a Japanese detachment to mount guard over his residence, and his urgent request was acceded to with sardonic readiness. Fully armed Japanese patrols thereafter proceeded to restore some semblance of order to the town, for whose control its cowering, humiliated governor was still at least nominally responsible.

Thus at a total cost to the victors of something under 60,000 men—plus such of the sick and wounded as subsequently expired—the Japanese regained Port Arthur. The haven which had been designed by the Tsarists as a forward base for an attack on Japan had proved no more than a self-devised trap for the Russians.

Although scarcely to be dismissed as no more than "a triumph of brute force and ignorance," General Nogi's capture of Port Arthur was less the outcome of military foresight and tactical genius than the reward of dogged persistence and an unswerving will to win.

The easy triumph of 1894, when a rabble of ill-armed, ill-led, and undisciplined Chinese had been reduced to submission almost in a matter of hours, had had the effect of persuading the Japanese general staff very gravely to underestimate the gravity and complexity of the task with which they were confronted. Furthermore, the quick victory at Nan-shan encouraged a mood of optimistic self-confidence that events were very speedily to deflate.

The first assault on the fortress was a daring but foolhardy attempt to apply the methods of field operations to the very different problem of siege warfare. Its failure brought home the lesson that fortifications constructed on reasonably scientific lines are not to be stormed even by the most intrepid soldiery. Even when Nogi sought to adopt the slower but more certain and conserving methods of formal siege, political considerations impelled him to make desperate assaults on the Russian works, at heavy expense to his long-suffering infantry.

It was only when the sap and the mine had accomplished their preparatory work that the Japanese troops were given the chance to get to grips with their opponents.

The fall of Port Arthur did not end the conflict, although taken in conjunction with the alarming increase in the opposition to the War Party in Russia itself, it undoubtedly helped to precipitate the end.

A wave of commercial depression swept the Russian community. Allied to a bitter resentment of the struggle with

Japan was a smouldering anger at the political restrictions under which so many of the ordinary people still laboured. This was a mood that the extreme Left was swift to exploit. Russian socialism had always been insurrectionary and violent in tendency, dedicated to fighting a class war without compromise. Thus the undercover activities of skilled agitators speedily resulted in a serious outbreak of public disaffection. On Jan. 18 the workmen employed at the Neva Shipbuilding, Putiloff, and other industrial centers in St. Petersburg went on strike. At the same time, secretly encouraged by revolutionaries who were not openly to declare themselves for another twelve years, the strikers drafted a petition demanding legislation to deal with poverty, the oppression of labour by the employers, guarantees of personal security, freedom of speech and of worship, compulsory education, equality before the law, responsibility of Ministers, and a representative assembly.

On the twenty-second a delegation, supported by huge crowds, and led by an unfrocked priest, "Father" Gapon, marched on the Winter Palace in order to present their demands to the Tsar. Their way was blocked by the military, and when the crowd disobeyed the summons to disperse, the order was given to open fire. Scores were shot and many others trampled to death in the rush to flee.

Two days later General Trepoff, a man universally loathed on the score of his harsh, dictatorial methods, was appointed governor general of the city, with plenary powers; and every demonstration of popular feeling was suppressed with great severity. Many confessed revolutionaries, including Maxim Gorky, were put under arrest; and although a handful were subsequently released, a high proportion was held for trial.

Nor was St. Petersburg the only scene of turbulent unrest. Lesser disturbances broke out in Moscow, Reval, Odessa, Riga, Warsaw and Lodz. Each was ruthlessly crushed.

Gloating over the news out of Russia, in his shabby Geneva lodgings Vladimir Ilyich Ulyanov—to be "damned to eternal fame" as Nikolai Lenin—rubbed his hands with well-founded satisfaction. All things considered, the long-planned Marxist revolution was incubating very nicely.

THE PORTENT

"IT IS A LAW OF NATURE COMMON TO ALL MANKIND,
WHICH NO TIME SHALL ANNUL OR DESTROY, THAT THOSE
WHO HAVE MORE STRENGTH SHALL BEAR RULE OVER
THOSE WHO HAVE LESS."

—DIONYSIUS THE YOUNGER

10   PORT ARTHUR surrendered "wisely, perhaps, but not well,"[1] and a defence which might have gone down to posterity as one of the finest feats of arms in all history was shorn of all its lustre. Rozhestvensky, still near Madagascar awaiting the arrival of Admiral Nebogatoff and the collection of maritime old crocks that constituted the Third Pacific Squadron, almost welcomed the further excuse for delay. Obviously, with the destruction of the vessels in Port Arthur harbour, he could no longer regard his armada as a reinforcing fleet. Instead, it was the only Russian naval force left to challenge Japanese sea power. St. Petersburg had issued no order of recall, and in the absence of any base in the Pacific to support operations at sea, it was impossible to suppress the dark thought that the Second Pacific Squadron was being utilized for political rather than for strategical ends, a suspicion that much-delayed news of recent events in the homeland went far to confirm.

Tidings of the strikes and demonstrations in St. Petersburg and elsewhere speedily provoked a spirit of unrest among the personnel of the fleet; and Rozhestvensky's training programme was as seriously interfered with by the measures taken to restore discipline as by the numerous casualties arising from dysentery and sunstroke. In the general atmosphere of uncertainty and gloom the only relief was afforded by the readiness of the French to render all the help in their power—but always at a price. Without such aid it is clear that the Second Pacific Squadron would have been unable to continue its passage.

When the news of Port Arthur's surrender reached Kuropatkin's general headquarters, Ignatyev records that "we heard a heavy sigh. The blow to our pride resulting from the fall of Port Arthur was felt with less force with the Manchurian Army than in Russia—the troops could not forget the blood that had been shed in vain to save it." Moreover, the long months of winter stagnation, with little but depressing home news, a heavy sick list, and unalleviated discomfort, had reduced the rank and file to a condition of sluggish disinterest in the conflict. This was largely attributable to the presence in the ranks of a heavy proportion of disgruntled reservists, in some units as high as 70 per cent, whose sole idea was to return to their homes. Nor were they inspired to patriotism by the example set them by their officers. Far from imitating the abstemious practice of the Port Arthur garrison, they guzzled the hours away over their endless hands of cards, and left the training, discipline, and welfare of their troops almost entirely in the hands of the noncommissioned officers. "Heavy drinking was not uncommon," the British military attaché noted; "and it had been a matter of conjecture whether the nerves of any of them would suffer in consequence."[2]

To Kuropatkin the collapse of resistance in the south could only presage a steady increase in the forces arrayed against him, as General Nogi's Third Army took its place in the line. Every military principle therefore urged an offensive before Oyama could benefit from this accretion of strength. The Japanese position on the Sha-Ho, thirty-four miles in length, was strongly fortified, with two lines of closed redoubts and a third line of deep entrenchments. But the territory between their left flank and the railway was thinly held. With the waterways frozen, a cavalry raid on Kin-chou might usefully disrupt the enemy line of communications and afford time for the Russian VIII and XVI Corps to arrive and detrain. A body of 5,000 horse, with flying artillery and a detachment of mounted engineers, was therefore placed under the command of General Mishchenko. After considerable delay, this force set out on its mission. Crossing the Hun-Ho on Jan. 8, Mishchenko's contingent passed round the extreme left of the Japanese screen and, in three columns, moved across the vast empty plain of the Liao. On the evening of the ninth a small convoy was captured. The next day some 500 Hunhuses were cut up and scattered. A fortified village was rushed, one or two more convoys rounded up, 500 yards of railway line destroyed, and shots exchanged with the garrison at Yin-kou station. Mishchenko could congratulate himself on accomplishing a useful, if limited piece of work. His success could have been far greater had he not encumbered himself with a baggage train that would have done credit to a travelling circus. Oddly enough, it did not include a single mortar.

The general action designed by Kuropatkin to anticipate the arrival of Nogi's Third Army was not put in motion, however, until Jan. 26. By this time at least part of the forces from Port Arthur had been transferred to the north. With the offensive under way, the I and III Russian Army Corps made a strong demonstration to hold the enemy attention, while Grippenberg's Second Army, supported by Shtakelberg's I Siberian Corps, sought to outflank the Japanese in the neighbourhood of San-de-pu.[3] At the outset Shtakelberg appears to have secured his right flank with some skill. This allowed the Second Army to concentrate against San-de-pu itself, the whole strength of the formation being engaged. But the operation was clumsily contrived. Attacks were hurled against unreconnoitered and strongly fortified positions without sufficient artillery preparation, with extremely costly results. Nevertheless, it was odd for Grippenberg, at the end of barely fourteen hours' marching and fighting, to order a day's rest for his troops. This inexplicable hiatus enabled the Japanese to concentrate considerable forces against the Russian I Corps. Threatened in front and on both flanks, the Tsarists retreated. It was the familiar story of unnecessary alarm, confusion, and wilful disregard of orders. Grippenberg himself had quibbled over every directive addressed to him. Shtakelberg had let the battle drift, and Kuropatkin had never succeeded in getting it into focus. Fundamentally, the fatal inactivity of the Russian Second Army was very largely attributable to the personal antagonism ruling between Grippenberg and the commander-in-chief. The feud ended when Shtakelberg reported sick and departed for Moscow. He was succeeded in command by General Bilderling.

Once again the Russian soldier had been forced to retire; and by this time "the knowledge that the fight would be bound to end in retreat," Soloviev recorded, "acted in a demoralising way. I have often heard the men ask each other, 'When is the order to retreat going to come?' This was done without any *arrière pensée*, and only from a consciousness that this had been done before and was going to take place again."[4]

Back in their prepared positions in front of Mukden, the three armies, totalling between three and four hundred thousand men, with 1,320 guns and 56 machine guns, were "extended in one continuous line for nearly a hundred miles. Kuropatkin's encirclement-phobia reached its maximum, and the more reinforcements arrived from Russia, the longer the front became."[5] Russian Intelligence had entirely failed to discover where Nogi's army was deployed; for once in his life Kuropatkin had failed to accumulate a strong general reserve, all the army commanders having refused to part with the necessary troops with which to form one.

Morale was shaky, and was not helped by rumours and reports of Japanese cavalry raids on the railway as much as 170 miles behind Mukden. All this activity, together with the Japanese-inspired forays by large bands of Hunhuses, so alarmed the commander-in-chief for the safety of his lines of communication that he detached the Don Cossacks and the whole of the 41st Division to reinforce the already numerous railway guard. Persistent reports from the Intelligence department that the Japanese were contemplating a combined operation against Vladivostok—carefully fostered by Oyama's agents behind the Russian lines—caused the detachment of yet another body of troops for the northern garrison's reinforcement.

The waning spirit of confidence was struck a further blow by the discovery that magnificent roads had been constructed through the kaoliang, all plainly marked "Rear-road for the —th Army Corps" and so on.

With 333,000 infantry still under command, to the Japanese total of 315,000, Kuropatkin was confident that the initiative rested with him. But on Feb. 20, while he was still mulling over his future plans, Oyama landed the first blow. With unfailing ardour, his men went into the attack against positions in which every device of field fortification had been incorporated. From Feb. 25 to Mar. 4 the struggle raged to and fro, with counter-attack following on each fresh assault. On the fourth, however, the Japanese at last succeeded in outflanking their opponents' right. The Russians were forced to fall back and form a defensive flank; the fighting front thus took the form of two sides of a square. During the night of Mar. 8–9 the Russian lines of communication north of Mukden were so severely threatened that retreat was unavoidable. A wide gap had developed between the two army groups commanded, respectively, by Bilderling and Kaulbars, and on the tenth these disconnected forces were caught between two fires and suffered appalling punishment, but at considerable cost to their assailants. Kuropatkin's defeat was virtually complete. He had been entirely deceived as to Oyama's intentions, and Nogi's whereabouts had been perfectly screened by the rest of the Japanese forces until the moment arrived to send forward the victor of Port Arthur to envelop the enemy right and cut the railway well to the north of Mukden.

The confusion that had set in during the final stages of the struggle was almost beyond belief. "Over the heads of their direct commanders Kuropatkin would pull regiments or even separate battalions out of the line, sending them away to block up gaps. The result was that no one had the slightest idea any longer whom he was to take orders from, the more so because, in the endeavour to secure unification of command on the new front, improvised units were created one after another."[6] On the fifth day of Nogi's hustling offensive, the only reserves Kuropatkin had in hand was a single company of bakers! Troops were hurried forward, but "the ebb was soon turning into a flow; new formations sent to reinforce the broken forward companies had to try and force their way through it,"[7] and many abandoned the attempt only too readily.

The sole line of retreat was along the Mandarin Road, where the narrow seven- to eight-mile avenue of escape between the converging horns of the Japanese encircling movement was rapidly contracting. It was a question of how many of his broken formations Kuropatkin could contrive to squeeze through the neck of the sack. "The Officer corps had vanished, doing its best to escape notice. It was powerless to restore order to the elementary torrent pouring northwards, as far as might be from the dusty fields of Mukden."[8] There was little Linevitch could do to stem the flood when, by direct order of the Tsar, he superseded Kuropatkin in command.[9] "Order was restored to the armies not so much thanks to the measures of the High Command, as to the company cooks and the field kitchens rescued from the general flight. To these flocked the soldiers dead-tired from hard fighting; from the soldiers companies were assembled, from companies—battalions, regiments, divisions, corps. It entered nobody's head to forsake his precious company field kitchen. The Japanese gave no trouble, they were so exhausted that they dropped off to sleep in the positions they had reached at the end of the Mukden fighting. In vain do military historians reproach Marshal Oyama with insufficient energy in pursuit. You cannot always make a Sedan with troops that have reached the limit of exhaustion."[10] When the final count came to be taken, it was found that the Russians had lost, in killed, wounded, and missing, some 59,800 men, seventy guns, and enormous quantities of ammunition and military stores. The Japanese returned their losses, from all causes, as toalling 53,500.[11]

By yielding all along the line the rump of the Tsarist army was enabled to get away and reassemble in and about Hai-ping-kai. No preparations were made for a counteroffensive. On the contrary, defensive positions were prepared for 200 miles behind Hai-ping-kai—as far back as the Sangari River. Nor were these self-protective measures interfered with by the

Japanese. With their recent heavy losses, the strain on their resources and matériel had become the cause of the most serious anxiety. Already the classes of 1905 and 1906 had been called to the Colours; and while their field strength was threatened with progressive decline, that of the Russians was increasing.

The Russians' sole immediate hope of restoring the situation in their favour lay with Rozhestvensky, who had been joined off the coast of Indo-China by Nebogatoff and his command of venerable "old shoes, squatty, short-tailed slow-pokes," as one foremast hand contemptuously described them.

With even his decks so crammed with coal that some of his guns could not traverse properly, Rozhestvensky might well have tried to reach Vladivostok by way of the Perouse Strait, or even by circuiting the Kuriles. But with a sort of defiant fatalism he ploughed directly ahead for the Strait of Tsu-shima. And here he found Togo's thoroughly refitted armament awaiting him, with the yards of the *Mikasa* aflutter with the admiral's signal: *The rise or fall of the Empire depends upon today's battle. Let every man do his utmost.*

The conflict which ensued was a classic example of the gun battle, in which the powerfully armed ironclad justified all that its sponsors had claimed for it. But where there was indecision, fumbling, and confusion on the Russian side, with the Japanese complete order and control prevailed, so the end was virtually predetermined.

The action opened with an indeterminate clash between Rozhestvensky's battleships and a detached Japanese cruiser squadron. It was not till 2 P.M., when the Russians were well in the Straits, steaming in two columns in line ahead, that Togo closed to attack with his heavy armament. He chose the port column as being the weaker, the light cruiser squadrons having received orders to steam southward and attack the enemy rear. The heavy Japanese vessels, circling on the left front of the enemy's advance, put on speed with the intention of recrossing the bows of the Russian battleship division—a manoeuvre known as Crossing the T. As the *Mikasa* led the Japanese line in its turning movement, Rozhestvensky swung round to starboard and opened fire at 8,500 yards. Waiting till the distance had shortened to 6,500 yards, Togo opened with all the heavy guns he could bring to bear. Following in succession, ship after ship came round to join in the cannonade, to which the Russians' ill-regulated return fire made woefully inadequate reply. Captain Semenoff, who was aboard the flagship, subsequently recorded, "It seemed impossible even to count the number of projectiles striking us. I had not only never witnessed such a fire before, but I had never imagined anything like it. Shells seemed to be pouring upon us incessantly, one after another."

But there was no lack of courage in the Tsarist fleet, where the crews stood manfully to their guns. Hammered and battered, the *Suvoroff* continued to fire defiantly until she was sunk. The *Ushakoff* replied to the Japanese summons to haul down her flag with a broadside, and sank with the whole of her crew, while of the *Navarin's* complement only two men were saved. But the unseaworthiness of the craft themselves, their tactical mishandling, and, above all, the unreadiness for war of both officers and men, were handicaps that gallantry could not overcome. With Rozhestvensky wounded and out of the battle, the flagship's steering jammed, and the engagement broke up into a number of scrambling, isolated actions, the whole affair degenerating into the merciless slaughter of a herd of blind, maimed, blood-crazed animals.

With the early morning of May 28 Nebogatoff was faced with the fact that nothing was left him but surrender, and orders were given to hoist the white flag. One fast cruiser, the *Izumrud*, refusing to capitulate, slipped the encircling Japanese warships and escaped to the north. Running out of coal, she steered for Vladimir Bay, where she drove hard onto the reef. Landing her crew, her captain destroyed her guns and then blew her up with charges wedged into her vital parts. The only vessels to reach Vladivostok and report the news of defeat were the destroyers *Grosni* and *Brawy* and the small swift cruiser *Almaz*. Of the twelve ships that comprised the Russian battle line, eight were sunk, while the *Oryol* and *Emperor Nicholas I*, together with two old coastal defence ships, were surrendered. Of the cruisers, four were sunk, one was run ashore and scuttled, and three made good their escape to internment at Manila. Three of the six special service vessels were sunk, two escaped to be interned at Shanghai, while one reached Diego Suarez. Of the remaining Russian destroyers, four were sunk, and one—with the wounded Rozhestvensky aboard—was captured and towed into Sasebo.

Togo's losses totalled three torpedo boats, while the damage inflicted on some of the larger craft put them briefly out of service. The Japanese toll of killed and wounded totalled 700, as against the Russian loss of 4,800 killed and wounded in action, or drowned, with nearly 6,000 taken captive, and 1,800 officers and men interned in neutral countries. It had been a victory almost as sweeping, and even more far-reaching in its consequences, than Nelson's triumph at the battle of the Nile.

Japan had clearly established her superiority over her opponent at sea; but on land she was faced by odds that were slowly but steadily increasing. The whole of the Russian XIII Army Corps, for example, had now joined the First, Second, and Third Manchurian Armies in the field. Moreover, Japan was now finding it difficult to raise money. "If they want more loans," the international financier Sir Ernest Cassel informed an acquaintance, "except for purely pacific purposes, we will not let them have them."[12]

In Russia, from the very outset the authorities had had to contend with a lack of popular support for the war, which quickly became a widespread movement against its further prosecution. Some of the ultraliberal newspapers openly urged the rank and file to revolt and do away with their officers; and the Moscow town council recommended "inviting the representatives of the people to consider the question of putting an end to the war." The moment had arrived when only an accommodation with the Japanese, accompanied by far-reaching domestic reforms, would serve to avert a national insurrection. Moreover, any further Japanese military successes might well end in the fall of Vladivostok, the abandonment of the eastern Ussuri Province, and the loss of Harbin—possibly in the complete isolation of the Pri-Amur District from the rest of Siberian Russia. And possession of Harbin would give the Japanese control of the minerally and agriculturally rich provinces of Fengtien and Kirin, and the fertile Ussuri, with its excellent fishing grounds.

It was at this moment of dubiety, reappraisal, and self-questioning, by both Tokio and Moscow, that President Theodore Roosevelt came forward with an offer to mediate. As an outcome of the negotiations that ensued, Japan was accorded the right to lease the southern part of Manchuria from China, and was ceded the lower half of the island of Sakhalin, together with the right to fish the Siberian waters of the Pacific. Dai-Nippon's paramount position in Korea was given full recognition. Enough pressure was brought to bear on her, however, that her claim to a substantial war indemnity was eventually dropped.

In neither country were the terms of settlement universally approved. There were ugly riots in Japan, while the Tsar voiced the opinion of many among the governing classes when he affirmed that he was "greatly dissatisfied not merely with the terms arranged, but with the cessation of hostilities."[13] He had calculated that the peace conference would break down on the question of an indemnity, and that the struggle would be continued until Japan could raise no more loans.

That hostilities were brought to an end must be attributed, in a very large measure, to the influence and skilful personal diplomacy of the President of the United States.

All wars are wonderfully well fought when they are over; although it is speedily discovered that while victory has a score of fathers, defeat is an orphan.

In most wars one side starts with certain advantages over its opponent. In the Russo-Japanese campaign Japan enjoyed the very great benefit of far shorter lines of communication, vulnerable only if command of the sea should be lost to the Tsarists. Russia had of course to be defeated on land as well as afloat, and with this end in view the Japanese speedily made themselves masters of Korea, possession of which was not only of great military value, but also of considerable political importance.

From the very outset it was the Japanese design to try and envelop their opponents at Liao-yang, and "the whole campaign forms an interesting example of a strategic deployment made with an avowed object of culminating in a decisive battle at a definite point."[14] Initially, the Japanese forces appeared to be dangerously separated. But Kuroki's thrust across the Yalu and his subsequent march to Feng-huan-ching rendered it impossible for Kuropatkin to fall on Oku's isolated army corps and beat him in detail. Any such move would have exposed his lines of communication far too nakedly.

Liao-yang did not prove decisive. It has been suggested that it was a mistake on the part of the Japanese to detach forces for the investment of Port Arthur and thus, by weakening their field army, forfeit the chance to secure overwhelming victory in their first major encounter with the Russians. Equally, it has been advanced that the Russians were in error to try and hold Port Arthur, since its garrison would have formed a valuable addition to the field army. These are arguments that seem to cancel each other. In any case, once the Tsarist fleet had sought the shelter of Port Arthur, the army had no option but to garrison it. Had it been possible to deny 203 Metre Hill to the besiegers, and had the fortress held out until Rozhestvensky had made the junction with Witgeft's armament, Admiral Togo's task would have been rendered infinitely more formidable. The Japanese can scarcely be faulted for seeking to destroy the naval armament in the port prior to Rozhestvensky's arrival, and, as it transpired, they achieved their aim in ample time to enable Togo fully to restore his fleet by a comprehensive refit. Moreover, on both sides the question of prestige in the eyes of the watching world was deeply involved. It is scarcely in question, however, that the Japanese fully expected to bring about Port Arthur's fall —and with it the release of Nogi's Third Army to other activities—long before it did in fact succumb. In the circumstances, Oyama had little option but to divide his forces, since Kuropatkin could not be left alone to gather strength while the Japanese concentrated all their resources on the reduction of the fortress.

Togo's problem was to secure and retain domination of the local waters, and thereafter to inflict as much damage as possible on the Pacific Ocean Squadron without risking capital ships he was in no position to replace. For the Baltic Squadron's potentialities could never be left out of his calculations. Economy of strength forbade the detachment of a force strong enough closely to blockade Vladivostok, whose naval forces could only be fended off by the detached squadron under Kamamura.

So far as the actual conduct of the war was concerned, Kuropatkin unquestionably had legitimate grounds for complaint over the unconscionable delay in the mobilization of reinforcements for the Manchurian theatre and the tardiness with which they were transported to the front. He was on equally firm ground in protesting against the folly of posting trained soldiers to the reserve while filling up the ranks in the East with raw recruits of the 1905 class and with large numbers of *opolcheni*,[15] so long out of touch with the army as to lack all knowledge either of current tactical doctrine or the proper handling of the latest weapons. Grave deficiencies in the supply of technical equipment was another cause for complaint. Moreover, there was no reason to maintain so large a body of troops in Vladivostok.

If Kuropatkin, in his memoirs, is indulgently reticent with regard to the shortcomings of the higher command and general staff, there were others who were not. Ignatyev bluntly describes the former as made up of "decrepit old men," and the latter as composed of "luxury-loving effeminates"; and adds that "in Manchuria every chief waited inactive until his neighbour was defeated, in order to have a justification for his own retreat under pretext of straightening the front." That may be a little sweeping, but the lack of co-ordination between formation commanders, from the highest to the lowest, was certainly a characteristic defect in every engagement to which the Russian forces were committed. Ignatyev adds that "Kuropatkin regarded his holding of reserves in hand as his greatest accomplishment," yet he seldom employed them to launch a counterstroke. At Mukden, on the one occasion when he could legitimately have made use of them "to plug the gaps with bodies," lack of control over the development of the battle had led to such confusion that there were no reserves available.

Russian Intelligence work was lamentably poor. The Tsarists' consistent inability to divine Japanese strength and intentions was a direct result. Not only was it hopeless for a Russian to try and pass himself off as an Oriental, but if Semenoff is to be believed, "there was not one person [on the staff] who was a thorough master of the Japanese language and characters." The Japanese, on the other hand, had been careful to train large numbers of men in the study of the Russian language and the Cyrillic script. Moreover, their agents could mingle with the native population with small risk of detection. "Their admirable espionage system had been organised many years before the outbreak of the war, and went smoothly into operation—or rather continued in operation with added zest. For the Japanese were fully alive to the fact that an 'Intelligence' service simply cannot be improvised with the outbreak of hostilities."[16] There were no "leaks" as to their forces' intentions and resources, whereas the carelessness of the Russians in this particular was so notorious that a popular camp ditty derisively affirmed that:

> You can't keep Russian orders dark;
> An owl will out, hid in a can;
> From Hun-Ho back to Volga's banks,
> The whole world knows of ev'ry plan.

Finally, "when it is remembered that Kuropatkin was not even supreme in his own province, it must be acknowledged that the commander of an army has seldom been placed in a more unenviable position."[17]

The most notable feature of the operations in Manchuria was the dominant influence exerted by quick-firing artillery, the machine gun, and the magazine rifle. To launch a close-order advance over open terrain was to court annihilation.

But it was a long time before the Japanese grasped the necessity of adopting a more open, extended order in the attack. It is difficult to shoot men out of well-dug earthworks; to force them out with butt and bayonet calls for a successful approach leading up to hand-to-hand conflict. Barbed wire was the obstacle on which the assault was first retarded and then blasted out of existence. Yet the idea of deliberately employing gunfire for the purpose of cutting a way through the wire was slow to develop and even slower to find general acceptance. Neither did the need for the adoption of this measure receive sufficient emphasis from the official military observers.

The grenade was enthusiastically adopted by both sides. Yet while lacerating cruelly, the proportion of fatal wounds from this source was only 2 per cent, as against 97 per cent attributable to firearms—rifle, machine gun, and quick-firing cannon. The Russians were faithful to the bayonet throughout, but it was responsible for no more than 0.4 per cent of the casualties suffered by the Japanese. "The average figures are about 98 *per cent* from firearms," Fischer reports, "and 2 *per cent* from all other weapons." The loss from artillery fire, he adds, "was the greatest ever known."[18]

Little advance was made in the respective communications systems; but the searchlight, employed as a defensive device, was a novelty that fully justified its introduction.

So far as the Russian navy was concerned, M. Burun was scarcely exaggerating when he affirmed that it was "kept up entirely for show." Russia has always lacked a numerous and virile maritime population upon which to draw for the manning of her mercantile marine and battle fleet. In consequence, a large proportion of the foremast hands serving in her navy were farmers with as little knowledge of the ways of the sea as they had sympathy for them. Given sufficient intensive training, they might have turned into passable seamen. But little time was spent afloat, even by the vessels on the active list; and it is seamen, not ships, that constitute a navy. "Our crews," wrote one discerning observer, "besides being unversed in the use of modern implements of war—such as automatic gun-sights, etc—were not accustomed to life at sea. Our

Officers were new to the crews and ships, which they had suddenly to command against a fleet trained in the stern school of war. Born sailors, the Japanese never left their ships, while our vessels had neither permanent nor full crews. Our Captains were unable, owing to the shortage of ammunition, to put their crews through a course of gunnery, or to test their training."

Not that the Japanese forces, either naval or military, were without defects. Almost too literally they had been guided by Admiral Fisher's precept, "Rashness in war is prudence; prudence in war is imbecility." There was nothing they were not prepared to dare; success was an offering on the altar of patriotism, reverse a spur to further effort; while to die in the service of the Mikado and the Fatherland was both an ecstasy and a fulfilment. From the outset they lost no opportunity to seize the initiative, and theirs was also the advantage of the side which consistently assumes the offensive. *They* made the plans and put them into execution; the Russians perforce conformed to them. But their bristling sense of aggression led to a reckless expenditure of manpower that was as unwarrantable in itself as it was heedless of the potential demands of the future. It is not the prime purpose of a fighting man to get himself killed, but to immobilize his enemy—and live to fight another day. Courage without prudence is like rhetoric without sense—more dazzling than constructive. Moreover, the Japanese never seemed to grasp the fact that victory without pursuit endows the enemy with a heaven-sent opportunity to reorganize. But they were easy and contented troops to sustain in the field; their technical services were excellent and their mountain artillery particularly alert and enterprising. As for their infantry, the British military attaché unreservedly affirmed that "a Japanese battalion has no equal in European armies; for upon the patriotism they have absorbed with their mother's milk the Government has been careful to graft initiative, quickness and intelligence."[19]

Had the Japanese army been compelled to make its way laboriously through Korea, Kuropatkin would have been given far more time in which to concentrate a more numerous body of troops to oppose it. This snail's progress was spared Oyama's men by the early successes won by the navy. It was, indeed, Japan's dominance of the ocean from the very outset which constituted the decisive factor in the struggle. For "He that commands at sea is at great liberty, and may take as much or as little of the war as he will."

To the surprise of many and the chagrin of not a few, Dai-Nippon had proved victorious in her contest with a nation that was less a Western people than a fringe-member of the Concert of Europe. ("Russia," the Princess Lieven had informed her English friends in 1814, "is not in Europe; nor, indeed, will it ever be.") The achievement was less startling and disturbing in itself, perhaps, than in the revelation it involved of the uncanny ease and skill with which an Eastern race could master Western techniques and adapt them to their own ends. It was an achievement which, however costly,[20] embodied a portent of the utmost gravity for the years that lay ahead.

"East is East, and West is West, and never the twain shall meet," save—for century after century—in mortal combat. In the age-old struggle between Occident and Orient the energy, resource, and inventiveness of the white races had ultimately brought them a predominance that the East came resentfully to accept as a virtual inevitability. Japan had broken the spell. Japan had demonstrated the possibility of assimilating all that the fertile Occident had made its own, without jeopardy to the essential ethos of the Asian. With Dai-Nippon's triumph in her conflict with Russia, it was clear that the weapons and modes of warfare devised by the West could be successfully turned against the very people who had perfected them. From the bazaars of Tashkent to the alleyways of Bombay, from the lonely khans of the Mandarin Road to the kasbah of Algiers, the exultant whisper ran that the white man was not invincible.

The fires of enmity, long banked, burned with new vigour; and although largely unheeded by the world in general, their sinister glow was not entirely disregarded. So early as 1906 General Kuropatkin noted down, "The cries of 'Asia for the Asian' and 'Africa for the African' are of serious import for Europe. The danger is approaching, and it is so imminent that the Powers of Europe will be forced to sink their differences and unite to withstand the attempt of these uprising peoples to drive old Europe home into the narrow shell she has long since outgrown." Halfway across the world William Greener was also writing, "Europe will have to fear when she is actually in close contact with the masses of pure-bred yellow-skinned —the people who do not, will not, and cannot change."

For the moment the dyke holding back the flood was still unbroken. British and native troops manned the frontiers of India, the cornerstone of Western defence against the trampling hordes of Asia. For "the Indian Empire," wrote that far-sighted little military genius, Homer Lea, "is the strategic centre of the third most important portion of the globe; . . . and in the future the power of its strategic position as a determinate factor in world politics will increase with every international readjustment."[21]

The "international readjustment" which followed World War II delivered India into hands demonstrably too feeble to preserve her freedom. Red China towers over her borders; her own State of Kerala is Communist-controlled; the lands to east and west of her are either openly Communist or riddled with the emissaries of Moscow and Peking.

Captain A. T. Mahan envisaged the dangers inherent in a situation such as this when he wrote, "the problem of India is a world problem, and one that concerns the people of the United States as acutely as it affects those of Europe."[22] Nor is the reason for this far to seek. The whole of America's Pacific strategy is dependent upon India's continued ability to maintain an impenetrable defence against Communist aggression. Small wonder that the Washington columnist George Sokolsky has given it as his considered opinion that "since India gained her freedom there is not a scintilla of evidence that her people have enjoyed greater benefits or security; and at the moment it appears that, sooner or later, Great Britain or America will have to step in and rescue India from either Russia or China, or both"—and by doing so sooner rather than later, be it added, take the first and vital step toward their own salvation. This is not a question of

seeking to re-erect an outmoded system of colonial imperial-
ism. It is simply a question of obeying Nature's first and
overriding law—the law of self-preservation.

The long-smouldering fire of Pan-Asianism and Pan-
Africanism that was fanned into flame by the Japanese victory
of half a century ago has become a raging conflagration, stoked
by eager Communist hands—and the West stands in its path.

The Present is the guardian of the Future . . . and the
writing is on the wall.

NOTES *&* BIBLIOGRAPHY

NOTES

CHAPTER 1

1. Japan's own name for herself.
2. *Decisive Battles of Modern Times*, Col. F. E. Whitton, C.M.G.

CHAPTER 2

1. *A Secret Agent in Port Arthur*, William Greener.
2. *Rasplata* [*The Reckoning*], W. Semenoff.
3. A *sotnia* is a body of mounted troops of, nominally, one hundred sabres.
4. Greener, *op. cit.*
5. Semenoff, *op. cit.*
6. Semenoff, *op. cit.*
7. *Before Port Arthur in a Destroyer*, Anonymous, trans. by E. Grant, D.S.O.
8. Greener, *op. cit.*
9. Ultimately the Japanese succeeded in mobilizing some 2,727,000 men, of whom 1,185,000 were actively employed at sea or in the theatre of war. Kuropatkin put the number against him in the field, from first to last, at 1,500,000.
10. See Appendix A for the strength of the respective fleets.
11. "Three line" indicates the calibre of the rifle, a line being a Russian measure equal to approximately .1 inch. Three lines = .299 inches. The Japanese rifle had a calibre of .256 inches. At the outset neither side employed quick-firing guns. The Russians had them, but they had to be transported laboriously from the West. Among their mixed array of field artillery the weapon of 3.42 calibre predominated. The Japanese

favoured the Ariska field gun of 2.95 calibre. The Russians had a certain number of machine guns, and the Japanese speedily organized units armed with the Hotchkiss.

12. Greener, *op. cit.*

13. *The Russian Army and the Japanese War*, Gen. A. N. Kuropatkin.

14. *Actual Experiences in War*, Capt. L. Z. Soloviev.

15. *The Truth about Port Arthur*, E. K. Nojine.

16. *My Experiences at Nan-shan and Port Arthur*, Lieut. Gen. N. A. Tretyakov.

17. Greener, *op. cit.*

18. Prince Arthur of Connaught, third son of Queen Victoria.

19. Nojine, *op cit.*

CHAPTER 3

1. Greener, *op. cit.*

2. *Official History of the Russo-Japanese War (Naval and Military)*, Committee of Imperial Defence publication.

3. *Official History.*

4. *Private and Confidential*, Brig. Gen. W. H.-H. Waters, C.M.G.

5. Bezobrazoff's tortuous machinations in furthering the interests of his Royal Timber Company are fully dealt with in the liberal review *Osvobojdenie*, no. 75, published in Stuttgart on Aug. 10, 1905, and in the September, 1908, issue of *McClure's Magazine.*

6. *A Staff Officer's Scrap Book*, (2 vols.), Lieut. Gen. Sir Ian Hamilton, K.C.B.

7. *Ibid.*

8. *A Subaltern in Old Russia*, Lieut. Gen. A. A. Ignatyev (trans. Ivor Montagu).

9. Soloviev, *op. cit.*

10. *Decisive Battles* (vol. II), Maj. Gen. J. F. C. Fuller, C.B., C.B.E., D.S.O.

11. Nojine, *op. cit.*

12. Semenoff, *op. cit.*

13. *Human Bullets*, Lt. Tadoyoshi Sakurai.

14. Semenoff, *op. cit.*

15. Greener, *op. cit.*

16. Ignatyev, *op. cit.*

17. Also known as Kin-chou Bay and Society Bay.

18. By mid-June most of the Japanese infantry had been reclothed in khaki uniforms, which had the effect of making them far less conspicuous targets.

19. It was calculated that the wall's destruction would have called for the use of 719,000 pounds of TNT, considerably more than the total amount of explosive available to the Russians in the whole of Manchuria.

20. Quoted by Semenoff, *op. cit.*
21. Nojine, *op. cit.*
22. Sakurai, *op. cit.*
23. Sakurai, *op. cit.*
24. *Port Arthur, the Siege and Capitulation,* E. Ashmead-Bartlett. Siberian rifle, or sharpshooter, regiments were normally of two battalions, but were expanded to three during March and April.
25. Greener, *op. cit.*
26. Semenoff, *op. cit.*
27. Nojine, *op. cit.*
28. Nojine, *op. cit.*
29. Semenoff, *op. cit.*

CHAPTER 4

1. *The Russo-Japanese War,* Col. Charles Ross; Kuropatkin, *op. cit.*
2. Details of the Port Arthur garrison will be found in Appendix D.
3. General Négrier, in his *Lessons of the Russo-Japanese War,* particularly emphasizes that "The most difficult problem all along was to obtain information."
4. Kuropatkin, *op. cit.*
5. Actually, Niu-chuang was put under martial law by the Russians on Mar. 27.
6. Of this force some 1,600 were cavalry under General Samsonov, and there were 100 guns.
7. Nojine, *op. cit.*
8. Semenoff, *op. cit.*
9. Greener, *op. cit.*
10. Nojine, *op. cit.*
11. Sometimes known as Inchenzy Bay.
12. *The Siege of Port Arthur,* David W. James.
13. Nojine, *op. cit.*
14. In one month roving bands of Chinese brigands, or Hunhuses, egged on by the Japanese, made ninety attempts to damage the railway.
15. *Official History.*
16. Captain Svechin, as reported by Ignatyev, *op. cit.*
17. Négrier, *op. cit.*
18. James, *op. cit.*
19. This brigade was put under the orders of Major General Matsumura, commanding Nogi's 1st Division. Later, a naval brigade was also included in the Third Army command.
20. Semenoff, *op. cit.*
21. Sakurai, *op. cit.*
22. Sakurai, *op. cit.*
23. *The Great Siege,* B. W. Norregaard.
24. Sakurai, *op. cit.*
25. Sakurai, *op. cit.*

CHAPTER 5

1. Kawamura, Commander of the 10th Division, was in temporary control during the brief absence of General Count Nodzu.

2. *Official History;* Kuropatkin, *op. cit.;* Ross, *op. cit.*

3. Samsonov and Rennenkampf were also concerned in these operations, but "did not show much ability" (Waters). They survived to bring heavy reproaches on themselves in the early days of World War I, Samsonov committing suicide and Rennenkampf being retired in disgrace.

4. *Official History.*

5. Nojine, *op. cit.*

6. Greener, *op. cit.*

7. Ashmead-Bartlett, *op. cit.*

8. *Three Months with the Besiegers,* Frederick Villiers.

9. James, *op. cit.*

10. Nojine, *op. cit.*

11. Redoubt No. 2, west and slightly forward of Erh-lung-shan (Fort No. 3).

12. Villiers, *op. cit.*

13. U.S. War Department, Reports.

14. Waters, *op. cit.*

15. Semenoff, *op. cit.*

16. The *Bayan* took no part in the action, being still under repair.

17. Semenoff, *op. cit.*

18. Nojine, *op. cit.*

CHAPTER 6

1. Greener, *op. cit.*

2. *Before Port Arthur.*

3. The Russians never had more than eight machine guns to a battalion.

4. Greener, *op. cit.*

5. Hamilton, *op. cit.*

6. Hamilton, *op. cit.*

7. "The cult of the bayonet had been pushed to such an extreme that, under all circumstances, it remained fixed to the rifle" (de Négrier).

8. Even with the reserves he had in hand, the army commander complained: "If we only had one more train a day we would have had present at Liao-yang the 1st Army Corps and the 5th Siberian Corps—sixty battalions." Kuropatkin, *op. cit.*

9. Hamilton, *op. cit.*

10. U.S. War Department, Military Information Division, Reports of military observers attached to the Armies in Manchuria.

11. *Official History.*

12. Hamilton, *op. cit.*

13. Kuropatkin, *op. cit.*
14. Waters, *op. cit.*
15. Sakurai, *op. cit.*
16. Villiers, *op. cit.*
17. Soloviev, *op. cit.*
18. Greener, *op. cit.*
19. Nojine, *op. cit.*
20. Greener, *op. cit.*
21. Ashmead-Bartlett, *op. cit.*
22. Norregaard, *op. cit.*
23. This was a new type of incendiary grenade.
24. Tretyakov, *op. cit.*
25. Ashmead-Bartlett, *op. cit.*
26. Nojine, *op. cit.*
27. Tretyakov, *op. cit.*
28. Tretyakov, *op. cit.*
29. Nojine, *op. cit.*
30. Nojine, *op. cit.*
31. Tretyakov maintains that the defence of Namako-Yama and 203 Metre Hill cost the defence 4,000 casualties, a total considerably higher than that given in the *Official History*.

CHAPTER 7

1. U.S. War Department, Reports.
2. At the current rate of exchange 2 roubles went to the dollar.
3. Nojine, *op. cit.*
4. Looking back on the course of events, Soloviev recorded his belief that "It may be remarked about the late campaign that the spade takes its place side by side with the rifle, the spade has become a purely fighting weapon," a dictum that the experiences of World War I did nothing to controvert.
5. In all, the force consisted of 75 battalions, 53 squadrons and *sotnias*, 190 guns, and 34 mortars.
6. In all, 62 battalions, 26 *sotnias*, 128 guns, and 2 sapper battalions.
7. In all, 24 battalions, 10 squadrons and *sotnias*, 56 guns, and 1 sapper battalion.
8. Hamilton, *op. cit.*
9. Hamilton, *op. cit.*
10. On the left bank of the Sha-Ho, between the villages of Sha-ho-pu and Sha-ho-tung.
11. A *camouflet* is a mine calculated to break down and shatter an enemy's underground gallery without causing any crater on the surface.
12. To *tamp* a mine is to fill up the gallery in which it is lodged with earth and other materials, so that the force of the explosion is not dissipated in an all-round burst, but is thrust in the desired direction.

13. Rashevsky's *Diary*.
14. Nojine, *op. cit.*
15. Nojine, *op. cit.*
16. Villiers, *op. cit.*
17. Ashmead-Bartlett, *op. cit.*
18. Villiers, *op. cit.*
19. Villiers, *op. cit.*

CHAPTER 8

1. Nojine, *op. cit.*
2. From Sept. 19 to Oct. 31 Japanese losses had come to 78 officers and 1,827 men killed, and 220 officers and 6,480 other ranks wounded or missing.
3. Apart from rice sacks, over 1,200,000 sandbags were incorporated in the trench system.
4. Norregaard, *op. cit.*
5. James, *op. cit.*
6. Norregaard, *op. cit.*
7. Nojine, *op. cit.*
8. U.S. War Department, Reports.
9. Norregaard, *op. cit.*
10. Ashmead-Bartlett, *op. cit.*
11. Command of the 11th Division was given to Major General Samijima, who had been sent out from Tokio to superintend the elaborate engineering operations against the forts.
12. The Twenty-seventh Regiment of the 7th Division had been in the thick of the fighting on the eastern sector, but the other formations had not been seriously involved.
13. Tretyakov, *op. cit.*
14. Tretyakov, *op. cit.*
15. Ashmead-Bartlett, *op. cit.*
16. Ashmead-Bartlett, *op. cit.*
17. Ashmead-Bartlett, *op. cit.*
18. From first to last, the defence of 203 Metre Hill accounted for close to 4,000 casualties.

CHAPTER 9

1. Semenoff, *op. cit.*
2. Semenoff, *op. cit.*
3. Nojine, *op. cit.*
4. Norregaard, *op. cit.*
5. Ashmead-Bartlett, *op. cit.*
6. Tretyakov, Nojine, and Norregaard all refer to this experiment. But it did not constitute the first attempt at gas warfare to be recorded.

At the siege of Delium in 424 B.C. the Athenians employed sulphur fumes against their opponents, and at Ambracia in 189 B.C. the Aetolians smoked out the besieging Romans by burning chicken feathers in their countermines. Lord Dundonald's offer to smoke the Russians out of Sevastopol with an admixture of coke, sulphur, bituminous coal, and tar had been rejected by the British War Office on humanitarian grounds.

7. Nojine, *op. cit.*

8. Ashmead-Bartlett, *op. cit.*

9. Ashmead-Bartlett, *op. cit.*

10. Ashmead-Bartlett, *op. cit.*

11. U.S. War Department, Reports.

12. Nojine, *op. cit.*

13. Kostenko was president of the military court of Port Arthur. For the evidence he adduces against Stössel, see his *Siege and Fall of Port Arthur.*

14. Nojine, *op. cit.*

15. Tretyakov, *op. cit.*

16. Sui-shih-ying village.

17. Nojine, *op. cit.*

18. Ashmead-Bartlett, *op. cit.*

CHAPTER 10

1. Norregaard, *op. cit.*

2. Waters, *op. cit.*

3. In general, the series of engagements lasting through January were referred to by the Japanese as the battle of Hei-kou-tai.

4. Soloviev, *op. cit.*

5. Ignatyev, *op. cit.*

6. Ignatyev. *op. cit.*

7. Ignatyev, *op. cit.*

8. Ignatyev, *op. cit.*

9. On petitioning the Tsar to be allowed to continue serving in any capacity, Kuropatkin was permitted to take command of the First Army.

10. Ignatyev, *op. cit.*

11. Fischer, *Kriegschirurgische Rück- und Ausblicke vom Asiatischen Kriegsschauplatze.*

12. Waters, *op. cit.*

13. Waters, *op. cit.*

14. *Official History.*

15. The equivalent of the German *Landwehr*, or third line of defence, usually employed on home service. "Everyone knew quite well," Ignatyev records, "that the reservists were not fighting-men, that they had been forced to come to the war, and that all they thought of was to get away from it as quickly as possible."

16. Négrier, *op. cit.*

17. *Official History.*

18. This refers, of course, to the Japanese ratio of casualties. Brentano gives the loss from artillery fire in the Russian forces as 20 per cent of the total loss; Schaefer puts it as high as 22 per cent.

19. Hamilton, *op. cit.*

20. Fischer gives the losses for the whole war as: JAPANESE: killed, 47,400; died of wounds, 11,500; *total,* 58,900; died of disease, 27,200; missing or prisoners of war, 6,700; *total* wholly lost, 92,800. (At Port Arthur the Japanese lost: dead, 12,500; wounded 37,000.) RUSSIANS: killed, 28,800; died of wounds, 5,200; *total* battle losses, 34,000; died of disease, 9,300; missing or prisoners of war, 39,500; *total* wholly lost, 82,800. (*Kriegschirurgische Rück- und Ausblicke vom Asiatischen Kriegsschauplatze.*)

21. *The Day of the Saxon,* Homer Lea.

22. *The Problem of Asia,* Capt. Alfred Thayer Mahan.

BIBLIOGRAPHY

Official History, Naval & Military, of the Russo-Japanese War (3 vols.).

The Siege of Port Arthur, Committee of Imperial Defence, Historical Section.

The Russo-Japanese War. Reports from British Officers (3 vols.).

U.S. War Department. Military Information Division. Reports of Military Observers.

The Japanese Army, 1904–5. War Office Publication.

The Russian Army, 1904–5. War Office Publication.

German Army, General Staff. The Russo-Japanese War.

The Russo-Japanese War. Official (Japanese) Reports. Compiled by M. Kinai (2 vols.).

The Times Historian's History. Vols. 17 and 24.

The Cambridge Modern History. Vol. 12.

The *Russkaya Starina.*

The *Militar Wochenblatt.*

Contemporary newspapers.

ASAKAWA, K., *The Russo-Japanese Conflict* (Boston: Houghton, Mifflin, 1904).

ASHMEAD-BARTLETT, ELLIS, *Port Arthur, the Siege and Capitulation* (Edinburgh: Blackwood, 1906).

BARING, M., *With the Russians in Manchuria* (London: Methuen, 1905).

BARRY, RICHARD, *Port Arthur, a Monster Heroism* (New York: Moffat, Yard, 1905).

BROOKE, LORD LEOPOLD, *An Eye-witness in Manchuria* (London: E. Nash, 1905).

BUBNOV, CAPT. M., *Vospominaniya.*

BURLEIGH, BENNET, *Empire of the East* (London: Chapman and Hall, 1905).

CAREY, C., *The Trans-Siberian Route.*

CHARQUES, RICHARD, *A Short History of Russia* (New York: Dutton, 1956).

CORDONNIER, COL. E. L. V., *The Japanese in Manchuria* (London: Hugh Rees, 1912–14).

FISCHER, H., *Kriegschirurgische Rück- und Ausblicke vom Asiatischen Kriegsschauplatze.*

FORTESCUE, GRANVILLE, *Front Line and Deadline* (New York: Putnam, 1937).

FULLER, MAJ. GEN. J. F. C., *Decisive Battles* (vol. 2; New York: Scribner's, 1940).

GATTSKI, J., *Tableau du Système Militaire.*

GRANDPREY, CLÉMENT de, *Le Siège de Port-Arthur* (Paris: Berger-Levrault, 1906).

GRANT, CAPT. R. (trans.), *Before Port Arthur in a Destroyer* (Anon).

GREENER, W., *A Secret Agent in Port Arthur* (London: Archibald Constable, 1905).

GREER, LT. COL. T. MacG., *A Short Account of the Russo-Japanese War.*

GRIFFIS, W. F., *Matthew Calbraith Perry* (Boston: Cupples and Hurd, 1887).

HALE, JOHN RICHARD, *Famous Sea Fights* (New York: Dial Press, 1931).

HAMILTON, LT. GEN. SIR IAN, *A Staff Officer's Scrap-book during the Russo-Japanese War* (2 vols.; London: Arnold, 1905–07).

HOLLAND, CLIVE, *Old and New Japan* (New York: Dutton, 1907).

HOUGH, RICHARD, *The Fleet That Had To Die* (New York: Viking, 1958).

IGNATYEV, LT. GEN. A. A., *A Subaltern in Old Russia* (New York: Hutchinson, 1944).

IMMANUEL, CAPTAIN, *Der Russisch-Japanische Krieg.*

JAMES, DAVID, *The Siege of Port Arthur.*

JAMES, COL. LIONEL, *High Pressure* (London: Murray, 1929).

KEYES, ADM. SIR ROGER, *Adventures Ashore and Afloat* (London: Harrap, 1939).

KLADO, CAPT. H., *The Russian Navy in the Russo-Japanese War.*

KOSTENKO, MAJ. GEN. G., *The Siege and Fall of Port Arthur.*

KUHN, L., *Report as Military Observer at the Russo-Japanese War.*

KUROPATKIN, GEN. A. N., *The Russian Army and the Japanese War* (2 vols.; London: Murray, 1909).

LAWRENCE, T. J., *War and Neutrality in the Far East* (New York: Macmillan, 1904).

LEA, HOMER, *The Day of the Saxon* (New York: Harper, 1942).

MAHAN, CAPT. A. T., *The Problem of Asia* (Boston: Little, Brown, 1905).

NÉGRIER, GENERAL FRANÇOIS OSCAR de, *Lessons of the Russo-Japanese War* (English ed.; London: Hugh Rees, 1906).

NOJINE, E. K., *The Truth about Port Arthur* (New York: Dutton, 1908).

NORREGAARD, B. W., *The Great Siege* (London: Methuen, 1906).

PARRY, ALBERT, *Russian Cavalcade.*

POLITOVSKY, EUGÈNE, *From Libau to Tsushima* (London: Murray, 1907).

RODZIANKO, COL. PAUL, *Tattered Banners* (London: Seeley, Service, 1939).

ROSS, COL. CHARLES, *An Outline of the Russo-Japanese War 1904, 1905* (London: Macmillan, 1912).

SAKURAI, LT. TADAYOSHI, *Human Bullets* (Boston: Houghton, Mifflin, 1907).

SEMENOFF, CAPT. VLADIMIR, *The Battle of Tsu-Shima* (New York: Dutton, 1907).

———, *Rasplata* (London: Murray, 1909).

SKRINE, F. H., *The Expansion of Russia 1815–1900* (Cambridge, Eng.: University Press, 1915).

SOLOVIEV, CAPT. L. Z., *Actual Experiences in War.*

STEER, LT. A. P., *The "Novik" and the Part She Played in the Russo-Japanese War 1904* (London: Murray, 1913).

TRETYAKOV, LT. GEN. N. A., *My Experiences at Nan Shan and Port Arthur* (London: Hugh Rees, 1911).

VILLIERS, FREDERIC, *Port Arthur* (New York: Longmans, Green, 1905).

WATERS, BRIG. GEN. W. H-H., *Secret and Confidential.*

WHITTON, LT. COL. F. E., *The Decisive Battles of Modern Times* (Boston: Houghton, Mifflin, 1923).

WRIGHT, H. C. SEPPINGS, *With Togo* (London: Hurst and Blackett, 1905).

APPENDICES

Naval Forces in the Far East

JAPANESE		RUSSIAN	
BATTLESHIPS		**BATTLESHIPS**	
First-class		*First-class*	
Fuji	Asahi	Sevastopol	Pobieda
Yoshima	Hatsuse	Petropavlovsk	Retvisan
Shikishima	Mikasa	Poltava	Tsarevitch
		Peresviet	
Second-class			
Chinyen			

JAPANESE		RUSSIAN	
CRUISERS		**CRUISERS**	
First-class		*First-class*	
Asama	Yakumo	Rurik	Pallada
Tokiwa	Idzumo	Rossia	Variag
Adzuma	Iwate	Gromoboy	Bogatir
		Bayan	Askold
Second-class		Diana	
Naniwa	Yoshino		
Takachiho	Takasago	*Second-class*	
Itsukushima	Kasagi	Novik	Boyarin†
Matsushima	Chitose		
Hashidate	Niitaka		
Akitsushima	Tsushima		

COAST DEFENCE VESSELS
Fuso   Heiyen*

* In addition to the above, there were 13 third-class cruisers of 1,250–2,920 displacement, 14 gunboats, 19 destroyers, 49 first-class and 29 second-class torpedo boats.

† In addition to the above, there were 4 gunboats, 6 sloops, 25 destroyers, and some 14 first-class torpedo boats divided between Port Arthur and Vladivostok. The Russians possessed eleven vessels fit to take their place in the line of battle; the Japanese could count on fourteen. Moreover, the Japanese could sail at 18.3 knots to the Russian 16.3. The Russians possessed forty-two guns over 6-inch calibre, the Japanese mounted fifty-five. In the Tsarist craft there were 138 six-inch guns, in the Mikado's ships 184.

APPENDIX B

THE JAPANESE ARMY

At the outbreak of the war military service was divided into four categories:

(1) STANDING ARMY (*Jobi*) subdivided into
    (a) Active Army (*Genyeki*), 3 years' service
    (b) First Reserve (*Yobi*), 4⅓ years' service
(2) RESERVE ARMY, or Second Reserve (*Kobi*), 5 years' service
(3) CONSCRIPT RESERVE (*Hoju*) subdivided into
    1st Term, 7⅓ years' service
    2nd Term, 1⅓ years' service

Men in both the First and Second Reserves were called up for annual training. Men of the Conscript Reserve received ninety days' preliminary training, and a further period of sixty days during the second and fourth years of service. The men in the Second Term exempted from service on health or other grounds—were untrained, and after completing their period of purely nominal service, passed into the Second Section of the National Army.

(4) NATIONAL ARMY (*Kokumin*) was subdivided into
    1st Section ⎫
            ⎬ Both formed of men up to forty years of age
    2nd Section ⎭

The First Section consisted of men between twenty and forty years of age who had completed their service in the Reserve Army or in the First Term of the Conscript Reserve. The Second Section consisted of all men between the ages of twenty and forty not belonging to any of the other categories. They were quite without training.

COMPOSITION OF A JAPANESE MOBILIZED DIVISION

Two infantry brigades of two regiments, each regiment of three battalions
1 cavalry regiment of three squadrons
1 artillery regiment of two battalions of three batteries
1 engineer battalion of three companies, with a bridging train
1 telegraph company of three sections
6 field hospitals
5 ammunition columns (three artillery, two infantry)
4 supply columns

In round numbers 11,400 rifles, 430 sabres, and 36 guns, with staff, 830 engineers, and 5,500 noncombatants.

In 1904 the Japanese Standing Army consisted of thirteen divisions, namely, the Imperial Guard Division and twelve territorial divisions, two cavalry brigades, two artillery brigades, with the garrisons of Formosa and of various fortresses, and certain guards in Korea.

THE RUSSIAN (EASTERN) ARMY

At the outbreak of the war infantry divisions did not exist. They were formed later by the expansion of existing brigades with reserve formations. In the theatre of war there were:

FIELD TROOPS
Infantry (96 battalions)
Cavalry (35 squadrons and sotnias)
Artillery (25 batteries = 196 guns)
Engineers (13 companies)

FORTRESS TROOPS
Infantry (26 companies)
Railway troops (11,450)
Frontier Guards (55 infantry companies, 55 squadrons, 6 batteries = 48 guns

This accounted for a combatant strength of some 148,000; with noncombatants added, approximately 165,000. Additional troops despatched in February probably brought the total up to 175,000.

APPENDIX C

PRINCIPAL WORKS—"FORTS"

No. 1 Fort (SE)	Paiyin-shan Fort; South Fort
No. 2 Fort (NE)	North Fort Chi-kuan-shan; Fort Kitohadai
No. 3 Fort (N)	Fort Erh-lung-shan; Fort Nirusan
No. 4 Fort (NW)	I-tzu-shan Fort; Yi-tzu-shan
No. 5 Fort (W)	Tayanko North
No. 6 Fort (SW)	

SUBSIDIARY WORKS—"FORTIFICATIONS"

Fortification No. 1 (SE)	Southeast Chi-kuan-shan Battery
Fortification No. 2 (E)	Dangerous Mountain
Fortification No. 3 (N)	Sung-su-shan Fort; Sho-zu-shan Fort Shojusan
Fortification No. 4 (W)	South An-tzu-shan Fort
Fortification No. 5 (SW)	Cha-kua-tzu

INTERMEDIATE, TEMPORARY, AND FIELD WORKS

Takhe Redoubt (SE)	Southeast Redoubt
Rear Redoubt (E)	
Kuropatkin Lunette (NE)	"Q" Work
No. 1 Open Caponier (NE)	
Redoubt No. 1 (NE)	East Pan-lun-shan Redoubt; East Banrusan
No. 2 Open Caponier (NE)	"P" Work
Redoubt No. 2 (NE)	West Pan-lun-shan Redoubt; West Banrusan
No. 3 Open Caponier (NE)	"G" Work; Hachimaki-yama
Water Supply Redoubt (N)	Fort Kuropatkin
Red Redoubt (N)	Railway Redoubt; Lung-yen; Rocky Redoubt
Temple Redoubt (N)	
Pan-lun-shan Redoubt (NW)	
Flat Hill, No. 1 Redoubt (NW)	
Flat Hill, No. 2 Redoubt (NW)	
Flat Hill, No. 3 Redoubt (NW)	
Flat Hill, No. 4 Redoubt, Stone-broken (NW)	
Double Angle Lunette (NW)	
New Lunette (NW)	
Fougasse Lunette (NW)	
No. 5 Redoubt (W)	Quarry Battery
No. 4 Redoubt (W)	
Timber Redoubt (SW)	
Salt Redoubt (SW)	
Quail Hill (centre)	

LAND BATTERIES

Cross (SE)	
Dragon's Back (E)	
Dragon's Head (E)	
"A" (E)	
"B" (NE)	
Zaliterny (NE)	"R"
Little Eagle's Nest (NE)	"M"
Eagle's Nest (NE)	Bodai; Wan-tai
Zaredoubt (N)	"H"
Howitzer (N)	
Wolf's (N)	"I"
Tumulus (N)	Sung-su-shan Auxiliary
Cemetery (NW)	Cemetery

"C" (Sapper) (NW)
Jagged Hill (NW)
Howitzer (NW)
Obelisk Hill (NW)   Obelisk Hill
Tea (W)   Stonebroken
Pigeon (W)
"D" (W)   South Tayanko
Salt (?) Redoubt (SW)

COAST BATTERIES

White Wolf
No. 1
No. 2   Tiger's Head
No. 3
No. 4
No. 5*
No. 6*   Chi-kuan-shan
No. 7*   Man-tzu-ying
No. 8
No. 9
No. 10
Lighthouse
No. 12 (S)
No. 13 Golden Hill (S)
No. 14 (S)
No. 15 Electric Cliff (S)
No. 16 (SE)   Six-inch Gun
No. 17 (SE)
No. 18 (SE)
No. 19 (SE)
No. 20 (SE)
No. 21 Long Battery (SE)
No. 22 (SE)

PLACE NAMES AND THEIR ALTERNATIVES

Kuen-san Hill (NE)   *Ken-san Hill*
Sia-gu-shan (E)   *Shokozan; Hsiao-ku-shan*
Ta-ku-shan (E)   *Ta-ku-san*
203 Metre Hill (NW)   *Royusan; High Hill*
Angle Hill (NW)   *174 Metre Hill*
Namako-yama (NW)   *Long Hill; 180 Metre Hill*
Akasaka-yama (N)   *Flat Hill*

* On Tiger Peninsula.

Wolf's Hills (NE)	*Feng-huang-shen*
Liao-tia-shan	*Laotsue-shan*
Kuan-tun Peninsula	*Kwantung Peninsula*
Te-li-ssu	*Telissu; Wa-fang-gu; Vafango*
Pyong-yang	*Niu-chuang*
Niu-chuang	*Newchuang*
Kin-chou	*Chin-chou*
The Yalu	*Turinchen*
Mo-tien-ling	*Moduling*
Nan-kuan-ling	*Nankwangling; Nagalin*
Sung-su-shan	*Shogusan*
Shui-shih-ying	*Siushuing; Shushien*
Yu-pi-la-tzu Hills	*Upilazy Hills*
Mount Ho-shan	*Hoshan*
Waitu-shan	*Witosan*

APPENDIX D

PORT ARTHUR GARRISON

4TH EAST SIBERIAN RIFLE DIVISION *(Major General Fock)*

First Brigade: Thirteenth East Siberian Rifle Regiment
Fourteenth East Siberian Rifle Regiment

Second Brigade: Fifteenth East Siberian Rifle Regiment
Sixteenth East Siberian Rifle Regiment

Fourth East Siberian Rifle Artillery Brigade (4 batteries)

7TH EAST SIBERIAN RIFLE DIVISION *(Major General Kondratenko)*

First Brigade: Twenty-fifth East Siberian Rifle Regiment
Twenty-sixth East Siberian Rifle Regiment

Second Brigade: Twenty-seventh East Siberian Rifle Regiment
Twenty-eight East Siberian Rifle Regiment
Seventh East Siberian Rifle Artillery Brigade (3 batteries)

Attached: Fifth East Siberian Rifle Regiment

Cavalry: Verhne-Udinsk Cossack Regiment (1 squadron)

Miscellaneous Units: 1 field howitzer battery
2nd East Siberian Rifle Division Telegraph Company

3rd, 4th, and 7th East Siberian Depot Battalions

Twenty-first and Thirty-sixth Companies of Frontier Guards

Kuan-tun Sapper Company

Port Arthur Mining Company

3 battalions of fortress artillery

The strength of the Russian regiment was normally of four battalions.

The Fifth East Siberian Rifle Regiment was less one company, serving as Legation Guard at Peking.

In all the garrison numbered approximately 41,000 officers and men.

APPENDIX E

PORT ARTHUR FORTIFICATIONS
Technical Terms

DITCH: A (dry) moat or fosse, dug at the foot of the ramparts; often as much as 20 feet deep and 30 feet wide.

CAPONIER: A defence work, or lodgment, sunk 4 feet or so under the counterscarp—i.e., in the forward bank of the moat, or ditch—with sides rising about 2 feet above ground level. The chamber thus formed was roofed with stout beams, supporting a heavy mound of earth. The forward face of the work was loopholed, as was the masonry wall facing inward to the moat. Communication between the caponier and the fortress interior was by a concrete-built passage, also loopholed to allow of flank fire along the ditch. In certain instances the caponier extended the whole length of the ditch.

CASEMATE: A vault or arch of stonework or concrete, in which the fortress guns were emplaced.

PARAPET: In a fortress a work raised on the ramparts and designed to protect the defenders from cannon and musketry fire. In the field a breastwork erected along the face of a trench, dug in sufficient depth to furnish adequate cover.

BANQUETTE: A bank of earth under a parapet on which the men stand to fire. A firing platform.

FASCINES: Faggots of wood, or bundles of withies, wattles, or stout cornstalks, bound together and used to strengthen fieldworks or fill up a ditch to facilitate passage across it. On occasion, small bundles would be set alight and thrown into the enemy works to fire the timber and sandbags in them.

FOUGASSE: or *fougade*. A variety of mine, made like a well, 8 to 10 feet wide, charged with explosive covered over with earth. The fougasse could be exploded electrically or "on contact." Sometimes referred to as a mine chamber.

PARALLELS: Trenches.

CONTRAVALLATION: A trench, with a stout parapet, made by the besiegers between them and a fortress or fieldwork under siege, to secure themselves against the fire of the garrison.

SPITLOCK: To mark out with a spade the lines on which a fortress or fieldwork is to be erected or dug.

CHAMADE: A parley, during which hostilities are suspended.

LUNETTE: A relatively small detached fieldwork, consisting of two faces making an angle inward, often sited so as to bring fire on any attack on the moat or ditch.

GLACIS: The sloping bank, almost but not quite perpendicular, that reaches from the parapet of the counterscarp to the level of the surrounding terrain.

SPLINTERPROOF: An earthwork supported by rails or timber, impervious to penetration by shell splinters.

SAP: A deep trench carried far underground, with steps cut in the earth to give access to it. Cover from fire is provided by roofing over the entrance with planks, strewn with a thick layer of earth. A sap can be dug under fixed fortifications to undermine them.

INDEX

Aiho River, 37
Ai-yang-ching, 62
Akasaka-Yama, 81, 110, 112, 113, 124, 137, 144, 145, 146, 147, 148
Akiyama, Brig. Gen., 64
Alexeieff, Viceroy Admiral, 14, 20, 25, 33, 35, 36, 39, 40, 42, 43, 54, 55, 56, 57, 67, 78, 90, 136
Angle Hill (174 Metre Hill), 81, 84, 85, 86, 88, 109
Anju, 28
An-ping-ling, 79
An-shan-chau, 79
An-tzu-shan, 151

Baikal, Lake, 19, 98
Bezabrazoff, A. M., 8, 36, 51
Biely, Maj. Gen., 43, 159, 160, 162
Bilderling, Lt. Gen., 100, 120, 122, 170, 171

Chefu, 25, 52, 58, 67, 83, 93, 116, 135
Chia-tou, 78, 79
Chi-kuan-shan (North Fort, No. 2), 22, 85, 86, 87, 108, 115, 117, 118, 123, 125, 126, 127, 128, 129, 130, 135, 137, 138, 140, 141, 152, 153, 154, 155

China, 5, 7, 8, 9, 20, 21
Chinese Wall, 22, 88, 130, 137, 157
Chiu-lien-cheng, 36, 37, 54, 64
Chu-tien, 120

Dalny, 20, 25, 26, 28, 42, 44, 49, 50, 51, 52, 66, 67, 71, 75, 83, 88, 98, 103, 115, 127
Deep Bay, 32
Diego Suarez, 175
Divisional Hill, 81, 84

Eagle's Nest, 130, 135
Eight Ships' Bay, 32
Electric Hill, 40, 115
Elliot Islands, 13, 42
Erh-lung-shan (Fort No. 2), 22, 85, 86, 87, 88, 108, 115, 117, 119, 120, 123, 124, 126, 136, 137, 138, 140, 141, 155
Essen, Capt. von, 66, 107, 150

Feng-huan-ching, 177
Fen-shui-ling passes, 36, 56, 76
Fillmore, President Millard, 2
Fischer, H. (quoted), 180
Fisher, Admiral Sir John (quoted), 181

Fock, Maj. Gen., 44, 45, 47, 53, 61, 68, 69, 70, 72, 134, 154, 161, 162
Formosa, 4, 5
Fort Kuropatkin, 108, 109
France, 3, 5, 7, 9
Fukushima, Maj. Gen., 99
Fushun coal mines, 120, 121

Gapon, "Father," 166
Gensan, 35
Germany, 4, 5, 8, 9, 18
Golden Hill, 12, 13, 14, 16, 22, 73, 84, 109, 115, 150
Gorky, Maxim, 166
Great Britain, 3, 7, 8, 9
Green Hills, the (Port Arthur), 51, 60, 61, 68, 69, 70
Gregorovitch, Rear Admiral, 91, 160
Grippenberg, Lt. Gen., 136, 169, 170
Gulf of Korea, 33

Hai-cheng, 12, 52, 56, 76, 77, 79
Hai-ping-kai, 172
Hakodate, 3
Ha-ma-tong, 37
Hand Bay, 42, 46, 47
Harbin, 33, 55, 97, 175, 176
Hon-tu-shih (port), 54, 57, 66, 76
Horoshima, 18
Ho-shan Hill, 71, 108
Hsi-mu-cheng hills, 77
Hun-Ho (river), 120, 121, 169

Idichi, Maj. Gen. K., 161
Irman, Col., 110, 113
Ivanoff, Maj. Gen., 120

Japan, 1–10 passim
Jilinsky, Gen., 55

Kagoshima, 3
Kai-ping, 76, 77
Kamamura, Vice-Admiral, 35, 60, 95, 107
Kaulbars, Lt. Gen., 136, 171
Kawamura, Maj. Gen. Baron., 76
Keller, Maj. Gen. Count, 76, 77, 78, 79

Kerr Bay, 32, 43, 60
Khilkoff, Prince, 98
Khvostoff, Col. 14, 114, 159, 163
Kiao-chau, 95
Kin-chou, 15, 22, 23, 25, 29, 42, 44, 45, 47, 49, 52, 168
Kondratenko, Maj. Gen. R. I., 29, 67, 70, 72, 85, 125, 134, 144, 151, 152, 154, 164
Korea, 5, 7, 8, 9
Korea Straits, 18, 30, 176
Korsakosk Bay, 96
Kostenko, Maj. Gen., 159
Kronstadt, 80, 124
Kuantun District, 15, 23, 33, 43, 44
Kuen-san, 60, 61, 68, 69, 70
Kuroki, Gen. Baron, 12, 17, 25; at the Yalu, 36, 37, 52, 54, 62, 76, 78, 99, 100, 101, 102, 122, 177
Kuropatkin, Gen. A. N., 30; assumes command, 33, 35, 36, 38, 39, 43, 52, 55, 57, 62, 65, 69, 76, 77, 78, 79, 89, 97, 98; at Liao-yang, 99–103, 106, 114, 117, 120; Hun-Ho offensive, 121–123, 136, 162, 168, 169, 170, 171; superseded, 172, 177, 178, 181; quoted, 182
Kuteynikoff, Engineer Officer, 28

Lang-tzu-shan, 79
Lea, Homer, (quoted), 183
Liao-tieh-shan, 13, 21, 22, 27, 30, 35, 40, 92, 114, 151, 158
Liao-tung Peninsula, 5, 6, 7, 19, 120
Liao-yang, 12, 21, 33, 41, 52, 54, 55, 56, 62, 70, 76, 77, 78, 83, 98; defences of, 99; battle of, 100–103, 115, 121, 132, 177
Libau, 80
Lighthouse Hill, 16
Linevitch, Lt. Gen., 136; supersedes Kuropatkin, 172
Liu-shu-tun Peninsula, 46
Loschinsky, Rear Admiral, 26, 159
Louisa Bay, 68, 83
Lun-ho Valley, 21, 155
Lun-wan-tun Valley, 69

Mahan, Capt. A. T. (quoted), 183
Maisura, 18

Makharoff, Vice-Admiral S. O., 26, 30, 32, 34, 35
Manchuria, 5–10 passim, 18, 20, 30, 33, 62, 92, 132, 133, 176
Manila, 175
Manju-Yama height, 100, 101
Matsamura, Gen., 110, 114
Mishchenko, Maj. Gen., 76, 77, 169
Molas, Rear Admiral, 31
Moscow, 20, 175, 176
Mo-tien-ling, 54, 77, 78
Mukden, 12, 20, 24, 55, 62, 78, 101, 120, 123, 162, 170, 171, 172, 179

Nagasaki, 12, 18
Nakamura, Maj. Gen., 141, 143
Namako-Yama, 81, 88, 109, 110, 111, 112, 114, 115, 118, 125
Nan-kuan-ling, 45, 46, 47, 48, 50
Nan-shan, 44, 45, 47–49 passim, 51, 52, 57, 60, 62, 84, 165
Nebogatoff, Admiral, 133, 167; at Tsu-shima battle, 173–175
Nikitin, Col., 70
Niu-chuang, 32, 33, 56, 67, 68, 76
Nodzu, Lt. Gen. Count, 51, 78, 99
Nogi, Gen. Baron K., 52, 56; at Pei-pao-tzi-ai, 60, 61, 67, 68, 69, 71, 72, 77, 81, 83, 84, 85, 88, 89, 96, 98, 105, 109, 110, 114, 117, 118, 119, 123, 124, 130, 131, 133, 136, 137, 138, 139, 140, 141, 143, 153, 158, 160, 161, 162, 165, 168, 169, 170, 171, 177
Nojine, E. K., 26, 39, 70, 123, 130, 134, 164
Nytonsu, 71, 72

One Tree Peak, 122
Okubo, Maj. Gen., 75
Oku, Lt. Gen. Baron, 41, 44, 45, 52, 56, 62; at Te-li-ssu, 63–65, 75, 76, 77, 78, 99, 177
Osaka, 120
Oshima, Maj. Gen., 63, 64, 127
Oyama, Field Marshal Marquis I., 74, 98, 99, 101, 102, 123, 133, 168, 170, 171, 172, 177, 181

Pacific Ocean Squadron, 11, 12, 15, 20, 26, 30, 33, 34, 35, 66, 69, 71, 81, 96, 107, 132, 133, 143, 148, 149, 151, 178
Pai-ju-shan hill, 134
Pan-lun-shan hills, 81, 84, 88
Pekarsey, Capt., 42
Peking, 5, 7
Pen-chi-ho, 121
Pen-hsi-hu, 121
Perry, Commodore M. G., 2
Peter the Great, 6, 15
Petrusha, Col., 28
Pigeon Bay, 35, 58, 105, 109, 114, 116, 151
Ping-tai-tzu heights, 123
Pingyang, 25, 36
Pi-tzu-wo, 12, 42, 44, 54, 98
Poland, 18
Polo, Marco, 1
Port Adams, 43
Port Arthur, 5–8 passim; first naval assault, 12, 13, 14, 15–20 passim; defences, 22; Old Town and New Town, 22, 23–28 passim, 29, 31–33 passim, 35, 39–45 passim, 49–57 passim, 58; Town Guard, 59, 60, 61, 66, 69–73 passim, 76, 77, 80; first land assault, 81–89; naval action off, 90–96, 102, 103, 105, 107; second land assault 108–115, 117, 118, 121, 123; third land assault, 124–131, 137; final land assault, 138–148, 153–159 passim, 161, 162; surrender, 163–165, 167, 168, 177
Pu-lien ten, 43
Pu-ling, 120
Pyongyang, 28

Quail Hill (or Signal Hill), 13, 21, 111, 150

Rashevsky, Col., 119, 125, 126, 134, 152
Reitzenstein, Rear Admiral von, 94
Reuss, Col., 152, 163
Reval, 80
Roosevelt, President Theodore, 176
Round Island, 12

Rozhestvensky, Admiral Z. P., 80, 106, 107, 118, 124, 132, 133, 149, 169; at Tsu-shima battle, 173–175, 177
Russia, 3–10, *passim;* discontent in, 19, 57, 165

Saddle Hill, 112, 118
Saigon, 95
St. Petersburg, 166, 167
Sakhalin Island, 176
Sakurai, Lt. T., 87
Samsonov, Maj. Gen., 65
San-de-pu, 169
Sangari River, 172
Sarnichev, Capt., 31, 32
Sasebo, 12, 18, 133
Satow, Col., 118
Second Pacific Squadron, 81, 106, 107, 118, 124, 133, 137, 167, 168, 173–175 *passim*, 178
Semenoff, Commander, 17, 43, 66, 90, 93, 179
Seoul, 12
Sha-Ho, 122, 123, 132, 168
Shanghai, 95, 96, 175
Shan-tai-ko, 60
Shan-tung Province, 7, 51, 96
Shao-ping-tau Island, 51, 67, 69, 71
Sha-tai-tzu, 121
Shimoda, 2
Shimonoseki, 3; treaty of, 5, 18, 120, 133
Ships:
  Alexander III, 107
  Almaz, 174
  Akaji, 45, 120
  Akasuki, 26
  Amur, 40
  Asama, 95
  Askold, 14, 32, 40, 68, 94, 95, 96
  Azuma, 95
  Barrackzi, 120
  Bayan, 40, 68, 69, 125, 150
  Blume, S. S., 83
  Bobr, 46
  Boevoy, 31, 67
  Bogatyr, 11, 40
  Borinsky, 120

Ships (*Cont.*)
  Borodino, 107
  Boyarin, 14, 31, 32
  Brawy, 174
  Burni, 96
  Charbin, 40
  Chailar, 40, 41
  Chitose, 96
  Chokai, 45
  Crane, the (trawler), 124
  Diana, 93, 94, 95
  Emperor Nicholas I, 174
  Gamecock Fishing Fleet, 124
  Giliak, 30, 40, 130
  Goya Maru, 35
  Gromoboy, 11, 95, 107
  Grosevoy, 67, 96
  Grosni, 174
  Hatsuse (flagship), 40
  Heiyen, 45, 109
  Hipsang, 24
  Hiroya, 95
  Hitachi Maru, 60
  Itsukushima, 69
  Iwati, 95
  Izami Maru, 60
  Izumrud, 174
  Kasuga, 18, 35
  Kinshu Maru, 35
  Kioto, 120
  Kniaz Suvoroff (flagship), 106; at Tsu-shima battle, 174
  Knight Commander, S. S., 24
  Koreëts, 12
  Koryo Maru, 34
  Lieutenant Burakoff, 67
  Manchuria, S. S., 26
  Mikasa, 173
  Miyaka, 43
  Navarin, 174
  Nesshin, 18, 35
  Novik, 13, 66, 92, 95, 96, 150
  Oryol, 107, 124, 174
  Osiva, 83, 94
  Oswa, 120
  Otvanjy, 30, 40, 42
  Pallada, 13, 68, 92, 94, 120, 150
  Peresviet, 94, 95, 115, 125, 150, 154
  Petropalovsk (flagship), 34

Ships (*Cont.*)
Pleiades, S. S., 24
Pobieda, 34, 92, 93, 115, 150, 154
Poltava, 91, 92, 94, 125, 150
Reshitelny, 40
Retvisan, 13, 16, 28, 92, 93, 95, 125, 150
Rossia, 11, 95, 107
Rundschau, S. S., 116
Rurik, 11, 95, 107
Sado Maru, 60
Sevastopol, 66, 91, 92, 95, 150, 161
Shilka, 40
Shirakuma, 13
Silny, 31
Steresguschy, 26
Strashny, 34
Tsukusi, 45
Tsu-shima, 96
Tzesarevitch, 13, 28, 66, 90, 92, 93, 94, 95
Ushakoff, 174
Variag, 12
Vnushitelny, 52
Winchow, 24
Yakumo, 95
Yashima, 40
Yenussi, 31
Yonemaro Maru, 33
Yoshino, 40
Shi-shan, 122
Shtakelberg, Maj. Gen., 57, 62; at Te-li-ssu, 63–65, 68, 76, 120, 121, 122, 169, 170
Shui-shih-ying village, 21, 85, 86, 108, 115, 148, 161, 163
Sia-gu-shan, 22, 61, 68, 72, 74
Signal Hill, 158
Sluchevski, Maj. Gen., 78, 79
Smirnoff, Lt. Gen. K. N., 15, 29, 30, 33, 44, 53, 55, 58, 61, 67, 69, 70, 72, 86, 89, 108, 114, 125, 126, 134, 135, 144, 151, 152, 154, 155, 159, 162
Sokolsky, George (quoted), 183
Soloviev, Capt., 38, 101, 170
Spiradov, Col., 43
Starck, Admiral, 12, 14, 26
Stössel, Gen. Baron A. M., 13, 14,

15, 23, 24, 25, 29, 30, 33, 44, 45, 47, 50, 51, 53, 54, 59; recalled, 69, 70, 71, 82, 84; again recalled, 89, 108, 134, 151, 152, 159; offers to surrender, 160, 162, 163, 164
Sung-su-shan, 20, 108, 126, 136, 137, 138, 141, 156, 157
Suribachi-Yama, 37

Ta-fang-shen, 64
Tai River, 51, 68
Tai-tzu-Ho (river), 78, 100, 101, 102, 121
Tai-yang-kou valley, 151
Takhe Bay, 67, 69, 158
Ta-ku-shan ("The Great Orphan"), 22, 52, 61, 68, 72, 73, 74
Ta-lien-wan Bay, 31, 42, 45, 54, 71
Ta-sha-Ho, 54
Ta-shih-chiao (railway junction), 76, 77
Ta-shih-chiao hills, 78
Te-li-ssu, 56, 62; battle of, 63–65, 68, 75, 76, 131
Temple Redoubt, 108, 109
Ter-Yama height, 122
Third Pacific Squadron, 167; at Tsu-shima battle, 173–175
Tiger Peninsula—Tiger's Tail, 12, 21, 22, 150, 158
Togo, Admiral H., 12, 16, 32, 66, 74, 80, 81, 91, 92, 95, 96, 109, 137, 151; at Tsu-shima battle, 173–175, 177, 178
Tokio, 5, 7, 8, 151, 170
Trans-Siberian Railway, 7, 19, 20, 30, 97
Trepoff, Col., 166
Tretyakov, Col. N., 42, 48, 82, 84, 85, 105, 108, 110, 119, 134, 144, 145, 147, 152, 160, 164
Tsintchow, 45
Tsuchiya, Maj. Gen., 73, 127, 143
Tsu-shima, Strait of, 12; island of, 18
Tu-men-ling pass, 121
Tumulus Hill, 140, 141
Tung-chia-tun, 76
203 Metre Hill, 22, 25, 81, 105, 109, 110, 112, 113, 114, 115, 118, 124,

136, 143, 144, 145, 146, 147, 148, 149, 151, 177
Uktomsky, Capt. Prince, 94
Ulyanov, V. I. (Lenin), 166
United States, 2, 3, 5, 8

Vasiliar, Maj. Gen., 100
Vershinin, Chief Commissary, 82
Vladivostok, 7, 8, 11, 12, 18, 31, 35, 60, 66, 81, 91, 93, 95, 96, 107, 132, 170, 173, 174, 175, 178

Waitu-shan, 69
Wan-tai knoll, 88, 157
Waterworks, the, 22, 108, 109
Wei-hai-wei, 5, 93, 96
White Wolf, 16, 22, 66
Wiju, 36

Wiren, Admiral, 149, 159, 160, 161
Witgeft, Rear Admiral, 35, 40, 43, 59, 65, 66, 90, 91, 92, 93, 107, 177
Wu-chia-tun, 64

Yalu River, 8, 9, 26, 29, 35, 36, 37, 39, 56, 57, 177
Yamaguchi, Maj. Gen., 63
Yenissi River, 98
Yen-tai mines, 78, 121, 122
Ying-cheng-zu Bay, 60
Ying-kou (port serving Niuchuang), 56, 68, 76, 77, 79, 169
Yi-tzu-shan (Fortification No. 4), 88, 148, 151, 155, 156

Zarubaeff, Maj. Gen., 101
Zasulich, Maj. Gen., 36, 37, 38, 39, 41